THEATER AS THERAPY FOR THE DELINQUENT

Top: Plaque for proscenium by Harry. Something useful to the group as a means of acclimatizing a stutterer and rejecting fellows to each other.

Bottom: Group motto. Result project of Overlapping. Irving, a skilled boy, with seven or more unskilled children made this. Every letter and part was separately hand-carved and polished and then cooperatively set together.

THEATER AS THERAPY FOR THE DELINQUENT

A Climate for Catharsis

Celia Avramo Rabinow

VANTAGE PRESS
New York Washington Atlanta Hollywood

The surnames of the children
have been deleted
for their protection.

Illustrations by the author

FIRST EDITION

Published by Vantage Press, Inc.
516 West 34th Street, New York, New York 10001

Manufactured in the United States of America
Standard Book Number 533-02668-7

Sing a Song of Cooperation

Written by the group for scene in end-year Group Theater Follies

Sing a song of cooperation—
That with which was built our nation!
Theater Group is our own creation—
We find joy in our avocation!

Swing the brooms and dust each table—
A clean workshop makes boys more able!
Then while around us tools are banging,
Make clear the stage for scenery hanging.

Unravel wires that shouldn't have been tangled—
Rehearse lines terribly mangled—
Last-minute touches to the painting—
By curtain-rise all near to fainting.

Our playwright climbs the peak of genius—
We're not bad, wait till you've seen us!
Though every ham actor thinks he's a Gable,
Any kind of acting makes us stable.

So sing a song of cooperation—
Everyone must do his ration—
Not always perfect to our sorrow,
But if not today, we will be tomorrow.

For once the work is begun,
We manage to have it done—
That's cooperation, folks!
One for all and all for one!

Contents

Forewords

I found Mrs. Rabinow's (nee Avramo) manuscript on "The Theater as Therapy" highly pertinent to the treatment needs of disturbed adolescent young people. Her technique of fusing the creative potentials of patients with their personal problems and as a means of revealing these problems is most effective. As Director of Re-Education at the Institution where Mrs. Rabinow had carried out her early experiments, I had an opportunity to observe her work and was convinced of the effectiveness of her procedures.

At a time when adolescents are generally more emotionally disturbed than ever before and when delinquency is on a rise at an almost alarming pace, her method of reaching them would be of great social value. A book such as this with its practical suggestions and details of operation should, and undoubtedly will, have wide and enthusiastic acceptance.

S. R. Slavson,
Consultant, Staff Development,
Brooklyn State Hospital, Brooklyn, N.Y.

Although Celia Avramo Rabinow's book on the theater as therapy is based on her work with youth whose behavior is antisocial and in conflict with their environment, there are much larger issues to which the report of her work addresses itself.

Behavior theory still imperfectly conceptualizes the unitariness or holism of personality and adaptation. The dichotomy persists in our theory between the psychic, inner life and the social experience of the individual person, in health and in illness. Individual psychodynamics and the dynamics of his group ex-experience are delineated separately with inadequate synthesis. Inevitably treatment efforts and schools of thought about treatment reflect this dichotomy.

The signal thing about *the theater as therapy* is its contribution to the challenge of synthesis of inner and outer, psychic and social, experience of individual persons and of therapeutic approaches to them. Mrs. Rabinow illumines the reciprocity and mutual reinforcement of the clinical and social therapy.

More specifically theater work is a particular kind of social therapy. The behavior-disordered children who are Mrs. Rabinow's subjects suffer from lack of ego integration, low tolerance for anxiety and externalization of conflict—or more aptly from fixated inability to internalize component features of their social experience during their developmental years. They war with the outside instead of warring with themselves. Instead of tolerating certain affects, they translate them into action and destructive behavior turned outward.

Mrs. Rabinow describes how in a carefully-nurtured process these youths are inducted further into the world of feeling and emotion, first, awkwardly and then with increasing commitment, by assuming the emotional mantle of *dramatis personae;* then using this as a bridge to the awakening of anaesthetized affects within themselves and to *owning* them as their own. The pseudo hard-boiled youth discovers tenderness within himself as he fumbles to express the tenderness of a dramatic role. The youth who fends off awareness of his own inner rage by immediate translation of it into destructive action learns through dramaturgy, and at first at vicarious arms length, to express anger through words and gesture, and comes closer thereby to connections to his own anger.

This is only one of the vital aspects of the total experience of the youth in the hands of the skilled, therapeutically-oriented dramatic coach. Mrs. Rabinow discusses the importance of the participation in a group whose members must effectively complement each other achieving a desired, *creative* effect, and of over-arching influences, there is the mutual engagement of individual youth and coach or teacher that gives meaning and coherence to the youth's efforts to feel and express another side of himself.

The book is important not alone to psychiatrists, psychologists, social workers and others in mental health fields who are concerned with delinquent youth, it contributes generic insights into work with the full range of ages and types of patients; the book is not to be viewed narrowly simply as a guide to resident facilities which are interested in use of forms of art as therapy (valuable as it is in this way), but as an inspired addition to the broadening understanding in all fields of the nature of personality, personality and behavior disturbance, and effective portals of therapeutic entry. I would like to see this book in the hands of every mental health practitioner.

November 30, 1976

Sanford N. Sherman
Executive Director
Jewish Family Service
of New York

This is an important book for every worker in the helping professions. Psychiatrists or psychoanalysts, psychologists or caseworkers all work with the basic concept of sublimation. This volume details with sublimation.

While the literature abounds with theoretical papers on the subject of sublimation it was not until recently that artists concerned with the therapeutic aspect of the creative process have begun to illustrate the process. To my knowledge this book is the first genuine attempt to detail the process as applied to the theatre. That this by itself new venture is also set against the background of "delinquent" youth makes the book particularly significant. The author takes the reader into her workshop, the stage and introduces us to the very particular young people who have participated in the development of her unique method. In the process she also manages to clarify, without ever theorizing, the long confused notion of "acting out," as distinguished from "play-acting" or "acting-in." It certainly makes it clear that "acting" as developed by the author can indeed go beyond a primitive mode of the ego to bring about reconstruction. Without this method and the trained director-therapist there will not be enough neutralized energy cathexis for higher forms of ego organization—hence sublimation would fail, while with the author's ingenious and truly original technique and sensitivity, an interim form of communication is made possible.

While this book is in no sense a research report it contains longitudinal follow-up studies of the youthful participants. This obviously validates the method for certain character types and, incidentally takes care of such confused derivatives as "psycho-drama," "role-playing"—none of which reach the level of sublimation.

The same careful and patient approach that was needed to evolve the author's method is used in the description. The book requires slow and careful reading, not because the language is difficult or the philosophical sections cumbersome, but because the concept of "Theater as Therapy" is complex and infinitely interwoven with all aspects of the human psyche.

It is hoped that it will find its way to all thoughtful and concerned workers in the behavioral sciences.

Dr. Rudolph D. Wittenberg P.H.D.
Child Analyst

New York,
June 15, 1976

Preface

It has been my privilege to make with some two hundred delinquent—and neurotic—children a five-year excursion into a little world we built together in fellowship, albeit in turmoil and with ups and with downs, but always with ahead of us a comparative goal to reach both in artistic achievement and in personal growth. This book is the tale of our odyssey.

These pages make no pretense at esoteric revelation; they are not written in the language of the clinical specialist, for the theater I present is the universal theater and the language I employed with the children usually was purposely the glamorous language of the stage and its working people. What is new are the techniques I used in taking by the horns all that was already there in old-fashioned theater and in turning it inside out for the maturing experiences each child could separately get in the direction of adjustment. Whatever happened through the theater process to or among the children seems simple and logical to me, and I have tried to write it this way in the hope that others will want to carry on the work, especially in schools where the predelinquent may be prevented from becoming the delinquent.

To the reader who has found wearying the normal putting on of a play with children my spirit may often seem utopian, but this will only be because I stress the results in terms of children, which even in my fifth year still gave me cause frequently for marveling. It may be he will have to reevaluate the reasons for putting on plays, also his knowledge of children, especially the adolescent, and also his personal equipment with which he has approached his task. I acknowledge that I am decreeing an even more trying job for the adult who must be director, technician, and manipulator of environment, the soul of kindness and a stern parent, standard-bearer, and a

Solomon of wisdom, a good fellow, and yes, often a bad "guy" shouldering hostility. But these are the *sine qua non* which though they frazzle the nerves leave the person whole and satisfied, for there is always the concrete evidence that a socially unapproved child is becoming an acceptable and accepting person.

Knowing the egotistical pitfall which often traps the experimenter into stretching the truth when he turns writer, I have checked myself in these pages by alotting a great part of them to what the children in their own words recount of their awareness of experience, changes, and adjustments, or of the cultural satisfactions which have widened their horizons. A letter, a poem, a page from a play, a dialogue, or a self-evaluation—these are authentic materials springing from the renascent spirits of socially maturing children, and it is necessary that their voices be heard as proof that theater used with a method and a plan becomes truly a painstaking tool for carving personality.

Because I want so much for children to be helped along a way I found useful, I answer a criticism about my work that what I accomplished was due not so much to techniques but to a special kind of personality which I possess. Well, this brings back to me two episodes of childhood, and my point will be that what the person *is* so does he *do*. The two are inseparable, and I am certain that only those whose personalities are prepared for coping with the task I describe will be inspired actively to undertake it and to add their own contribution. I had a drawing teacher in public school whose method of criticism was to punch, with muscular abandon, a tearing hole through one's precious drawing; the tool was a sharp pencil, the very symbol of what I hoped one day to be—a teacher of drawing. It changed my plans for life, for more than rejecting her children she rejected the arts themselves, both the art of teaching and the magic we were supposed to learn to create with mere lead on paper. But in high school there was an English teacher—hallowed be her name, Miss Perkins—whose greatness, revealed in a split second of time, taught me all of pedagogy and of the child-adult equation I have ever learned: respect for the child as a person. Whatever I was able to do later with children derives from this principle.

It happened thus. In the oral English period, I stood with shaking knee introducing the class to a discovery I had made—Walt Whitman. She stopped me to correct a mispronounced word. "Please wait till I have finished; you are disrupting my thoughts," I answered.

My heart had almost stopped beating, for never had I been so disrespectful. But no word came from her, only a gesture, a lowering of her head. I remember the corporate amazement of the class because authority did not mark me down and send me to my seat as I continued my trembling but ecstatic report on the poet. I am sure Miss Perkins had no special philosophy of education. From the flush on her face she was going through an ordeal, for she had a position to maintain before the class. But apparently, too, she saw a child driven by a creative impatience to go on with her subject. With swift insight she read the girl's true attitude; out of fairness and out of respect she capitulated and by her humbled head acknowledged her own error. That silent resignation affected me poignantly. I seemed suddenly to understand the adult's part in the world. Could this teacher have done this beautifully difficult thing if she weren't as she sat there a totality of qualities which made her personality a "special kind"?

On such fragile influences do we grow, and this I have always tried to remember in my relationship with children already blighted in their regard for the adult word or action. Delinquent children are world-wise in their years; they see through to the core of us, make their judgments on our deeds, they decide by what we are whether or not maturity is a hoax or a state worth climbing to. If people specializing with delinquents would but know it isn't they, but we, who are under examination. Thus it has been my privilege to have passed the scrutiny of their shrewd young hearts and to have been accepted as their adult leader on the road to better things.

If I have helped them, and if by this theater experiment I have contributed my bit to the treatment field of delinquency, I have two men to thank. In this practical world rare are the men with vision enough to give ear and a hand to the newcomer fresh with an idea or a plan for something untried. Dr. Harmon S. Ephron, psychoanalyst, proved to be such a man when as an inspired and inspiring friend, despite my position as lay-person unschooled in the psychiatric or casework field, he encouraged my ideas, gave me faith in myself for the task, and introduced me to the Hawthorne Cedar Knolls School. The other was Prof. Harry Shulman, then the director of the school, whose warm acceptance of my outline of work made possible the organization and the continuation of my experiment.

I dedicate this book to these two men; and to all those who in their various functionings give of themselves—and will give—beyond any conceivable line of duty and worldly recompense, to achieve the high goal of recreating boys and girls considered the spoiled, the doomed and the wastrels of society. Many of these will have better destinies thanks to Barney Beryl Rabinow, my departed husband who combining talent for planning with deep caring, shed enlightenment into the dark corners of slumbering educational and treatment systems by pioneering and perfecting programs for the training of teachers of emotionally disturbed and socially maladjusted children. To this end he labored as the supervising principal of the Hawthorne Cedar Knolls School of the Jewish Board of Guardians, and as program director of Children's Village. As writer, and as guest lecturer in various colleges, he opened new vistas of helpful performance to student-teachers and others who would have these children in their care.

And so to him I tender this book IN MEMORIAM; to him, educator, innovator, humanist, and latterly New York City Planner, whom, for his knowledge in many related fields, his wisdom, and his caring for the younger planners, all looked upon as their "Guru." His spirit lives on!

Celia Avramo Rabinow

PART ONE

1

Orientation

Humankind, long before Aristotle named Catharsis as the goal of drama, had out of a profound necessity gropingly evolved for itself theater, for which I should like to substitute the word "therapy." Whatever forms or expressions the devised theater took throughout the centuries, its impulse sprang from a need for, and remains eternally a way of climbing out of, mundane living to a loftier sphere in which the repressed human spirit may expand, may face and rebuild itself. Since the immemorial time when the rewarding harvest called forth ecstatic paens of thanksgiving for the reprieve from elemental anxieties and in the yearly ceremony man reversed upon another creature—the sacrificial goat—his own long-endured cruelties from nature, dramatic expression (through participation or through identification) has brought solace, release, periodic cure, and has helped man to live. Such theater as folk participation has always been ritualistic, charging man's physical manifestations of song and dance and costume and ceremony with his subconscious fears, yearnings, and hopes.

Today, despite our modern outlook and our oft irreverent themes and our rationale about seeking the theater for entertainment, we obey the same impulse and seek the same reprieve. We have not the naïveté of past ages and so we have lost—except for going to church—the spontaneous folk movement in search of our catharsis. We do not participate in theater, but we go to it and get something from it by identification. We go, not consciously but actually, to a darkened auditorium in the same mystical spirit of our ancestors who crowded sanctified places, to find ourselves in a larger life by losing ourselves to the singleness of purpose, experience, and perception of the large multitude. The blackness but illumines by accentuation the portion of life enacted on the stage, and by this same alchemy withdraws the individual body and personal mind on a receding tide and releases instead in every darkened seat a poised and aware spirit cleansed of self and charged electrically to complete the human circuit of universality. Like one body, heart, mind, and soul we absorb the sight, the sound, and the meaning and live through the sorrows and joys vitalized on this pivotal spot of light and shadow we call a stage. Cleansed of our petty mundane cares, we perceive clearly good for good and truth for truth, and we leave the place when the lights at last go up a little better, a little wiser, and a little more confident about living than when we entered. If this is not what happens then the fault is with the play; it wasn't great enough and our discontent is only proof that we have gone to the theater for purification and for learning and that the best in us has been trifled with.

But even the next to a great play has something of the author wiser, profounder, and more intrinsic than all of himself as known to his wife, his friends, or his children, something which has been exacted from him at the price of utmost giving regardless of personal returns. This is true of the director, the actor, the designer, the stage hands. Despite bickerings and cares, jealousies, ailments, and all the gamut of individual human weaknesses, all together submerging self combine to weld into a product of beauty so fragile and insubstantial a thing as a night's vehicle for catharsis. Each contributes his vision and his truth from the depth of his knowledge and his art. Each gives that by which he lives, for the bread—or the luxuries—earned by it are incidental to the spirit's prime necessity for its most honest expression. It is remarkable that so temperamental a group as actors are can accomplish to perfection so complex a thing as a production. As a class, too, they are more benevolent to their fellows in need than any other; it must be that the common experience in an exacting—and in the final analysis a selfless—profession brings them close together in their common humanity. Together they do, separate they fail. They travel the same ship over which there are many masters—the author, the director, the public, the producer—whom to serve well, all at the same time, requires a capacity for adjustment to situations and to people greater than is asked of most of us; and though these personal masters change in face and in name, always is the actor in abnegated service to a never changing, imperious, and impersonal master—art.

Art, or theater, like the church or like all bigger than personal spheres of performance, imposes disciplines but balances them with an unbroached bargain, to wit—by giving yourself wholly shall you grow abundantly, meaningfully. And this, too, like the multitude's search for the meaning of life is in essence a catharsis. Something unusual happens when the actor sweats beneath the klieg lights to understand and interpret his role. All of the human vanities fall away, for the mood is one of consecration; and in that moment when he has achieved his best, something of awe, something shining like very great love comes to him from the eyes of his fellows who have been watching. Actors have frailities like the rest of us but what is often called temperament and pettiness are "nerves" from giving too much without the chance for recuperation. Very profoundly, behind the tensions are fine emotional attitudes of tolerance, respect, cooperation, service.

This theater which I describe as rooted in the needs of mankind and which today we self-consciously seek for "entertainment" has for these very reasons an authentic claim on the imagination of the adolescent. The delinquent adolescent has lost his way, but he is at the time of his life when regeneration may come if new experiences charge his personality with vivid and aware excitements more meaningful and more pleasurable than his delinquencies have proven to be. The delinquent is a trapped spirit seeking yet rejecting his surrounding world of form and order because something in his immediate world is all wrong. He is the epitome of man in his primitive beginnings seeking warmth, security, well-being, and receiving instead a burden of pressures and pains.

Mankind as a mass found instinctual recompense in blood sacrifice to appease the cruelties of the gods; might this not have been the folk way—to vengefully transpose man's role, anthropomorphizing the animal to assume in a mad holiday the pleasurably cruel powers of the gods, thus rejecting them? As an individual in a more complicated world, the delinquent reacts as primitively. He rejects authority and assumes powers. He takes his instinctual revenge by also calling a holiday against fate. A creature, he plays at being a god; and his doings pleasurably chaotic, secretive though guilt-laden, nourished by the fire of rebellion, are in the nature of mysteries to him, rituals by which he seeks to balance the turmoil he can neither understand nor cope with. Actually he is evolving theater by which to live, albeit while making us the goat he further entraps himself.

It is so unsound and so unfair to pigeonhole him into a classroom to tell him to be good by precept. We tell him to be honest while we approach him with our first dishonesty, the whitewashing our world of "form and order" which we so often ourselves find intolerable. We ask him to emulate the spoken virtues when watching us he has learned about lies and backbiting and greed. What are the things we ask of him? A dull honesty which packs him in poverty or in rejection in what is supposed to be a home. Working for a living which earns him yearly less than one hour's gallant thieving. Attention to studies when truancy teaches him so much. Gentleness, decency, high-thinking which to his knowledge either do not exist or pay the least rewards. Courage to face reality when actually life nets you only what you take out of it by force. How farcical to expect his return to us from his transposed role filled with private and thrilling ecstasies! What do we offer for his return to authority, to law and to order that does not seem cowed, dull and uninteresting by comparison? What do we plan for him to induce a *need* to "behave"?

I continue the analogy of man and his catharsis, expressing first the hope that nothing will be read into my thinking which I do not intend, as for instance an isolated evaluation of the theater as man's supreme accomplishment, or an undue matter of factness in the identifaction of the delinquent with the folk. But there is this similarity between the modern child of man and the ancient childhood of man—the process of adjustment to life. The adolescent child and the adolescent race are similarly narcissistic, solitary, ritualistic, shaking an angry fist at the heavens. The race acclimatized itself to fate, making its relative conquest by meeting it halfway. This is what we want to happen to the delinquent for his good and for the good of the future generations whom he will sire. Mankind groped its way slowly through the ages, speeding up the process with its maturing; we have no time to wait with the delinquent and all depends upon what we do *with* him and *for* him *today*.

I see mankind with progress changing its attitudes and expressions (despite all our ills) from the self-centered to the universal, from the mystical to the humanistic. I see these changed attitudes evolve the social theater of identification out of the mystically ceremonial theater of participation. Man's experience in awareness and in human solidarity made the modern theater where he now goes to see himself in the universal stream as one *inseparable* from the common destiny, to get through tears or laughter a reiteration of his belief in the goodness and dignity of himself and his fellowmen. But still the people *of* the theater remain participants, call them actors and stage crew, or priests and priestesses in a cult dedicated to the cathartic needs of their fellow people; because this consecrated service which they render apparently to art is actually, remote as it may seem, an obeisance to the mass without whose need they could not professionally exist. So modern participation *in* theater is in essence identification with those *outside* the theater. To each other, to the audience, stage folk are obliged by their dedication to man's need and by their consecration to their art to live more profoundly than the rest of us *in identification*.

When some years ago I undertook the work described here, I took my inspiration from the total picture drawn above—from man's cathartic history, from the theater's present form and the special all-engrossing service it exacts from its servants. From its mystical appeal to imagination and its embracing hold on the total personality, I took the cue which led directly to theater as a milieu and a process where and by which the adolescent delinquent through *intensive* participation might work out his personal catharsis, that is, might achieve his identification with the world or make his adjustment to life.

It is well here to define the world "catharsis" as not used in the clinical sense. Clinically, a patient is said to have a catharsis when he discharges pent-up emotions after he has been helped to recall forgotten and painful experience to which he did not react with adequate emotion at the time. I use the word in its truly dramatic meaning in that the child entering the theater will be a wayfarer into a new life and as such will be a protagonist in the classic sense in which time and experience—and the suffering through the conflicts of one's negative and awakening natures—will be the factors in bringing harmony finally to the disquieted spirit. In this meaning there is the ultimate catharsis or the rebirth of the being and this is like a mountain peak to reach which one needs to climb in slow succession many minor peaks, or impacting moments of searing and healing, or small catharses. Simply it is the climax of a process of learning to live by living; in which process one goes through the step of blind, rebellious tearing at knots that bind, then slowly climbs the steps where oneself unwinds them by making certain acknowledgments and concessions to life in a spirit of complete consciousness and personal responsibility. In the complete experience dormant memories are stirred and painful emotions discharged along the way; meanwhile, newer memories are impressed upon the psyche as a result of cleaner emotions born of purpose and of hope never experienced before.

Using a theatrical concept, why do I speak of theater as

therapy? The misery and the guilt, the entanglements, the frustrations, the vulnerability, and the withdrawals of the delinquent—and the neurotic child—are in essence the failure of his instinctive seeking his catharsis or the balancing of his life and the quieting of his person. The salutary experiences necessary for this he has not been able to make for himself as a substitute for the guidance he has needed from those about him. In theater—in its exalted yet human environment and in its enticing engrossments—lie the treatment potentials for guided salutary experience. Herein, if the adult leader but knows how to fashion it, is a new, wholesome climate in which the child may become well.

The virtues of this new climate for the newcomer are a new ground to trod and a fresh air untainted by the past to breath. Without questions asked a beautiful world in entrusted to him to build bigger and better. Here the child finds unexpected springs for nurturing his new roots and unforeseen springboards for experimenting with new emotions. The theater atmosphere abounds in unheralded surprises, not the least of which for the delinquent is the visible enlargement of himself as one endlessly variable, capable and decent; for the treasures of this engrossing world must be dug for, sought by trial and error and by the sweat of one's brow, and when found and accumulated must be shared with one's fellows. And all the findings and the doings, he learns though they lead ahead toward a bright horizon never bring one to the goal except by the pooling of efforts to the same purpose and in the same direction. So he starts with his troubles and discontents and learns from the inherent ethics of the theater process something about the rules of life. He learns slowly, but he learns the lessons with his hands, his eyes, his mind, his emotions, and his nerves. His subjective experiences mirrored in the objective world built by himself give him in time two staves of support, *awareness*–learning, knowing, weighing, and choosing; and *solidarity*–the sense of belonging in weal and in woe, thus repeating the history of man.

It is evident that I do not speak of a clinical theater, which may be good for the very young and for the adult who *wills* to have himself cured of emotional disturbances. The adolescent, as soon as he will have grasped the purpose of such treatment, must rebel, for on top of all his rejections he finds himself treated like a "nut"; besides which a stage for acting out a role, no matter to what good purpose of a clinically oriented director, is not an environment for learning how to live by living out one's patterns against the patterns of others. Nor do I mean by theater what some call dramatics, which allows for narcissistic satisfaction through an occasional play for such a nebulous goal as culture or for what is called the expression of creative energy. These are anticlimactic goals since they are inherent, along with other factors, in all theater activity, and the good they do as the be-all and the end-all of theater work—besides the pleasurable preoccupation they afford—is accidental. They set a temporary sparkle on the outer personality, perhaps add slightly to the child's knowledge of literature and people, but rarely touch the inner being. The error of such activity lies in the fact that both leader and children have the same aim, the producing of the play, when this in the adult should be merely his apparent aim for the purpose of incentive, guidance, and stimulaiton.

His orientation should be, not to the mustering of children into a play, but to the individual child as a totality in relation to the other children, and in relation to the complete enterprise which will result in the producing of a play. Such orientation has for its goal not the expression of creative energy but the *tapping* of creative energy in the forgotten child that from its unexpected flow and exercise he may gain satisfaction in himself and in his world. Dramatics as given in the schools rewards the talented and the well behaved; the children who need it most never have a chance. Pity the withdrawn child, the stutterer, the physically awkward, the troublesome child with energies which might be directed into healthy channels.

Theater as therapy is theater in capital letters, a glamorous place, colorful and richly human, a world to work in and to build up with props and scripts and makeup and construction; where time is a determining factor in the accumulation of experiences which are to form positive habits and attitudes. Here the director is the understanding person, as well as the theater person, resourceful and consecrated to the arts as though the creative life were the only possible one. He has a double set of techniques. He wields one set as high priest of the temple of Thespis, imposing high standards and an obligation concerning the date set for the play as a holy responsibility. He wields the other set as a therapist observing needs, trends, situations, attitudes, originating—within the great plan—other plans to meet these needs, situations, trends, and attitudes. He invents work meaningfully related to the group project, or he builds a project around a piece of work. He rewrites parts or lengthens plays on the basis of observations. He casts on the basis of the child's personality and frequently allows talent to take a back seat in order to be active otherwise if that will be a better experience for the child. He is the leader of a small democracy, disclosing his plans with their reasons and encouraging the same in the children. As a giving person he represents the best of the adult world. He invites a transference to him as the alter ego who supplants eventually the antisocial heroes of the delinquent era.

To conclude, the theater in organization, multiple interests, and basic appeals has everything useful for the reeducation of personality provided that the director's orientation is always centered on the child. The production then serves in the dual role of an art expression for the group, and as a way by which the individual learns to live. Thus the theater hall, room, or stage is a controlled environment; it is a community for living; it is a workshop for self-discovery and for the development of work habits and social attitudes; it is a family group united by a common cause, sustained by mutual problems and uplifted by cooperative success. It is a consecrated place where the adult asks nothing but gives all and where the production asks everything and the child gives all. Here in behalf of the great cause, the play, ignorance is accepted as a starting point for learning; ability is accredited the responsibility of being useful. The attitudes "I'm afraid"; "I don't want to"; "I can't"; and "I don't care to" are discouraged, coped with, and changed. Finally, not immediately, the child stands forth stronger and surer of himself as he learns from the daily living situations courage, social approval, and the joys to be had from his changed pattern of behavior. And thus the art process called theater gives a cumulative spur to the life process. Sharing the responsibility for the fate of the group, step by step, day by day, the child is himself re-created.

PROGRAM
Hawthorne Group Theatre
Hawthorne-Cedar Knolls School

In our open-air theatre on the campus

June 12 At 3:45 p.m.

THE HAWTHORNE GROUP THEATRE

PRESENTS
A MUSICAL FANTASY
"THE CLOCK SHOP"

Cast of Characters

The Clockmaker .... *Harry*
False Alarm .... *Hyman*
Cuckoo Clock .... *Morris*
Hans .... *Isadore*
Gretchen .... *Mollie*
Grandfather Clock .... *Nathan*
Modern Clock .... *Rose*
1st Dutch Clock .... *Doris*
2nd Dutch Clock .... *Sidney*
3rd Dutch Clock .... *Abe*
4th Dutch Clock .... *Helen*
5th Dutch Clock .... *Mollie*
Little Boy Blue .... *Irving*
Father Time .... *Jack*

SCENE

A Clock Shop—A world of Illusion in which clocks live a glorious short life of their own.

PROGRAM NOTES

All prop clocks and costumes for "Human Clocks," all the effects in the staging of the entire production have been made by the cooperative labors of twenty-two boys and girls.

FOR THE HAWTHORNE GROUP THEATRE

Construction Crew . . . . *Jack*
Harold
Jack
Hymie
Sidney

Art Crew . . . . *Morris*
Abe
Hymie
Bernard
Rose
Mollie
Lillian
Mollie
Doris
Helen

Stage Crew . . . . *Harold*
Irving
Jack
Hymie

Costumes . . . . *By the girls in the Group Theatre*

Piano Accompaniment . . . . *Anna*

Director of Group Theatre . . . . *Miss Celia Avramo*

ACKNOWLEDGEMENTS

The Group Theatre thanks the following staff members for their co-operation. For their musical contribution in the orchestration: *Miss Unger and Mr. Barney Rabinow*
For her patient instruction of the pianist: . . . . *Miss Mary Horn*

Three boys speak about the Group Theatre

I.K.

"The Group Theatre is not only for the correction of the boys—their behavior, that is the creation of Morals and giving them a backbone and confidence; it is something to fall back on, and not to feel downhearted, and the correction of their speech, and the experience not to stay 'I can't,' and to lose self-consciousness and their nervousness through going on a stage before an audience. Also the theater work includes several trades which are of interest to the boys now, and for the future too. . . It has helped me conquer my biggest enemy, stubborness! And gee, when I remember the first batten I cut. . . . And now I feel I can hold down a job."

M.S.

"I want to publicly thank the Theatre Group for all the things I have learned. I don't mean only acting and scenery. I mean especially that I want to thank our director of the Group Theatre for what it has taught me for now when I am going home, and for the future, in the different ways, how to live."

H.B.

"I loved words so I signed up for the Group Theatre because it had a nice sound—Hawthorne Group Theatre. Though I wasn't aware of it, I believe it was my salvation. . . . My speech improved. I am an active participant in various activities. No longer do I slink off into corners. Conversation is a fairly easy matter now, I am less self-conscious. . . . Hawthorne Group Theatre, I am fervently for you, with three cheers and a few huzzas thrown in."

All quotations are given with permission of the boys.

2

Theater As Appeal

There may or may not exist a racial memory of mystical ritual or of orgiastic catharsis. Still, children—out of what instinct?—clamor for theater or its popular version, the movies. To break their hearts just take away their periodic privilege of sitting for hours in the stale halls, in the smoke-filled balconies, immobilized, wrapped up body and soul in what is happening magically on the screen. Or, wherever there are dramatic groups for children, see the noble importance child actors assume; or more revealing, observe the absorbed wistfulness of other children peeking in at a rehearsal, or hanging around stubborn against appeal and dismissal alike, or bartering with some humble gesture of helpfulness to be allowed to stay.

The first weeks of my work at Hawthorne I had evidence of this attraction in a negative way. There were boys of stern loyalties on the campus. An office clerk had been sponsoring theatricals of the variety theater type. These were quickly gotten together affairs of noise and doubtful jokes and pranks, the choice over which the adult showed little leadership. My presence and my plans for a real theater were a threat to the status quo. I was a stranger with a new idea. The other lady was a known quantity who led the boys as they led. A handful had been won over by our conversations, here and there on the campus, as a preliminary to my organizing the theater group; the others remained enemies. With the several—we were not yet using our permanent quarters—I began rehearsing a play in the Assembly Hall to warm up a feeling for the stage which needed building up, and for the properties and equipments called for by the manuscript, which I hoped the boys would be inspired to make. Crash

. . . bang . . . crash . . . a pounding of fists . . . a stone. One day, a second, a third. Another pane in the glass door broken. Day by day for two weeks there was this violent ritual against us from some ten or more youths who by the school program were supposed to be elsewhere, in various classes or on work details. Why were they doing it? I could get no answer but a mute shamefacedness and once more a stone or a banging thrust of the door or a forced chaotic entrance, and at my questioning a withdrawal in a chaotic wave. At last I challenged them to stop or I would have to report them. I said, "I have let this be a man to man fight between us (embarrassed smiles) hoping you would stop if you realized what you were doing. I have purposely not called in the supervisor, although the director thought I should have a guard. Make up your mind that we will build this theater no matter how many doors you will break."

At last one of them spoke up for all. "We want to see what you are doing. We want to watch the rehearsal."

"Okay," I said, "but if I hear as much as a pin drop out you go."

The future members of the Group Theater entered. Tense, watchful, absorbed, they did not dare let a pin drop. Then at the end one sound escaped them, a composite sigh or deep intake of breath, and at the door one word, "Thanks."

Theater isn't ordinary fun to youth. Deep streams in the psyche rush them toward it; for each age it has a varying attraction, but altogether it is the same attraction. The drives are complex and often contradictory. Perhaps partly, it is the play instinct for indulging in make-believe—what is outside of one's own ken gains beauty and glamor and is more real to awakened awareness than the mundane realities one seems to know too well. Make-believe, too, as for grown-ups, is escape, well, from such annoying trivia as doing one's lessons, minding the baby, obeying parents. Partly, perhaps, theater is an instinctual directive for growing up quickly, an opportunity for taking life by the forelock and for peeping into its mysteries, something otherwise not permitted to youth except through the drawn-out process of passing time and tide. And, too, theater holds the wonderment of the limitless variations of so great a world, offering vicarious participation in it, that its sounds and colors and personalities and ideas, like unusual toys from exotic lands, are provocative to heightened emotions, to the senses, and to the searching mind. Also, heroes and heroines are furnished, ideal personalities to emulate or to worship and—in egotistical contradiction—to measure one's stature by, not in humble comparison but in the envisaging of identical traits of beauty, skill, charm, daring, strength, or nobility.

Thereby youth finds its courage. The drab little girl imagines herself the queen, or the black witch if the latter role fits her emotional necessity. The big girl sees herself the enchanting siren, or if she is at the age of goals and causes, as the selfless nurse assuaging the pains of the world. The boy identifies himself as the gallant and fearless detective or as the equally gallant and fearless bandit. All this is specially true of the adolescent whose feelers are out to touch and discover every possible perception of life while, meanwhile he is also deeply inward turned to assailing troubles and conflicts which come with growing up. He needs a medium for understanding, comparing, justifying, resolving his uncertainties, desires, hopes, frustrations, his plans childish and grandiose at the same time, and his aspirations often beyond the margin of reality. All unconsciously then, theater is to him what it was to unsophisticated man—and what it still is to us but not so clearly—an escape, an identification, a seeking, and a catharsis or way of rehabilitating oneself during blessed periods of psychic uplift.

I believe the delinquent has even a greater instinct for theater than the average child. His delinquencies have been retaliations, manipulations of the world which attempted to manipulate him. All his acts have been a play concocted by himself, enacted by himself; in his role of protaganist he has held at bay—heroically in his own estimation—father or mother or both and the *greater authority* of the *people;* sometimes outwitted, most often outwitting, but always getting a thrill out of the chaos he has been able to cause. Or, in the guilty and lonely moments when facing himself, self-pity, hate, undue circumstance have given him enough material to color the situation with exaggerated drama. I have observed him in the darkened movie house, for example. When he is present in numbers a play of living actors unfolds itself against the play of shadow actors on the screen. While the average child sits quietly entranced, corporeally lost before the flickering vista, the delinquent becomes overactive, noisesome. He doesn't laugh where others laugh with simple enjoyment of what is funny. His is a pattern of assumed superiority which pretends to scorn the nicer emotions, the tender situations. His mockery is raucous and vulgarly worded; his comments are cynical; he catcalls, whistles, makes the explosive sound of lusty kisses. This moviegoer is a scoffer, and under cover of the black auditorium he concocts his peculiar ritual to punctuate his feeling about us, to shout to us what he feel about himself that *he* is not soft, *he* cannot be fooled by trumpery theatricals. And truly he is sensitive as the other children are not to forced situations, to poor acting; he has lived too much; regardless of his expletive reactions, he knows the real from the false.

But still he is a child, no longer naïve, but beneath the brittle bearing a hurt, woebegone child. Sometimes for long minutes he, too, is silent in his balcony seat; he withholds the clamorous devices of his distraught ego, gets lost in the emotions and manuevers of the screen people, identifies with them despite himself, so identifies with the aims and hopes of all the human family. Short though these periods be—he evens the score by exploding more riotously afterwards—he belongs at these times to eternal youth gleaning through the theater's enactment of others' lives the hope of a complete rapport with life itself. His feelings and his thoughts—unless he is past all help—must be more inward than those of the average adolescent, because his guilts are actual, his doubts drawn from poignant experience, his longings made questionable by his history, his concealed need to belong to the world great.

Theater speaks to him in some very special ways. To him as an American, because publicity is part of our culture, theater is glamorous because theater people are success people. To the delinquent boy, the song-and-dance man, the crooner, the pugilist-actor, the leader of the orchestra spell socialized applause and monetary reward for the jigging, musical noise-making, and corner singing for which he himself has been cornered by the cops and branded by his family a no-account. To the delinquent girl, by a similarly devious logic, the beauty, clothes, fabulous salaries, and fame of sex-appealing stars spell society's approval—if one reaches far enough—of her own professionalized femaleness. In this aspect theater—though not consciously—has a direct personal appeal to the insecure ego, standing as a solid bulwark of proof of one's own rightness.

From this vantage point it can be seen how theater as an unusual world removed from sordid reality, yet holding forth justification and hope, must awaken in the delinquent personality a driving curiosity. The spotlight on Benny Goodman is the spotlight on one's own hallowed person. The light assumes proportions. Where does it come from; how is it done? The chairs obviously golden or silver, the trappings and unusual backgrounds, tricks of scenery, the clothes of the women, the tailoring of the men, and more lights and more scenic effects. A subjective interest becomes an objective study, an unworded wistfulness to see, to touch.

To all children, theater—the chance to partake of it

intimately—rings a bell more thrillingly invitive than a fire alarm. As against the subconscious urges which make them go *to* the theater, the response to participation *in* it is a very conscious self-centeredness and so expressed frankly in words or in the subtle alertness of the person. They see themselves in movement, in a complete abandonment, to pleasurable exhibitionism. Every child wants "a big part." They see the stage sets as a background for themselves. It isn't as simple, of course, as I have just put it, for dimly in the psyche is the memory of all the other meanings theater has for them. But it never means hardship, work, planning, skills, slow processes, doing things together, sharing with others their successes. It never means order, cooperation, obedience, responsibility, and never fortunately adult interference or authority.

Upon this last *never* rests paradoxically the adult's power to make theater mean these things to the child after the universal appeals of theater have brought him inside its portals. Every child is an opportunist in getting what he wants, the delinquent more than others. When he seeks participation in theater he envisages no tedious trials for himself; he swims in a sensory flood of anticipatory delights pleasurable to his ego. Hence he accepts the adult, as he would not a teacher. The adult is merely an agent through whom to gain one's ends—a rather glamorous agent because of his glamorous knowledge and experience. Herein lies an unusual condition in the child attitude toward the adult. This one differs from other adults in that his requests are not interpreted as authoritativeness but as authority in the ways and means of organizing and perpetuating pleasure for the child. He is a *special* adult outside one's usual reactibility to adults. It is this unguarded softening in the child which makes it possible to *lure* him—why not use an honest word?—gently by the indirect route of clearly egotistical anticipations into the direct and intricate bypaths on which life and theater go together, assume in fact the same form pointing imperiously to the same rules on a single scale of balances. The director's power to make theater a socializing catharsis lies in the fact that he does not remove pleasure or any of the anticipated satisfactions; but his point of contact with children or his specialness permits him the necessary strategies for changing the values or meaningfulness of pleasure and of the anticipated satisfactions.

How explain the swift obeyance of that unruly group which tried to break down my door? If we recall Liliom, a slap, too—or a stone—may be love. The breaking down of doors, interference with rehearsals, destroying stage property (this happened often), mocking the efforts of other children, was not dissimilar behavior to what these same children would show in a darkened cinema. Actually I was five feet one and half inches standing up to ten hostile stalwarts; but I was that special person! Afterwards I could make them literally sweat their bodies and break their backs even on a long Sunday when in the field there was a ball game on; I could make them—rather the change of values about pleasures and satisfactions could make them—remain tied to labors and to duties when the blood was quick with the desire to run away, when restless urges beckoned from the open road promising heady, quick indulgences.

We have seen that the appeals of theater do not necessarily prompt children to accept active participation in a theater. The delinquent personality blankets in one bed differing individualities. The exhibitionist, the intellectual child, the talented and the ambitious child rush to register enthusiastically. The withdrawn child, the self-conscious, the diffident, and the dull show wistful faces but dare not act until a number of plays with their attendant excitements have so roused the community that their own timidity, reserve, or lethargy has been broken down; just as often they do not enter at all unless encouraged, urged, pushed; but these are the children hanging to the periphery of theater ready to serve in humble ways, watchful, the hunger in their eyes. The lone-wolf type, though he goes in packs, we have already met above.

All children cannot participate in the theater project, for practical reasons. But—if only a portion of the population belongs to the theater *directly;* the majority also belongs, vicariously. Theater is not an isolated thing; it is for and of the community. If the smaller group constitutes the inner circle, initiates to the "mysteries," the outer circle constitutes the important audience whose approval and pleasure cause the nice things on the stage to have social value. And though the project aims specifically for the adjustment of its inside members, its educative, cultural, and human influences enrich the larger, peripheral mass. A theater in an institution is a living essence binding all its members, at least periodically despite difficulties and differences into one common humanity. It lifts the level of institutional life out of the humdrum plane, for its very existence *dramatizes* life. Everybody knows of the ups and downs of the forthcoming play; everybody sighs or makes merry over the troubles and triumphs respectively; everybody is keyed up, everybody awaits the "date"; jealousies, antagonisms, and other attitudes notwithstanding, everybody weeps, sighs, or laughs together.

3

"Bad" Boys and Girls

We are at the Hawthorne Cedar Knolls School on the tree-bordered path which leads between the boys' cottages and the school buildings. A "bad" boy walks beside me. He moves, speaks, and gesticulates in rhapsodic abandon to the high mood which goads him. To an outsider the vignette may present a too free attitude on his part as with unabashed gesture he interlocks his arm in mine. But come closer, stranger! Apelike this boy may seem, and small for his almost seventeen years, and in need of a shave, and indeed, in need of a bath, for he is just returning from the farm. All the more do I marvel at his blue eyes star-filled with a trace of tears. These eyes and his voice are melodizing an inner harmony it has taken most of a year to build.

Words, phrases, pauses come in a rhythmic ebb and flow in the effort to articulate a discovery he had made about himself. At this moment Milton is closer to felicity than virtue can ever be; he has stood at the foot of the burning bush; he has earned his portion in the promised land. It is true, slightly below the border of awareness, the boy's possessive arm is charmingly masculine, but it isn't for me at this time to let him know it, for this, too, is a symptom of growth. Homosexual activity has been one of his serious troubles. Another has been ungovernableness. But here he is in friendship with an adult, uncovering his secret heart.

Milton gives a happy laugh, part irony, part whimsy. "Ha! To think," says he, "that I'm a gentleman now. Eight months ago before I joined the Theater House, what a bum I was. Now I open doors softly. I say thank you. I think of other people. I used to do things, you know, and not care. Now I suffer if I do anything wrong. Now I think about everything—it's funny because I just used to do things without thinking, I just *did* them." A weighted silence, then, "Do you know what I think? Maybe it is because I have learned to love somebody outside of myself." He wants an answer, so I say, "But you love your mother [the father is dead]." There is no hesitancy in the reply which comes with a self-scornful "Ha!" "Yes," he asks, "that is selfish love, isn't it, loving your mother, like loving yourself?"

How far has Milton gone, and others, since that first evening when on this same path I stood with the director of the school observing the passing file of boys on their way to supper! July, a mellow five o'clock, not too warm, a poised silence in the air bringing quietude and peace. The youths came by, not too noisily, in fact subdued in movement and in voice. But they brought something with them—the delinquent personality! En masse, shorn of individuality, it reproduced its character boy by boy along their tenuous approach, like a monstrous thing less than human. It showed itself in eyes which could not look straight into ours, in faces shrewd and secretive yet willful, in body rhythms either restive or lagging; it spoke in the sound of shuffling feet—whenever a boy was stopped to be spoken to—or feet shifting the body's weight incapable of keeping a poised base.

These were the boys, and Milton among them, for whom I had burned my bridges behind me, to whom I had come in a consecrated mood to work with and for! I was horrified. It had sounded easy on paper, but face to face with this sick gutter personality I upbraided myself with the hopelessness of the task. I accused myself of windmill heroics in having assumed my plan was good for anything. Why, these were the same boys from whom I pulled my skirts away and called bums when as a young girl I was molested by them on the streets! I had been afraid of them; now I had chosen of my own accord to live with them; it would be impossible! Their passing had changed the climate. The quiet air seemed shattered with boding, the sunbeams playing through the trees accentuated a hovering gloom. Then I remembered something, one of those experiences given us rarely, when in an unusual situation, despite ignorance and fear, we happen to do the one *right* thing by which we grow wiser. Bums! A flock of them throwing snowballs, in a very bad neighborhood, and myself, about fourteen years old, wearing glasses and carrying a heavy bundle. There is another girl of the same age with me and both of us are at the mercy of the flying missiles. We are trapped on all sides by the prancing and shouting and pleasure-drunk boys. What makes me do it I do not know, for I am afraid. I put the bundle down; I face the gang; I address them by saying something about its not being sporting to attack a person with glasses. Certainly I expect nothing of what happens. First, open-mouthed amazement in that male army; then not a word in response; and finally, like the waters of the Red Sea for the Hebrews, there is a recession, a movement backward in slow retreat. We proceed in freedom on our way and my friend says cryptically—"Boy-tamer!" I walk silently with mixed feelings of a victory scored and a knowledge, a wondrous knowledge growing on me that "bums" aren't really bad, not when they're treated decently and when you show no fear of them. Later, through the years with this type of boy and girl, what has always struck me is how little they differ actually from other children, how likeable most of them are, how scintillating and vital many of them are, how sensitive to beauty and good all of them are. The exception, a certain type of psychopath.

Of girls I will not have as much to say as of boys because for various reasons the theater experiment did not include them completely enough. For instance, eight months in Milton's experience with the Theater Group meant daily exposure to the activity, with weekends and holidays included. Milton and all the boys were given a concentrated dose of the theater environment in which time, cumulative experience, exposure to situations, and a growing relationship with their leader—myself—were the essential ingredients. This was not usually possible with the girls.

The Hawthorne Cedar Knolls School was predominantly a boys' school. Seven out of ten children I worked with were boys who all lived on my side of the campus. The girls lived at its extreme end some three blocks distant from the central school and cottage buildings. Their daily routine, the special character of their delinquencies (in most cases), their accentuated neurotic narcissism, their mass incorrigibility made a permanent working arrangement impossible. Girls with sex offenses especially are unbridled women, at thirteen, or at eighteen; they are not as amenable as boys to constructive enduring activities, except in individual cases where there is a strong drive because of some talent, aptitude, or very personal interest. Theater work had to be introduced to the girls on the basis of their vanity, that is, under the thesis that they could learn to speak and walk better, that they would develop their personalities, in short that they would be helped to become more pleasing females. A few girls like Sylvia were the exceptions (Suicidal Sylvia, pp. 27, 111, 185). The majority followed the same pattern year after year. They left; others came; it was always the same. In contrast to the most outspoken, the most overactive or aggressive boys, the girls were the extroverts, each one looking upon the theater experience as a stepping-stone to glamor, as a means of learning how to take the place of a preferred Hollywood or nightclub darling.

My meeting with the girls was in the nature of a bolt from the nether regions. My plans and my arrangement with the school called only for my working with boys. For a week, in their cottage, the former had indulged in a beauteous nightmare of rioting. They had to be segregated, kept from our end of the campus, even from attending classes. In an institution the slightest tremor of a shakeup of morale, in one corner, steals its way in some underground manner to all the corners of the place; immediately there is sensed in all the children its unstabilizing effect. The director appealed to me to see what I could do.

When I crossed their threshold I entered a seething ocean in which I was not prepared to swim. I am not dramatizing. Literally, the eighteen or so girls were the incarnation of the furies. Most of them with bulbous breasts and wild hairdos moved about like lashed billows hither and thither, yelling sounds which were incantations, for the words could not be made out. A few sat listless apparently without nerves. Our appearance increased the storm. There were no inhibitions. Vile imprecations were hurled at the director. I believe I learned more street language in the first ten minutes than I ever heard in all the years from the boys. My knees felt pretty weak. How was I going to handle this wild mob? Any of those girls topped me by a head. But we had arranged between us that the director would leave me with them, alone.

Somehow the tension subsided, somehow they quieted, sat and listened. The noisiest of them placed a chair for me. Why? Was it because my visit changed the monotony of life? Was it because I talked quietly as though nothing were wrong? In a few words I brought them the gift of the theater project. They weren't all interested in that, but they listened and soon the girls were taking sides for or againt the expediency of self-control that they might be allowed in a day or two to come to the Theater House. Marie, the girl who gave me the chair, was the loudest against the idea. She was also the loudest to hush the others down when *they* threatened, with *their* excitability, the comparative lush tone of our conference. What a mixture of incorrigibility and the need to make a good impression! It was do or die, and I did. I criticized her—not in a moral tone, not on her behavior, but in that vulnerable domain, her feminine vanity. Surely, lipstick alone does not make a girl attractive, I pointed out, and then spoke of her sitting position—how ungainly; her raucous voice—how hard on the ears; her flamboyant gestures—how disquieting. This was in relation to the theater which could teach her how to sit, walk, speak, and generally could improve her personality.

My attention had the effect of flattery which the others would not be deprived of. They called for, struggled to be the next in turn to get, criticism. Thus did we have our first theater session, our first lesson in awareness. This lesson proceeded actively in exercises in walking, sitting, etc.—actually, in the major exercise of learning control over one's outer actions. I had expected I do not know what terrible outcome from my visit. Instead here were the girls, this boisterous, uncontrolled group, rehearsing over and over again, for instance, how to say with ladylike quality the mundane sentence, "How do you do." On leaving, a sedater group saw me to the door, called out friendly and hopeful greetings about seeing me on the morrow. They were going to become a part of the theater project.

Had they rioted because life wasn't interesting, wasn't purposeful? Sick children they were, but to a large extent, yes, that was the reason. Despite their anxieties, despite their drives, would they have had to release their energies in this way if they had had an overwhelming interest with which to ward off boredom and futility, if they had known what to do with time heavy on their hands?

Such was the human material around which was organized the Group Theater, an art theater which incorporated all the possible arts, skills, and interests inherent in theater or devised especially to interrelate with it. They were children with experience in pilfering, truanting, begging, prostituting, and even in a case or two with a close relationship to rape, arson, and murder. They were children shrewd in the sophistication gleaned from the sordid corners of life—suspicious, adult-hating, rejected and rejecting, callous or too easily vulnerable, guilt-driven, insecure. They were boys and girls from thirteen to seventeen and sometimes eighteen, neurotic delinquent, pure delinquent, and with a sprinkling of the psychopathological to season our group sessions already salted and peppered with clashing personalities. They were children, likable, stimulating, vivid, charming, and challenging.

How stimulating and how challenging to a person bent on helping them one may see from the completer description of a number of the children I encountered among that early batch which made up the group. Milton, whom we have already met, was sixteen, undersized, ugly, oversexed, and practicing homosexuality as an outlet ("What my father could do, so may I . . . I saw him myself in Russia playing with the maid."). Milton was left-handed, nearsighted, had not been in the country long, was a truant, could not read, had a dominating, wilful personality ("That's why I'm up here, because I mixed into my mother's affairs when we lived with my uncle. After all I had to take my father's place since he's dead."). This boy engaged in excessive introspection, suffered guilt beyond bounds. He had a shrewd insight into human behavior. There came a time when a mere lift of my eyebrow told him my meaning or intention or thought. Milton had a poetic and an aspiring mind, a sensuous love for words, genuine goodness of heart.

Harry was sixteen, gangly-legged, boned like Mahatma Gandhi, wore glasses, was a stutterer and a victim of all the inferiorities concomitant with his speech defect. Like the village idiot, he suffered untold mockery and abuse from his very effort to escape this by hiding away from his peers under tables, in corners, behind curtains. The one thing which gave him a sense of harmony was his intellectual escape to books or whatever reading material his hands laid hold of. I soon learned from his rapt silence or his abandoned chuckle coming from beneath somewhere whether he was lost in the funny paper or in more enduring literature. In our private conversations, very painful to the ears but very enlightening, I found he had a sense of humor and a rich appreciation for ideas and for values of beauty. His intellectuality gave him no common ground on which to meet the boys, but it did give him the compensatory sense of superiority for living in his nutshell world of fantasy. With the proper background and care, he could have amounted to something.

Joseph built like a pugilist and, looking twenty, was fourteen. Apparently an insensate clod without interests or desires, he was generally submissive in a lazy and softspoken way. One must imagine the sphinx vocalizing without change of facial expression and its lion's body surging suddenly into action—that was Joseph ready with his fists when the clod stirred at last. He had no mind at all but instead a chilly, self-indulgent, sadistic humor which took advantage of situations when others were tired, troubled, or trying against time or obstacles to finish a job; for example, he would tap me on the shoulder in a repeated rhythm at the height of my making a point to the engrossed children on the stage; or he would whisper close to a boy's ear in the same repetitious rhythm some silly sound just when the other child was anxiously leading his paint brush along a fine line in danger of being smeared. Observation proved to me this was his technique for getting attention and for compensating for his lack of intellect and his clumsiness with tools.

Irving was fifteen with a thick-set body and a stolid unsmiling face; his entire mien was that of a middle-aged gentleman without humor, impassive toward life, but on a very rare occasion there did break through a sunny quality of boyish friendliness and well-meaning. Irving had been as a child an inmate of an orphanage. He came to us for ungovernableness in his home where he had refused to accept a stepfather. His stubbornness had the quality of irrationality; he had to do things his way and under the urgency of receiving immediate satisfaction. He could work with no other child and when crossed threw down his tools with a rush of temper and withdrew into bristling uncommunicative silence. But Irving liked to work. Also he had a profound sense of loyalty not found in such abundance in other delinquents. Irving had a streak of insane, uncontrollable jealousy.

Bert, aged seventeen, was dark, handsome like a screen idol. He was intelligent, cold, and inaccessible, with a charming connivance toward adults. He had a superior air safe in the knowledge that he "put it over" on people. Anger flushed his face darkly, made him seem inhuman. I was warned never to be alone with him as he was a "killer."

Sidney was thirteen and spoke of his brother who was in Sing-Sing. His personality was dull bordering on the mental defective, but by some developed shrewdness from his background, he knew how to outwit suspicions or accusations concerning his behavior at the school. Sidney was restless, incapable of application, moving about constantly as though under compulsion. He had a dogged loyalty to an adult whom he liked (when he broke into my room he took nothing, thus remaining loyal to me and also to the pal who needed help in breaking my lock). Sidney was a burglar and petty thief.

Oscar was seventeen with a large head and bulging forehead which often, with the tendency of his body to slant forward in walking, suggested a less-than-human creature. Oscar was a psychological homosexual, and the others either knew it or sensed it from his movement and the soft curvature of his flesh. This caused hostility from the other boys. To boot, he was a coward, edging always to my protection under the merest gesture from another boy. Ridicule and physical attack were his lot. Mental defective he was, too, with ambitions beyond his capacities, for Oscar had a beautiful voice and wanted a stage career!

Sylvia had been given up by the psychiatrist as unreachable by his method. He said, "See what you can do with her." About fourteen she was ugly, and to make life more unbearable nature had endowed her with talent and with intellect, two attributes which put her

Outdoor Theater: *Aim of project was to develop long-time interest. Materials used were dowel sticks instead of natural wood; the latter would have meant a short-time interest. Dowel sticks allowed for skills in cutting; shaping; and simulating logs through proper painting after observing nature.*

outside of easy companionship with peers. With sexual delinquency she had attempted to compensate for bad looks and for loneliness. But mainly her ugliness gave her a deep sense of rejection which made her suicidal, existing always between two extremes of emotion—an unmovable apathy and a driving, uncontrollable restlessness. In rational moments, perhaps because someone in her family was a pattern maker, Sylvia disclosed her ambition to become a costume designer.

These eight children exemplify merely eight variables, among the many, of individual patterns and problems which were gathered about me in that early group with whom I started off the theater venture. Many other children will pass through these pages, some in a fragmentary way, others to sum up into complete portraits as I see fit to incorporate them with the material of the several chapters. In the end the passage of time, the shared experiences, innumerable intangibles too tenuous for perfect description—but which the reader may sense—and the effects from the techniques I devised to reach and reeducate them will show wholesome happy children no longer "bad" boys and girls.

For with the months, what started as a producing unit to create plays and entertain the campus became, except for eating and sleeping together, a family of struggling-upward youngsters. The Group Theater in the consciousness of these youngsters and in the mind of the community became a symbol for many fine things; it was a house of ardent larbors, a shrine of new ideals, a place for self-expression, a fraternity, a source of learning facts and faults and dreams for the future, a way of unlearning the troubles and traumas of the past. With the years it took on the nature of an ancestral edifice gathering substance and beauty and piling traditions and memories, each passing group handing all this over in trust to succeeding children to nurture and to be nurtured by. With joys and nostalgia, the reeducated or the re-created ones passed on to the newcomers, with the goods they had fashioned, by articulated phrases or by rhapsodic admonitions or by the fulsomeness of their attitudes their cherishment of constructivity and their faith in its love principle as the self-discovered tools with which to face and handle life.

DON'T WORRY TEACHER; PLE—EASE

Apology in verse by a refractory boy

In our chosen club
Work we do not snub.
Work piles thickly,
Hours go quickly,
And we always say
At the close of day—
Don't worry teacher, ple-ease.
Forget your sorrow,
You'll see to-morrow,
Though I acted poorly,
I'll make up surely.
As we always say
Before the great day—
Don't worry teacher, ple-ease.

4

Reeducational Goals

Between the noble moment when Milton yielded to the supreme necessity to communicate to me the phenomenon of love, or unselfishness as he put it, by which he felt himself cleansed and closer to the world, and my own proper orientation which made possible this moment there had to exist a structure of planning based on clear goals by which I guided my activities in his behalf—or in behalf of any of the children. Reeducation, a way of life, adjustment of personality—these may easily be mouthings if they are not translated into working words with action behind them based on analyses of the child's needs, of the employable values which lie in theater and of the potentials which exist in the adult privileged to put a sick rabbit into the theater hat and to pull out a healthy child. All aims, all therapeutic attitudes and manipulations, all plans, all results stem from this principle of delicately interlocking trinity—the child, the theater activity, the responsible adult.

Any socially minded person would, however, have arrived at a basic attitude toward the delinquent child's needs, hence to basic aims for his reeducation. One doesn't need book knowledge of the child, only human understanding and an intuitive approach or a sense of situation. One cares about what is passing on inside of a child or one doesn't; one does something about it or one doesn't. One reaches children eventually when they recognize our attitude of unconditioned sincerity. Here I must in truth make a heartening confession to the lay reader lest the job I outline in later paragraphs frighten him from also attempting it. My plans for the project were not founded on studies in either pedagogy or child psychology. The Hawthorne

Cedar Knolls School was open for experimentation with delinquent children. My interest in them was the interest of a socially minded citizen. Besides, I vaguely felt that there was something intrinsic in theater which had not been plumbed and analyzed for its full exploitation in behalf of children. This came to me after I had observed the amazing human change in a man, a truly dead soul with dead memories and with no life zest, whom by some vague intuition I had forced into a play I was rehearsing with adult amateurs. I found in me the necessity to probe myself—without benefit of hasty reading—to find out what I knew *within me;* what I myself thought about troubled children, the theater, and our imperfect adult world.

It followed that I became concerned with my position as a representative of the adult world rejected by the delinquent. How could I make the world acceptable to him? What would I have to be or do for him to accept my leadership? I reasoned that whatever might be the differentiated symptoms or expressions of delinquency, it was universally a disease of the child ego rooted in the sins of omission or commission of adults; that I as a stranger-adult would stand as a bridge between the child and all adults; that as a class we had made demands and given punishments and ordered respect for us failing to see that only the untrameled spirit or the secure ego can find in itself the faith necessary for obedience and the ardor necessary for respect; that therefore, my first and perpetual task or aim must be, as though I were repaying the debt the adult world owes him, to establish *status* for the child—that is, repair his ego losses by an unconditioned acceptance of him as a person. For acceptance I laid down five essentials to follow: (1) respect the child as a person with individual needs, feelings, point of view; (2) never pry into the past; (3) establish an honest person-to-person relationship free of authoritativeness but also free of sentimentality so that affection may grow in freedom and without obligation; (4) reestablish his faith and build up his ethics by exemplifying in myself the attitudes and actions I would demand of him; and (5) establish by removing the artificial wall between child and adult in the position of authority our common humanity. Status in this meaning is the child's by natural right, and this had been the delinquent's first deprivation, even where overpampering seems to point otherwise.

But there is a status which one earns for oneself in one's natural environment. It is self-esteem, a need of the ego for its constructive fulfillment. Normally the standards for self-esteem, even among one's peers, are tied up with adult standards; the blessings we bestow upon the child and our dependable guidance make him go our way. The troubled child has made his own standards; he has not found by them the contentment of self-esteem, and this is his second deprivation. In questioning how I might make our world acceptable to him I was wondering about the kind of world he could build through theater which would approximate the real world, with himself a secure participant acting upon emotional incentives similar to those which normally propel youth to "make his mark in the world." I concluded that the qualitative aspect of the theater environment should not be simple or down-to-child level, but complex with problems and with challenges like the real world, with just enough edge to difficulties to teach necessary lessons and with enough visible successes to encourage constructive effort. Oh, we would go slowly and acceptance would make this world warm and safe. But its industry for art's sake would be mature enough to set standards and would teem with opportunities for earning self-esteem. The interesting and engrossing hurdles one would have to jump would be by their demand of personal investment precious milestones in the retrievement of those ego losses which no adult could make up for one. Ignorance, personal inadequacy, lack of confidence, shame, guilt, etc., had to be made up for by oneself; the being entrusted a world to fashion, the thrilling difficulties of this world to conquer, the prod of succeessfulness would be the normalized emotional incentives to forge ahead. With the piling up of satisfactory experience and the gaining of status by standards which were ours but have become his, the child would naturally be entering our world, its acceptability no longer being in question.

So the first thing I asked of the school's director was not an equipped stage, but space large enough and bare enough for children to take over and build up from scratch. Fortunately, there was an empty cottage with two rooms downstairs and two dormitories a flight above. The director showed anxiety about my handling so many rooms at one time, and later there were, of course, some difficult situations. But how could children acquire status if they weren't placed in positions of trust? The lower rooms became my office and general sitting room of the Theater House. Upstairs, on one side, was a workshop; on the other side, the long room was marked off into a rehearsal area and space for tables and chairs for small project work. Small projects might include play-writing, discussion, carving, small-size prop-making, typing, doodling, or frank lazying, all things best done a wall away from the din of hammers or from entanglement with precariously placed larger works in process. Fortunately, too—and I say this advisedly because later I had always to plan how to prevent a too great heritage from one group to another—the auditorium stage was a mess, bare and poor and small, with not a foot or side or top strip of lights, with but one hanging bulb from above, without curtains, and with the loudspeaker for the movies thrust into its connection on the back wall. We had absolutely nothing, nor can I deny the effect of this poverty upon me who came lately from the theater. I had to remember my goals, from which point of view this was wonderful. Into the empty cottage and onto the barren stage about sixteen boys and perhaps eight girls were thrust, depsite their sophisticated outcries, to create, out of nothing and practically with their bare hands, the things we needed and which they knew and I knew could much more easily have been begged for or bought cheaply. Their protests required good salesmanship on my part to down, especially in the case of the girls, who had their knowledge of things theatrical from moving pictures versions of the glamorous life and from night spots.

I could hardly blame them. They came from poverty, and here in the name of glamorous theater I presented them with worse. But this would be a splendid lesson in resourcefulness; as most of these children would eventually return to poor homes, they ought to learn the thrill and acquire the knowledge of squeezing both beauty and utility out of little. Instead of easy satisfactions from things ready-made and gotten usually from the manipulation of other people, I aimed for them to learn to enjoy the hard-won satisfactions from self-exploitation in planning and in creating the things they desired. My best argument was an acknowledgment of my own weakness and of our united strength; I admitted that every boy present knew more about actual carpentry, even to the names of tools, than I did; that I, too, never had to build or plan for things as I would have to do now; and that I expected we would make many mistakes but doing them together ought to prove lots of fun. It was here at the beginning that I laid down a principle which became a slogan: "We are experimenting." I meant it for—and it did indeed become, growing from our practicing arts and skills into a new attitude toward life—a yardstick for measuring patience with oneself and tolerance with one's fellows. The idea "We are experimenting" or "We failed this time, but then it was an experiment," was stressed over and over again to knock finally at the innermost door of the psyche with the clearly understood message—"The past was an experiment. I failed. . . But then it was only an experiment. When we fail in the theater or in life we don't worry or fret, we start over again. *I* am starting over again. Hooray!'' The concept of experimenting or the concept that all successful people had first to go through a struggle in which failures and resourcefulness were natural factors cemented our relationship: (1) by it I was revealed to them as truly tolerant towards their faults and appreciative of their efforts; (2) it placed us together in common humanity before a universal law or fate.

That we had been experimenting even in our organization and without success we agreed after the first week. A primary gratification anticipated by all the children and freely voiced was the getting together boys with girls. Behind the frankness about the satisfactions of working in a mixed group—and how, too, could there be plays without one or the other sex?—had been surreptitious expectations of delightfully free moments in an environment not so sharply supervised as a classroom, a cottage living room, and so on. But. . . there were the clean-smelling lumber and the brand new tools and a freshly inspired ''vision.'' Most of the boys were hankering to build their world. Before this tangible, promising material they forgot the ''big parts'' they had craved for; and as ''busy'' men with a purpose they found the noisesome girls with their attention-getting devices in their way. Most of the girls clamored for the immediate satisfaction to their vanity. They wanted only to act.

And truly it was desirable to have separate groups if I intended to work intensively with the individual child within a group frame. The problem of sex would add a burden while lessening the effectiveness of my efforts to reach each child on the basis of his needs. The difference of attitudes already shown toward work, the fact that actually it was a situation of placing ''women'' together with boys, that also in terms of my goals I had a too large number of children to handle in acceptance—these were practical reasons for a change in the original plan. However, a basic need for development in some boys and in some girls—Harry, Irving, and Sylvia, for example—was the learning to be together, the acquiring of status from satisfactory contact with the opposite sex. Harry who stuttered, Irving who needed prodding into youthfulness, Sylvia who needed male approval had to be considered. The following plan solved all problems.

Both groups constituted the Group Theater and though each one fulfilled a plan of its own, unity was kept intact by the all-over plan for the production of a play or a program of plays. The Group Theater might be planning a boy's play or a girl's play or a program of two plays. Naturally the cast requirements of such plays were predominently male or female. Once the girls began rehearsals for their play, reality prodded them into physical work in its behalf. Meanwhile both groups were able to work without the obtrusion of sex as an added problem and I could make headway with the individual child in an atmosphere of relative calm. When the time came for the entrance of guest participants into either group to fill the roles requiring children of the opposite sex, the relationship between boys and girls was on an earnest co-worker level—boys participating in a girls' play or vice versa were rendering a needed service. Very subtly this kind of togetherness lessened the flagrant sexuality of the boy-girl attitude toward each other. The fruitful labors of the workshop contributed to this. Without the presence of boys, the girls settled down to projects of work and soon the things about the shop were the tangible symbols of *workers;* speaking nicely for them in their absence. The boys saw the designs or sewing for costumes or curtains or the lighter properties for the stage, the handiwork of the other group. The girls beheld the heavier equipment, the lighting constructions and bulky flats, etc., the work of the boys. This decent evidence of constructive activity useful to both groups and contributed to by both groups, arousing attitudes of appreciation and gratitude, established a common meeting ground of interests between girls and boys. Finally a mixed group met with me weekends. A few boys and a few girls as they became my dependables working on things that needed finishing, or on plans that needed revising, or on any thing I could devise as a reason for their coming together to get from each other the easing of tensions and status from their boy-girl relationship. The theater was organized; the children were engrossed in a community venture; the adult was now in theater language their director. But this director's real problems were now starting. Good salesmanship had organized this orderly state or group with its industries planned and outwardly flourishing and its moral atmosphere of consecration to a "cause." But we have seen from the description of the eight children the emotional and mental bankruptcy of this state's citizens, all sick, daily on the verge of secession, destruction, or overdoing or of sowing discord. It was natural that under the first flush of excitement before a new experience children should conceal their personal difficulties but that soon enough the living situations fostered by the work situation should bring them out with a clash of cymbals and a clatter of swords as atypical personalities came into conflict or habitual patterns came into play. My problem was what to do about the negative qualities revealed. What plan could I make for each child's need as revealed by his negative qualities or what could I do to help him win back his ego losses for which he had compensated with his special assortment of ill behavior?

I observed the children; I sought to learn their positive qualities—a trait, an attitude, an aptitude, or an interest—something tangible to use in the establishment of immediate ego satisfaction, using it as the potential for the gradual building up of permanent status. Or I studied the negative qualities to understand what external methods I might employ to establish status by a direct attack upon weaknesses. About the children I have mentioned, for example, I came to the following conclusions, from which I had then to manage with psychological devices and environmental manipulations or techniques that each separate child receive all the help necessary to him for his status growth. (See Chapter 7.)

In the cases of Oscar, Sidney, and Joseph I saw how narrow—because of their defective or limited mentality—my scope of planning would have to be. But surely Oscar could be encouraged to put up his fists in order to live less painfully with his peers. In various ways the portrait of Oscar in the eyes of the others could be changed and this would lessen their hostility to him; as also a greater security might stiffen him morally to stand up against ridicule and attack. His positive quality, his voice, could be of aid through his appearance often on programs, to establish public status and that ego satisfaction which might spur him to make efforts in other directions. As perhaps partially his mental inadequacy was the result of insecurity and fear he would need to be stimulated, through close proximity with friendly children around a simple project, to both express and assert himself. Definitely Oscar should not be the boy to be sweeping a floor or to be working in solitude. Work jobs having the external picture of masculine strength or aggression should be chosen for him. Sidney would need experimenting with. Perhaps trusting him, placing him in charge of stealable materials would remove his guilt somewhat, give him something to live up to. Heavy labors like climbing ladders, rigging stage curtains, hauling things would spend his restless energies while showing him dramatically to others as a useful, dependable member of the group. Joseph would need to work on a project or a plan having some pretense to demands on intelligence and skills but not too far above his capacities, since these were limited. It might lessen the aggressive hostility he felt toward better equipped boys if his job were showy, bearing quick results and requiring no special care so that praise and approval could fall upon him abundantly.

Milton belonged to another category. He would need responsibilities as the opportunities for developing his latent powers of leadership. His restless energies would have to be deflected into ideational channels; he would need to be introduced to books, to poetic expression, perhaps to play writing. These interests might be the incentives for a return to study in the schoolroom, particularly for his immediate application to learning how to read since actually he was ashamed of his illiteracy. For him ego satisfaction could not be manufactured but would have to come directly from the use of powers.

This last conclusion would be true of Harry. But he would need to be thrown almost bodily into group situations, forced into speech, enticed into discussions and contacts with children. He would need to be torn away from his escape compulsions by work at a bench with other children on a project requiring painstaking application and a long time for completion; it would have to be a job very much needed by the group, for its production or for its accumulated properties. For Harry acting in a play would be a *must*. Another must would be the development of his intellectual leadership—for the full expression of his powers as well as for the value his peers would put upon him.

Irving were best not tampered with at first. A one-man project should be his, one requiring skill and planning initiative and its eventual incorporation into the major project of the entire group—a lighting fixture, for example. Companionship should not be thrust upon him but could be encouraged by asking him to help less skilled children. Where haste or wilfulness should threaten the success of his job it might be necessary, even at the cost of time and materials, to let things come to their ultimate conclusion—for Irving would have to learn his own lessens by his failures. But bad results would need kindly and unperturbed handling. As soon as possible Irving should be given a role in a play, a light part needing some quick action, some youthful prank and laughter.

What could one do for Bert? Except for his cold temper he revealed little of himself. His asset, his intelligence, could bear responsibilities; perhaps opportunities to be helpful in a mature way would accomplish a rapport between us. But as his egotism was fed on the fear people had for him, he would have to be approached fearlessly and directly. Two facts would have to be established immediately: the adult had no intention to put something over on him; he would not be permitted to put something over on the adult.

As to Sylvia, the answer lay preponderantly in her ugliness. Prove that her face may be interesting or vital or handsome in its own way, and Sylvia would be encouraged to do something with herself. Until I found what to do about it concretely the girl could be given a sense of importance, a feeling, even if a fictitious one, of being popular. She could be invited to the mixed group on weekends, and here, because of her ability to draw, she could work directly with some of the boys, designing their stage scenery. To take her outside of her self-preoccupation I might give her a richly emotional role in a play, to live out someone else's grief or troubles. I could give her personal attention by means of private lessons in costume designing. It is obvious that so much varied activity must eventually reflect in Sylvia's mirror a changed face happier in expression and more alive than before, therefore a prettier and a more acceptable one.

To sum up—this observing and planning with a view to building up status took into account the fact that growth cannot be imposed by education (merely the reading and acting of plays or the making of theatrical goods); that change or *re*creation or *re*education must stem from positive, subjective experience which will cause a child to say inwardly—"Can this be me?" or "Is it possible—did I accomplish this nice thing, do this fine action or have this good feeling?"; that for such results tools, materials, all aspects of physical and work activity as well as children, need to be studied like coins for messages or helpful clues on their obverse sides.

Tools and paintbrushes, for example, may be instruments for destructive or constructive expression; the hostile smearing of walls or the mischievous scratching of property may be the fitful energy capable of painting scenery or of painstakingly carving wood or clay; or in behavior patterns aggression may be the external gesture of insecurity as likely as it may be the misdirected expression of unhusbanded powers; and quiescence or yielding may actually be a guarded hostility, or it may be the outer mien of fear, etc. All physical and emotional manifestations have their black and white sides to be studied for their meaning in any specific case. But universally pride and guilt come from the same source; destroying and building, accepting and rejecting, hating and loving the adult or his world, are the obverse assertions of the struggling ego, the reactive "*I am.*" In the growing child expected to become a social being the positive color of his ego's assertion is determined by the positiveness of external impacts upon him. Because the delinquent has been negatively impacted we must make up to him with positive influences by substituting attractive experience for that which has been painful and ego-destroying, to his detriment and to ours.

After acceptance, the first attractive experience he encounters is the fact that the new environment is truly open for his pleasure and awaiting his convenience. Thus the smearer gravitates to the paints, the noisemaker to the tools that clatter—or to the idea of making a wind machine or pounding a drum, the "digger" to the tools that cut deeply or to the hammering of nails; the bully poses and assumes prerogatives; the solitary boy initiates a job with enough variety to legalize his aloofness from other children; the habituated leader of a gang takes charge of affairs; the inadequate child makes no choice or movement but waits or causes trouble surreptitiously. Such spontaneous attractions and behavior may not be proof of ability, real interest, or actual character any more than lack of spontaneity in choice of self-expression is a proof of special character or a lack of ability and interests. But for the beginning they are clues on how to start a child off into constructive channels; they are the individual foundations upon which to erect start-afresh opportunities for the child to earn his needed status, that is, to make up his ego losses. To this purpose I laid down the following essentials as guides.

Generally, substitute tangible, ego-constructive and socially applauded experience through some aspect of work and of child-to-child and child-to-adult situation for the negative, anti- or asocial or self-preoccupational experience evidenced in the individual behavior pattern. This does not call for the forced obstruction or the repression of the individual pattern but for its immediate *employment* in some similar channel which can be made to prove itself equally ego-satisfying and meriting applause.

Specifically (1) give the obviously inadequate and insecure child something to do in which the learning process shows quick visible results in work and human relationship; (2) where traits are outstanding and natively useful, employ them where they promise progressive fulfillment; (3) for negative traits substitute, for example, for physical aggressiveness the use of aggressive energies in constructive ways such as the use of muscular strength on heavy jobs requiring the wielding of heavy tools or the carrying of heavy burdens which will get a show of respect from other boys; or detour this aggressiveness, if there are potentials for it, into leadership—perhaps in the bossing of a crew where verbalization can take the place of fists; for begin-

Example of a Purposely Created Project to Enlist Interest and Bind a Boy to the Group. Stove for Albert Bein's Little Ole Boy, *given at the 92nd Street YMHA; holds the story of the adjustment of a non-conforming; indifferent; impatient and lazy youth permitted to work on a group "need" under free expression. Humor helped. "A-a-a-gh!" The expression of disgust with which he threw away his tools was changed by my suggestion to* A-agh-yuch-nem, *etc.; from the Russian song until it became the habitual refrain accompanying his work. Jealousy of the stove; concommitant with pride of investment; had next to be dealt with; etc.*

ning experience in acting cast this kind of child in a bombastic noisy role in the play; (4) keep the children busy, busy, and more busy so that the results of their usefulness will show and will help them discover good things about themselves; and (5) give guidance and praise but never easy praise. The delinquent has worked hard on his delinquencies, he will get satisfaction only when he works as hard to merit applause; he is shrewd; he had been around; easily handed-out praise will make him suspicious of the adult's sincerity; he will suspect patronage; emotionally he is on the other side of the fence and wants no favors; allow him the dignity to really earn his winnings. For full discussion of differentuated children in the heterogenous environment see Chapter 7.

5

Theater As Socializer

One of my older boys, Max, once welcomed a newcomer, sotto voce and with his eyes twinkling—"'Come into my parlor,' said the spider to the fly." Max knew after two years the "tricks" which lay behind the play-producing. Himself, hadn't he been sweetly lured into the theater fold only to be enmeshed into its ardouous toils and disciplines to stand now at my side a grown person planning the welfare of other boys? He knew the rugged steps he had had to climb from easy pleasure to responsibility, from self-centeredness to social vision! His quoting from the child's tale was a forgivable conceit part introspection, part the warm anticipation of being in his turn helpful to another child. He was saying, "Enter, naïve fly; you are now going to meet your true masters—Work, Social Pressure, Authority."

We know about theater as an attractive web. Let us see now what factors in its structure can make it as Max found it to be, a maturizing or socializing agent. An art theater functions to an integrated plan made and accepted by its membership. Its useful and beautiful works are the intentionally best works of a consciously cooperating group. All its arts and skills and other miscellaneous offerings are necessary to the plan, and no capacity or skill or person is less important than another for this very reason. All give what they possess within themselves and give more as they possess more through the learning and experimenting participation which the innumerable needs of theater exact from them. Here are no stage stars, and no humbler workers in service to an elite class. Necessity—and the director's purposeful planning—makes a child a participant, in as many areas as possible, in a beehive atmosphere in which no effort is too insignificant for the total good and in which the gratitude of the group falls equally upon the child without as upon the child with talent or special ability.

A plan made with other people, no matter how lofty its inception or its goal, brings one down to earth. Thus *the* plan immediately changes the egocentric, amorphous concept of theater into a concrete and definite reality of shops, stage, materials, and above all people who need to be worked with harmoniously. Theater becomes a workaday world similar to the rejected outer world where all men do some kind of socially acceptable work; where big ventures are dependent upon ordinary people's pooling together their little ventures; where a person's effort is valuable in proportion to its fitting in with the standards and efforts of all the rest.

At first the delinquent is too disturbed emotionally, too lacking in simple education and in skills, to carry through so intricate a plan as a play production. But the discussion of a plan of work so glamorous and so challenging to one's feeling mature has the psychological impact of one's making choices and decisions in freedom. Who does not gird his loins to make efforts when a goal has been shaped of one's own free will? Later, naturally, there will be many "I don't want tos" and "I can'ts"; but the mass decision, "We have made a plan, we want to see it through" will carry affairs to success even when individual children fail. Psychologically, no one will have failed, for in every mind will loom big his own tiny difficult effort by which he has conquered something in himself in the attempt to win through to success. Merely finding oneself trying in a way and in a direction so opposite to past experience engenders a constructive emotional reaction to the new experience. One may not love work, but the plan—yes; for it gives purpose and meaningfulness to existence; it gives direction for the use of energies, direction which heretofore one lacked entirely or had painfully to seek. The *will* to see the plan through is the beginning of the *capacity* to see it through.

The living situation abets this development. A group of children separately faltering in the application of the individual *will* to necessary duties is simultaneously an entity, an authoritative force exerting pressures upon the individual. From the minute that a decision has been reached collectively and a date set for the play a discovery is made; though one has conceived a plan in freedom one is not himself free. The group is obsessed with a "cause," if not that of beauty and great art then with the cause of not failing in the eyes of the community. Like any social unit the group wants survival crowned with dignity and honor, and aware that its fate rests on the selflessness and industry of its members it exacts these standards from them. Despite any personal problems and incapacities, the individual is socially tied. Does he want truly to belong to the group, to be appreciated, to be befriended, he must lose himself in the group *will;* do his share, give more than his share, put controls on himself to do his job well enough—or court censorship and the kind of punishment children know well how to mete out to each other. This isn't so different an experience from the keeping in line with a crowd hell-bent for trouble. Only the direction is different; it is a positive substitute for a negative. The group has a creative inspiration promising positive social reward; hence long before its individual components it has pride and the standards to protect this pride. In the mass of children, awakened to hopeful fulfillment of something good, exist all the virtues and the critical standards tying correct behavior to work performance. And though the exercise of these is not consistent or constant, it works out that the offenders against one virtue or standard paradoxically rise up in wrath in defense of an other and the ball is kept rolling. The group pressure prods the child into social habits, attitudes, and capacities. The group is the adult's ally—against the individual—from the very beginning when he seeks to refashion the clues children have revealed into substitute work opportunities and behavior channels beneficial to the plan.

Work, the concrete aspects of theater, then introduces the true authority of the environment, whose recognition gives right to the group attitude and above all to the director in his constructive stand. This is the undisputable authority of a system of laws which governs the slightest endeavor in the arts, or the skills, or in human relations for the sake of work to be done. These laws are impersonal and all-present; they exist and that's that; they point to a correct way for a successful way to do things, accepting no alibis for failure.

For Theater, the benign and beckoning abstraction, proves to be an imperious lady. Once signaled by the will or the imagination because of the plan she does not abide except as a martinet laying down laws for her perpetuation. The most rigid law is that one who goes in pursuit of her must serve a hard apprenticeship—and in this way only may he master her. Give, sweat, labor, climb hurdles taller than oneself, break the heart a little, get dog-tired—all for some glimpse of theater's possible perfection! The child approaches a catharsis. This glimpse he has himself created! He owes it to himself to work better, control his negative actions. But this authority exacts so hard a price, demands such utter servitude! Yet, how deny onself the daily cup of satisfactions, the rich reward of mastership over something so much bigger than oneself? And in the struggle which ensues the adult, the director, stands blameless for if his is the voice which corrects, it is the voice of the Supreme Authority which speaks through him.

The adult speaks wisely if sometimes sternly—out of love for that which he the child, too loves . . . by gosh! This special adult whom one is tempted to reject because he refuses to turn tricks for easy pleasure making one work for it, this person is in deeper service than oneself! Something of a conscience awakens a struggling loyalty in the child. How can he deny the adult when before this Absolute Authority of Law (high standard of perfection in Chapter 7)—justified by the good and bad results seen about the shop—both of them stand in common humanity exactly as before fate (concept of experimentation)? The picture of the adult changes; he is no longer the special person useful for gaining swift pleasures, nor in moments of suspicion the grown-up on the other side of the fence, opposed to children. Warmly, now desiring this, the child looks upon his director as leader. The teaching and guiding principle of adult authority over children is established.

The plan ties children to the workbench. Group pressure keeps them there. But the creative process thrusts them into experience, painful and pleasant, depending on the degree of acceptance or rejection of its operative laws. What the eyes see and the hands touch cannot be gainsaid. Soon enough what has been carelessly done, breaks, hangs loose, or hurts someone. An error in measurement proves the hair's-breadth difference between waste of effort or perfection—or, as important—acceptance or rejection by peers. Haste, laziness, putting off what must be done, using the wrong tools or mishandling them, etc., exacts penalties in materials, time, disproval, and above all in self-disgust. The director was right, is always right. One has had to learn the hard way—but now the children are willing to follow their leader; the golden era of status-earning opens up. In freedom children acknowledge workmanship as of paramount importance, not merely for the sake of the play, but for oneself to avoid frustrations and defeats, to have the right to say, "I did this fine thing." To learn through doing, to be proud of what one is doing, to plan, to consult, to visualize—idle, lazy, quarrelsome, ignorant scoffers of work are on their way to become artisans. Or—because the structure of theater is made elastic by its many needs—to become fair workers on a simpler level since some children, like Oscar or Sidney for example, are not endowed for the development of work skills or discoverable capacities.

Status is earnable from any effort which is useful and requires some skill. It does not matter what a child does if the result is a feeling of pride or if the approval of others lifts him into grace. A theater is a studio of many parts in which the humblest child may find his niche and his halo. Among the assorted labors going on in a variety of miniature shops simple tasks are as important a part of a linked chain of endeavors as the most finished piece of work. The child with neither ability nor talent, the limited child, also the one too disturbed to make status-earning progress in areas fitting his aptitude, may fill these humble tasks and feel worthy doing their fair and needed share. For examples—the cleanliness of the shop and the orderliness of materials arranged in their proper places effect so much the total result of the production that sweeping and keeping materials sharp and clean and on their shelves or hooks have the character of essential, dignified labors. Neatness and orderliness are preventatives against fire hazard, against loss of time and materials, against nerve sieges in fellow workers anxious over their products. They are skills in which one may become more skillful because perfection is inspired by their fundamental relationship to other work and other children. One may not raise dust or it will settle on wet paint; one must be conscientious about movable projects; one must use his head remembering about the minutiae of unfinished work—what to throw into the dirt pile, what to gently put away. Caring for materials one must keep an inventory, report shortages for the necessary replenishments, improve one's writing and arithmetic on the way. Such is the elasticity of the theater environment that any human effort or expression can be turned into a status-earning asset.

Status-earning or status growth may be divided into before and after—the cathartic struggle—periods. The before period is rooted in curiosity, some fun, a halfway achievement in application to work and in the management of human relations. The after period is rooted in awareness. Awareness of the function of law and of the adult as leader, of the nature of materials, of the sense of personal potentials, of the stirring of love for the environment and for the goal of production—these make the beginning of a genuine willingness to cooperate in breaking down personal liabilities, from the simple lacks in education to the more complex blockings and problems of atypical personality.

From now on the child's activities and developments under the creative process of theater become activities and developments away from the infantile level—that childish plane in which wilfulness engages itself in a swift seeking of satisfaction of immediate desires, brooking no interference nor obstacle to self-gratification. The desire may be for an ice-cream cone in the midst of class, or in a generous moment for helping someone—in one's *own* way—or in a frenzied rush, for building the entire theater world in a day. No reasoning comes with this desire, no sifting of pros and cons or consideration of time or place. The infantile pattern does not distinguish between subjective desire and objective problems or barriers; it cannot bear being thwarted.

A proportionate patience, reasoning, good work habits, learning capacity, dependability, stick-to-itiveness, attentiveness are symptoms of maturity in a growing child. The delinquent—and the neurotic adolescent—may seem to be dependable in some area, may stick to some kind of a job, may be outstanding in a particular work or a particular kind of learning. Observation will generally reveal an apparently positive trait, or engrossment or ability to have a narcissistic base or to be disproportionate to normal requirements—overdone at the expense of other expressions or ways of being. The delinquent pattern shows the deprivation of those directed disciplines leading to self-discipline by which children are normally matured. Delinquency itself is a disproportionate growing up, a lacking of or a pulling away from the intermediary steps by which habits and emotions and intelligence are trained. Even when the child is outwardly knowing, assured, charming, poised, well-spoken, the psyche is obsessed narcissistically, the intelligence is blocked by emotional performance below the level of his age. He does in haste, as he desires also in haste and without duration. He dislikes work; he has no stick-to-itiveness; he lacks patience; he lacks a forethought and hindthought; and all sensations and all doings are of the moment—for the span of interest at all times is short. His intelligence has a helter-skelter functioning which parallels, like the wayward line of a graph, the disharmonies and fluctuations of his emotional state. We test his intelligence quotient and find it below par, or if high not of helpful use to him constructively.

Yet it is amazing how capable he has been in the realm of his past activities! His "work habits" in that field must have been ''sound,'' for he has had to know how to plan, how to fulfill the job hatched by himself and his pals, how successfully—until caught up with—to reap his harvest against the supposedly shrewder authority of society and law. It must have taken will, purpose, engrossment and application to evade the truant officer, to break into an apartment, to make off with a locked car. In his private world his intelligence seems not to have been blocked; it needed to be used adequately to permit him to be on his own against the world; surely for his escapades he had to size up the situation, learn something new from each experience, develop a certain sagacity over the adult, know how to judge and make choices. He did well what he *wanted* to do. The only thing missing in his ''sound'' pattern was the ability to accept the consequences, but that is in the emotional sphere.

Desire, then, is the pivot for any kind of constructive activity—for who can gainsay that but for the standards of society a successful delinquent act has most of the elements of constructivity—even that ace of social standards, cooperation. Delinquency is something accomplished as nearly perfectly as the child can because strong emotional incentives prod him to take pains. Rebellion or hate against the status quo is a strong stimulant to acts of self-assertion which we call negative behavior. But hate is the obverse of love; like it, it stimulates the child to great effort, and under the hazard of his situation to noble feelings and behavior—see him with his pals who carry the same banner and sword, how helpful, supporting, sacrificial, understanding, and loyal he is! Toward his own kind his pattern is social! Apparently his emotional infantile level is a specialized level of expression *for our midst* because with us he is confused, harassed, and conflicted.

Or we may view it in another way. Lacking the intermediary steps of training (educational, emotional, mental pretty much interlinked) for going the way we ask, the delinquent feels inadequate with us. The swift desire, the rush for satisfaction, is a way of covering up the painful consciousness of inadequacy, also a way of making up for it. He is more lost in our midst than with his kind because in any finished act or action of delinquency his lacks are made up for him by his mass of cronies—as in the theater environment in the beginning the group covers up for him with its sum of standards and virtues needed for achieving the finished play. Of course the gang judges and condemns sometimes, but it is more tolerant than the group. For the latter has had a revelation of its creative and status-earning powers and is in love with what it is doing, as well as with its present mode of existence; therefore it is a little impatient with traits and lackings in knowledge or skills which stand in the way of its progress. We may say that the spirit of the gang is negative constructive; its work toward its goal, though organized as harmoniously as possible, has a compulsion rooted in hate or rebellion and cannot therefore generate a righteous intolerance against its members to force them into growth. The spirit of the group may be said to be positive constructive so that its pressures like a tide swirl the individual round about forcing him forward to give a self-accounting by new standards.

Under the creative process the infantile pattern is intolerable; it is destructive, it wastes time, it interferes with those less infantile at the moment; it causes conflict because the crowning affront in this pattern is the child's inability to accept consequences; whereby he blames everything and everyone for his own actions and results from actions. Though he is still with his own kind in the group this trait is resented as a negation of the usual support, understanding and loyalty the children have given each other in their delinquencies. There is now a breakdown in the gang type of solidarity based on the united front that a guy and his pals are always right; everyone else—or society—always wrong. The group is refashioning its united front. Whatever it is separately, as a mass it is rational; it weighs matters, it is self-critical and self-corrective. Like all human patterns, the delinquent pattern has in it a preponderant portion of inertia. Aside from the original logic of causes and events which sends one in a certain direction there is the tendency to continue that way and to find reasons or make excuses against fate for one's lack of will to change the course. It requires an unexpected push to disturb habits and attitudes and to orient one elsewhere. It needs frequently the force of a catapult to agitate the psyche into looking upon a new horizon, to shock energies wakefully into unprecedented actions and emotions, or to create an entirely new awareness of the shape of one's world. This the glamorous, creative inspiration of theater does to the group when it presents it a world to build with hands made skillful, hearts refreshed, confidence born, tensions of self-doubt and insecurity relaxed. This the group does to the individual when in a new united front it insists upon striving for and reaching its goal.

Mea culpa is never spoken by the intelligence alone, nor by the heart alone. Love frees the intelligence as hate blocks it. This is why I emphasize work which leads to the appreciation of workmanship, or work to which one is bound by love—because of its goal and the opportunity it gives to change one's course—which leads to the complete psychic acceptance of personal responsibility as a major factor in the working out of consequence. Too simple work does not make demands on one's pretended maturity. What is beyond one and difficult is a spur to the ego, a challenge to the desire to earn status on the new road; it creates a conflict about returning to the old state of affairs. The goal, once the child experiences ego satisfactions from a new kind of conquest, becomes a "cause." As objects stand about having the vivid power to denounce or acclaim by their beauty and usefulness or by their ugliness and wastefulness one's consequential part in it, the most deep-seated self-centeredness cannot withstand, unmoved, the pointing accredit or rebuke to work habits or the lack of them, to the right or the wrong behavior, which may be held to be responsible. As work methods and work materials reveal their secrets to erstwhile ignorant and unhandy children—while they daily rise in personal stature—the apperceptive mass of the touchable world, and through it a world of ideas, enlargens, giving fresher and ever more stimulating opportunities for intelligence to function. All about satisfactions lead to greater love for the "cause," for the environment, for the servitude of work which reveal the child to himself as capable of judgment, choice, forethought, reasoning, self-criticism. It may be said that intelligence is developed, or that, certain stresses having been removed by the makeup of ego losses, it functions differently on a more even keel, less subject to emotional ebbs and flows. In the eight months, for example, which it took Milton to learn to "Love somebody as much as myself" he also rose from absolute ignorance of any work skill and the lack of the three R's to a fair workmanship in the construction and painting of scenery. Before entering the group Milton rated under examination by the psychologist an intelligence quotient of 76. I could not accept this percentage against the evidence of my personal observation. From a human point of view I believed him more intelligent than other children. He could not write but he had a language sense. He composed poetry and was alert to ideas as no other child. He had an analytical capacity which showed as much in his understanding of people and situations as it did in the comprehension of the central idea of a play. He was a thinking and a judging person. I insisted upon another examination; this time the IQ was 90. The busy psychologist put off my later requests for reexamination. Milton's performance in behavior, mental application, and workmanship was continuously progressive. Were he tested later, after he had become an active ideational group leader, writer of play skits and an outstanding actor—as well as a graduate from the academic school—I am certain he would have been found a little higher than average in intelligence.

Slowly the intermediary steps of training fill up the hiatus in the delinquent psyche. The child loses his sense of inadequacy because inadequacies are removed. He, the erstwhile truant, reads, writes, does sums better and better. Tools, books, new ideas do not frighten him. He gets along with his fellows, he has friendship with the adult; he doesn't fear the shadow of himself lest a word or deed, compulsive despite himself, get him into further trouble. He has lost fear and lost guilt. He faces a task no longer afraid he will bungle it or simply quit. He faces the adult with direction in his purpose, to consult with him, to speak his opinion, or voice a hope or an ambition. Adult words and ways are understandable to him—there is no reservation now of suspicion for the former or of the sense of being always suspected and blamed. He can take criticism, he is self-critical. He gets pleasure from learning and facts and ideas are his possessions. His span of interest in performance and in participation lengthens. He tries of himself for better work habits, better skillfulness, more and more self-control—because he likes himself better, because he likes his world. As he and the world are now one he is no longer confused, harassed, conflicted. He is less ego centralized, having less to cover up of inadequacies, less to compensate for. Hence he cooperates, identifies, serves.

The workshop alone does not do all this for him. Rehearsals, too, have maturizing influences, especially as they make sense for the building of the theatre world. Rehearsals embrace scenic men, actors, stage crew, all interlinking their efforts for the great day. Who is an actor today will be on the stage crew tomorrow and vice versa, so one man's job is a learning experience for all. It is true that rehearsals gratify the original egocentric appeal of theater, but they are hard, disciplining work. The give and take of lines, the proper timing for movement, actions, or speech, for entrances and exits, all demand the full attentiveness and the complete cooperation of the individual. One may not yield to personal desire; one must give oneself over completely. The ideational aspect of a play script must be considered; irresponsibility with lines, especially cue lines, may change the meaning of the play or just as easily be a wrong signal to backstage workers to ring down the curtain, blackout the stage or do whatnot detrimental folly. Creating a role imposes identification—with what the author feels about life and with a character whose motives and expressions differ from one's own. Rehearsals impose application through cooperation, the capacity to take criticism, patience with oneself and one's fellows, tolerance for people's mistakes and self-denial—in time and in painstaking—for the necessary experimentation which is to integrate all efforts into a finished work of art.

In conclusion, all the working and striving and growing together creates what may be termed a family spirit among children who have not in the past been able to get along with parents or peers. One day Milton whispered to me during a rehearsal, "I have such a strong feeling. . . . I'd like to do big things . . . help others . . . only I don't know how." Another time Joseph, that insensate clod and erstwhile teaser, trying to make peace in a trouble with a newcomer, said, "Don't you know that in the Group Theater we are all brothers?" Such expressions of human awareness bespeak the mature, socialized spirit in which the children eventually function. In the environment in which beautiful and clever works are created and individual developments acclaimed, a parent, the director is mutually shared, loved, and listened to. A group which met together hoping for swiftly gotten pleasures is united by the struggle to conquer obstacles, is tied together in affection by its mutual history of troubles and triumphs. The near-defeats and the almost successes are in its memories linked to the sorrows and regrets of comrade-fellows. Trials and errors, learnings and discoveries, high moments of joy are in its traditions, in anecodtes, in madeup songs, in every board and bit of cloth which is its created property. Even the English language gains special nuances understandable only to the Group; words and phrases sounding their literal meanings to others, to the family emanate their special comic or tragic connotation rooted in the cathartic history of children who have "made good." When in a group of differing ages and potentials a boy says, "He's only a kid; I'll help him," or a girl says, "She can't work today, she's had bad news from home. I'll do her job," and there is in this kind of expression an integrity incorporating confidence, responsibility, workmanship, protectiveness, and thoughtfulness for another child, then Max's "fly" after entering the "parlor" does very well indeed.

Now in Max's concept of theater as a web lies an unintended innuendo of the ominous hovering of a master weaver over the environment; and the fantasy is true enough but in a more benign sense because the director, to make certain that the lure of theater will culminate in the child's socialization, does play the part of an enticing warlock. It bears repeating that all aims, all *results* stem from the principle of interlocking trinity—the Child, the Theater Activity, the Responsible Adult. And the responsible adult has a bit of treachery to perform—he may not be merely the glamorous director of a theater! Having decided on reeducational goals, he has a duty to fulfill as an all-seeing, all-pervasive, omniscient, and persuasive presence in control of the environment. Hence. the first control which he practices is the employment of himself in the suggested difficult-to-maintain role of duality—that of artist-therapist.

6

Director As Artist-Therapist

A very delicate balance must be kept by the director to maintain his dual role of artist in love with the theater and therapist molding children, not plays. If he is the artist only he will deteriorate into a producer-manager in control of an external form of theater, bringing good to children accidentally but not intrinsically and permanently. If he is the therapist only he will not know how to create the essential environment of vivid and enthralling interests the adolescent needs to captivate his spirit and body in the direction of the constructive way of living. To keep the balance requires a constant vigil on oneself, for it is obvious the creative personality has rarely the calm collected impersonality of the clinician. Too, the very nature of stage production is a driving one demanding that things be done well and on time regardless of individual vagary; the very nature of therapy is the tranquil study of this vagary and the leisurely search for its corrective medicine. The one calls for an environment which is warm, often hectic, exacting a great wear and tear on nerves; the other calls for the cool clinic where judgment is kept serene, unobtruded upon by total giving of physical and psychic energy.

Nevertheless, an essential part of therapy through theater is expressly this warmth, this hectic doing, this adult giving without stint. The child revels and grows whole in such physical and spiritual atmosphere. Its volatile essence gives wings to existence. It's giving by the adult—not in sissy sentimentality but in ardent and honest selflessness—attains in the child heart that most needed and desirable (but not hitherto found worthwhile) capitulation to adult leadership. The director must give to his job as only the artist can give. To keep the children vitalized, enraptured, in love with the creative life, he must himself be in love with it. He must be resourceful, have a pride in his labors, know the things of the theater, exude the enthusiasms of the creative person for creativity. As artist the director has to be a never-ending source of inspiration; what he does and says and teaches must be eloquent of his complete personal surrender to the work at hand—with the attitude of accepting the children as his collaborators—in a kind of mystical search for beauty and truth.

This search for truth and beauty occurs simply in the everyday practice of accomplishing a little bit of beauty (toward the structure of beauty which will be the play) in the best devised and most painstaking, hence truthful way. But the attitude for such accomplishment can be awakened only where the arts are something to live for and where the leader, because of his artistic ideals, knows how to imbue every minor process or portion of labor with a radiating effulgence to light the way over ignorance, indifference, or inaptitute. I have said elsewhere that delinquency is self-made theater and self-dramatization in search of a catharsis—as growing up is to a greater or less degree. To the extent to which the artist-director can make himself a high priest of Thespis, sanctifying the workshop as a holy of holies, to that extent can he spur a new kind of self-dramatization to work toward a new kind of catharsis in the child. Only an artist—not a person who just does plays—will get down on his knees to work by the side of the children, will himself wield the broom or hammer or needle, will get his hands deep into the mixing of paints, will check his own impatience with the concept "We are experimenting." These are the acts and attitudes of participation and sharing in something so great that the individual is submerged. They are the deeds of priesthood which by example make proselytes and workers out of "I can't" and "I don't want to" skeptics and scoffers.

In this role of high priest which as the artist the director naturally assumes lies his power to make ethical demands, to insert a code of behavior, to make work—hard work up to one's fullest capacity—the habit and goal of existence in the group. He does these things not in behalf of himself but in the name of the abstraction Theater whose daily demands are concrete enough. He doesn't accomplish these with authoritativeness but with the evidence supplied by the art process, and perhaps with a good deal of the ritualistic mesmerism of the medicine man. But actually he applies to art-producing his insight into the adolescent personality. He does not forget that the adolescent delinquent has been out in the world, that he thinks himself grown up, that he cannot be given childish plays, for instance, and that he cannot be patted on the shoulder for labors too easy to fulfill, that he *must* be given that sense of unprecedented achievement his feeling of grown-upness requires. He remembers, too, that though he is infantile in certain emotional spheres, the child has tasted emotions deeply and should be given an equal opportunity for deep feeling. And so that artist-director needs somewhat to be a fanatical rider on horseback, carrying a blazing banner, pointing a shiny sword to somewhere beyond the horizon.

He plans projects beyond the child but possible of achievement by the cumulative talents and abilities of the entire group. He motivates big doings whose intrinsic value is the call upon desire, by intrigued imagination, to overcome obstacles; for the more apparently

MODEL STAGE to scale of actual stage. Has complete lighting system and set for Scene in ROPE. This represents cooperative job by unskilled children with the skilled in brother-leadership. Below is Harry's PROSCENIUM ARCH.

difficult the job, the more zest will the child throw into it. He plans *intricate* projects; the more threads there are to weave into the fabric of a successful venture, the more gallant and victorous will the child feel as after a rich adventure. The director's artistic vision must be high, wide, and handsome. The high priest may demand perfection where as mere adult he may not. His demands are in the name of theater, of high adventure and high purpose, and there is therapy in that as long as he stands by with moral and substantial support. These demands are of course sheer trickery to instigate interest and engrossment, for the director as therapist will not permit the threat of the perfectionist's whip over the individual child. It *is,* however, good therapy to increase the demands in proportion to the child's love for his work and when it is evident that he is not using the full quotient of his capacity.

The high priest—and the therapist, too—knows the power of suggestion. He knows the potency of such things as banners, songs, slogans to build esprit de corps. As medicine man he exploits these things, casually of course, but with spirit as though he himself were one of the children. For instance, the slogan: children do not listen to admonitions or precepts, but they love the repeatable phrase, dramatic in essence, short and terse, which carries the kernel of an idea or situation, especially if imagination can make the message applicable to self as the central protagonist. Hence the director not only speaks the theater language but emphasizes theater ethics in tellable, vivid phraseology. After a while good slogans originate from the children themselves quick to apply good-naturedly and even humorously catchy bons mots to check, avoid, or rectify difficult situations. The following phrases attain the subtle values of an esoteric code, seeping under the skin and accomplishing more than a hundred scoldings: "We are experimenting"; "Remember, cooperation!"; "The play *must* go on"; "It may be a hit—it may be a flop"; "It can't happen with us" (about a boy running away); "Not a Group Theater boy!" (about unseemly behavior on the campus); "Rush never finished a job"; "Speak English" (about poor diction or speaking from the corner of the mouth); "You may be right, but you'll have to prove it" (about avoidance to measure correctly, quick decisions, etc.); "I'd like to believe you, but . . . ." (a reminder about habitual lying); "If not today, why then tomorrow" (for encouragement over failure). Children bandy these about to admonish and to warn each other, to remind or scold themselves. How often have I heard Milton or some other child, in differing moods and under different circumstances, sing out, turn away in annoyance, or start up in self-censorship with the expression "Remember cooperation!" or a variation of it "So that's cooperation." Better than long-winded speeches, slogans are the mystical bells to duty, the reminders of a cause lost or won according to individual action, the alluring prods to push and pull and sweat upwards toward the chosen goal.

It becomes obvious that the director acts out an esoteric love for theater in order to enliven the environment, to make it intriguing enough for children to follow on an unaccustomed path. Intrinsically he loves more the human potentials around him; he looks upon theater not as an end but as a gateway to real life. His responsible orientation is toward the child in the same way as the priest's who cherishes his church but deals with human salvation. Behind the beguiling trickery of lights and settings, behind the miracle of changing worlds with each change of play, despite the driving necessity to fulfill on a date the promise of a completed show, the director must see the child, what he is and why, what he needs and wants and can be, and *what* from all the trickery and miracles can best be used, and *how* used *for* the child to resolve his inner problems—not sentimentally but realistically with a finger on his pulse, with an eye on his acts, with interpretation for his vagaries, with, most important of all, flexibility in his handling. Here is where the therapist holds sway, although the place or time where the artist leaves off eludes being pinned down.

The therapist observes and manupulates; when the artist is tempted by his vested interest in the arts to demand authoritative obedience and perfection the therapist calls a halt and reminds him—"Remember the child." The artist plans the production—scenery, lights, costumes, and so forth. The therapist plans where to fit the child in, with whom to pal him, how to reach him, what to do and say to encourage, discourage, let alone, inflate, deflate him, according to what may be correct day by day for each child. The artist plans for the complete art work, the therapist plans for the mental hygiene of the group and of the child within the group. The therapist manipulates the environment, the children, *himself;* and in so doing effects often drastically the best laid plans of his artist self (although both see to it that the group venture progresses to its successful finish). But the artist is nothing if not responsive and resourceful and so he falls in and rearranges his pattern of work; it is the artist then who manipulates under great challenge. Within his major plan he makes smaller plans or adjustments to fit the case of the child; he initiates projects which will link the individual ultimately with what is happening en masse; he not only rearranges scenes, rewrites plays, builds up or adds parts, he *creates* all kinds of miscellanea not really necessary for the production but related, even if artificially, to it so that the child may always be sure of belonging to the whole.

The combination of artist with therapist in charge of the pulsing life of theater gives the child his first genial picture of an adult. What he sees within the frame of a growing relationship is a more natural picture than the one he has been permitted to see at home, in a classroom, or behind the desk of his social worker. He sees a person capable of enthusiasms very much like himself. The picture gains stature when he sees the adult gives of himself by deed not mouthings, and it grows by the examples of good humor, fair dealings, and unstinted labors. The child feels closer, too, for the frailties he discovers—the times when weariness shows, when disappointment is not concealed, when on occasion temper is not controlled; what he observes is human and understandable and again so much like himself but with this distinction that weariness and disappointment are expressed not for self-centered reasons, and that anger so unusual in a loving and patient person assumes by this contrast the role of irreproachable and irrefutable justice. Instinctively the child sums up and balances against this show of displeasure all the enduring loving attitudes and he *knows* this is the extreme expression of the same feeling for him, come to a state of explosiveness from the accumulation of many, many untoward acts of misbehavior on his part. Rare anger from the adult is vastly important; the emotional accompaniment to a beyond-patience judgment brings to a climax the drama of living in that all tensions are finally eased—the child is always aware of his part in the situation and he is brought up with a start to face himself and to face also the possible loss of affection from one he loves, respects, and follows. Too, displeasure is guidance *against* just as praise is guidance *for* something—the delinquent child more than any other is a floundering child and craves guidance though he fights it. The genial picture of the adult bringing welfare makes the child immeasurably thankful. The genial picture of the adult bringing riches in color and sound, in skills and in ideas, and in unprecedented satisfactions of the spirit adds to the thankfulness and totals up in a feeling of warmth toward and in acceptance of that adult authority which could not be forced upon him.

The adult can be all things to the child in his needs when he is a whole and natural person; only a busy workshop dramatic with constrasting elements contains the tangibles and the intangibles, the order and the confusion, the leisure and the haste, the waste and the constructivity, the impulsiveness of inspiration and the sobriety of painstaking to show up the adult in his natural reactivity to life, that is, in the wholeness of his person. It would be too bad, of course were he not an intrinsically honest, aware, and responsible human being. For the major function of the artist-therapist is to effect out of the loving, guiding, teaching situation an ultimate child transference to himself as ego ideal to this end that his person symbolizes, all the more for the evidence of a similar humanity between them, a total of beloved and respected qualifications of adulthood worthwhile and possible to strive for.

For this reason I stress the concept *without sentimentality*. The ego ideal may have nerves but he may not lack justice and wisdom. His judgments, and his actions which stem from these judgments, must be far-reaching beyond the mere moment of the situation, and even some situations must be accorded individual treatment because of differing psychic material. It is sentimental to yield before a child's momentary hurt, for the chances are the adult is himself emotionally involved though unaware of his private motives. For of course the ego ideal is himself a sentient and normally egotistical being getting a full satisfaction out of his central position of the beloved and the looked up to. But this is a luxury he better enjoy in his privacy. The stern stuff of leadership may not be weakened by subjective calculation or by personal identification with the child at the expense of what is good for him. As the therapist the director may have to say no when as a person involved in affections he would be tempted to say yes—or the other way around. As therapist the director must give warmth to the child not in love with him, too; he may not be sentimental over himself like the doting parent who has favorites. The director must differentiate between heart and emotionability. He must act with courage—the show of fear or insecurity abnegates his position, gains disrespect from and confusion for the child—like for example, the wise parent who withdraws financial support from his spendthrift son to give him the chance through hardship to become a man. Such parent may not luxuriate in tears over the hard words his son speaks, nor enjoy self-justification in the eyes of his family. But sincerely and honestly while standing by his position he explains in order to enlighten this son and his sisters and brothers.

The theater environment precludes secrecy or reservation. In the interrelationship of all things human and material because of the work, no change in plan, no action in behalf of a child can occur without notice and without reaction from the assembled family. As children have their feelers out to probe the simplest situation the adult must forestall negative interpretations with honest, simple, and direct statements. He will of course not publicize a child's secret problems to shame him—this would deny his original acceptance of the child—but will give an externally true statement acceptable to all yet privately bearing its intended message to the guilty child.

An example would be the necessary decision that Milton and Oscar should not continue on a job they are doing together. The reason—both boys painting a set for the forthcoming production and doing exceptionally well to the praises of the thankful group have gallivanted to a corner not assigned for the purpose yet a seeming place for work of this kind; but they have off-guardedly revealed signs and actions of unhealthy familiarity. Knowing Milton's proclivities to aggressive homosexuality and Oscar's weaker trait, the director has two facts to face: one, it will be difficult to replace the boys on the job because of their acquired skill; also, such action will seem unreasonable to the group and will destroy for the two status satisfaction they have from the work; two, Milton and Oscar must be separated immediately.

This is handled despite the hue and outcry from the two and from the group, which sees a shambles of its coming play due so shortly—truly it *is* late in the schedule to makes changes and it does tax the director who says he is not worried about the production, oh, no! The simple announcement, "I am separating Milton and Oscar for their good" has a secret connotation both boys understand. But face is saved by a plan which continues to earn them status. At this odd moment the director believes, for such-and-such reasons, that Murry a tough, virile boy should have an opportunity at scenic painting—and in fact he instead of another aggressive child will have been chosen for the good it will do him. Further, as Milton is fairly adept in his skill he will save the director trouble by assuming the role of teacher—the two will work as a team and this fits in with Milton's need. (See Milton and Oscar, pp. 25, 26.) As to Oscar, there is a job for him at the curtains, he has not yet had that experience, and in order to run them smoothly he had better tackle their problems at once, grease the pulleys, unravel the knots, and so forth. Cries Oscar, "But I was doing good . . . and it's my painting!" "Whose painting?!" asks the director righteously of the group. A clamor arises, a shout answers, "Our painting, the painting belongs to all of us." And Joseph says in his drawling voice, "Better listen to the teacher, Oscar. Our teacher knows what's what." Oscar shows some feeling, then brightens up suddenly—the curtain idea, the ropes and pulleys are summing up in his fantasy a pleasurably heroic picture of Oscar as virile, nimble, and strong, the master of the stage area. He grins. "Okay! I'm going to climb up to the ceiling, way, way up to the roof and fix that———miserable knot!" But a battle will have just begun. Oscar will not be permitted to make the dangerous climb but will be teamed up with Irving more sober, careful, and adept for work in dangerous zones, who will in turn protest against leaving his lone job of work at a lighting equipment. (See Irving, pp. 34, 37.) Murry will surely challenge Milton's leadership, and the latter, inwardly aware of the reason for the new arrangement, will be strained in his relations with the adult. Despite this, benefits will accrue to all of the boys; the lights, curtains, and sets will be managed in the nick of time; and with mounting well-being the involved children will again love their leader. The play will be shown on the boards—but not at the expense of continuing for one moment more than possible a situation drastic for two children. Such is the procedure which must take place if judgment is to supersede feeling, that is, if a child problem is to be solved by thoughtful appraisal rather than by emotional floundering. This case does not exemplify, however, a serious group involvement with a child trouble where a stand, for therapeutic reasons, must be taken which may actually threaten group morale or even the entire enterprise.

Sidney and Hal represent cases of flagrant disregard and wilful lack of cooperation. (See Sidney, p. 36.) They are samples of external similarity requiring dissimilar handling because of differing psychological factors, and in both cases, for the sake of one child's need and out of necessity to teach the other a permanent lesson, the real punishment had to fall upon the group and its director. Guilty children like Sidney deliberately provoke, destroy, pick quarrels to bring down punishment upon themselves—but let us see the situation from the beginning of the session when he loosened the nether regions upon us all.

He had come in quietly, too quietly. He brooded over his job for a while then deliberately irritated the boys by jostling them, finding fault with their labors, etc. Nothing in our midst had happened to explain his mounting fury climaxed by the hurling of a hammer, the flinging about of materials, the startling of the peace with shouts and recriminations. The children, anxious about their work and recognizing his mood, tried hard to avoid entanglements, looked hopefully to me to handle him. He was a demon who finally succeeded in straining me to the point of anger which would definitely have lacked therapeutic objectivity had I not in time a revelation of what it might all be about. The boy was deliberately baiting *me* through the boys! At my first show of temper there was in him the look of a successfully stalking animal, his eyes too black and brilliant in an overly flushed face. It was the practice at the school for adults to write out referrals for misbehavior, blue slips which went into the office for record and which brought down upon a child punishment or deprivation. Sidney knew well that I preferred to work out recalcitrant problems among ourselves if possible. It was a tradition of ours that the infrequency of my "tickets"—perhaps half a dozen a year—got for that reason the special consideration in the office of being the last possible recourse on my part for unmanageable, therefore severely punishable behavior. Sidney was provoking such action from me. He was restive with guilt over something he had perpetrated elsewhere; most probably he had broken into an apartment. Did people know; did they suspect him; what would happen to him? The inactivity of the authorities made incertitude unbearable; he wanted immediate retribution upon himself to relieve the unbearable burden of his tension.

I told him he could break the shop to smithereens, he would not get the "ticket" he was aiming for. I calmed the clamorous protests of the others by an appeal that it would not be to Sidney's welfare—explaining the problem to them—if we banded against him to give him the easiest way out. Against the cries, "We don't want him, he's a trouble maker. . . .But you gave *me* a 'ticket'. . . .Look, he broke up my job on purpose. . . ." There were yells from Sidney, "I'm getting out of the Group Theater for good, see if I care," and this with a hammering of fists on the table! The voices pleaded, "Give him a ticket. . . . Why do you have to care what's good for him?" Other voices answered, "She knows what she's doing . . . . Forget about him, get back to work . . ." Sidney was at the door throwing a last defiance, "Okay, then I'm taking a trip. . . . I'm going to disgrace you all, I'm running away straight from the Group Theater . . ." I answered, "Not today Sidney, you're in enough trouble. However, I'll not stop you . . . but on the way down take a look into the sitting room; you fixed it up, maybe it'll say something to you." The boy was sobbing suddenly, and then with his whole person tensed like a fist about to strike he threw all of his suffering into a hysterical shout, "I'm running, I tell you, and nobody and nothing can stop me." The house resounded to his violent clatter of feet! The group resembled waxwork figures in their abrupt and silent immobility.

It was dark outside and no one would see or stop Sidney if he did "run." I was taking a chance! In the shop the buzz of tools and voices arose once more. As in an expressionist play a dialogue of dual content passed among us. "Look what he did to my easel! . . . Ha! some cooperator, Sidney!—how do I mix this crazy green?" "I'm not sore, but you gave me a 'ticket' for *less*." Answer: "Try adding more of that yellow to the ultramarine, not the new blue . . . The 'ticket' I gave you did you good, you were new here and tough, you had to learn that I could be tough, too. . . . It wouldn't have done Sidney good, he's not tough enough." Another boy—"I'm disgusted! The corner doesn't fit, he shook it just when —(with anxiety) do you think he will "run"? . . .I'll kill him if they ever bring him back, to do that to us!" Answer: "Tee-square, ruler, pencil—now let's check—see? Half an inch here, an eighth there. Sideny had nothing to do with plain carelessness. No, I don't think he ran." Another boy: "He was angry; he would have slammed the front door. . . . Teacher, I'm having trouble. Could you help me?" A shout interrupts us! "Teacher! Look who's here!" Could this be the same Sidney, pale and hesitant in the doorway, unsure of his welcome, asking to see me alone? He wanted to apologize for everything; and could he go back to his work? Yes, he understood that a person had to bear the consequences and guilt was a consequence just the same as punishment. Yes, he understood that it didn't help matters to add bad action to another bad action. Yes, he would ask to see his social worker tomorrow. My refusal to discipline Sidney in the usual way had furnished a cathartic opportunity for some slight start at facing himself and facts; this once he had been stopped in his rolling-stone proclivity to gather guilt from crime and more crime from guilt.

Paradoxically, while I was most lenient with Sidney I was cruelly strict with Hal, who committed no similar disorder but simply omitted the correct behavior. (See Hal, pp. 62.) Hal had been given a prognosis by his caseworker as impossible to reach. He had been in the Group Theater almost two years; from an awakening through acting to other interests, from friendship with me to other adult relationships, Hal had become a personage in the community. It was a week before an event at the school when several hundred outsiders—judges, educators, other prominent people—would be present at our outdoor production, one of vast proportions including the participation of many boys and girls not members of the Group Theatre. Hal had a major role and innumerable smaller ones, luscious parts of great satisfaction to a boy enamored of the theater as he was. Because he had become a responsible person, I had given him the strategic parts or the connecting links which tied the action together. The morale of the entire acting company of some fifty children depended especially on his many short interpolations, introductions, etc. And this was the time Hal—who had never done this before—chose to absent himself from rehearsals! For two days he knew about the crowd of children awaiting his arrival and failing in their work because of him. The boy had a perfect transference to me, a complete identification—he knew what his absence was costing.

In defense of Hal there was this; he had been told he would be paroled immediately after the play, and no doubt he was in a state of confusion between the joy of freedom and the anxiety for the future naturally aroused in connection with freedom. No doubt these last rehearsals spelled slavery to a boy suddenly confronted with an eternal stretch of servitude to real life, the looking for and holding down of a job, the buckling down to come-what-may future circumstances. There was a need to have a last fling, to be carefree and footloose; and the ball games on the field beckoned, offered release from tensions, forgetfulness, and animal fun. On reproof from his fellows his answers were really messages signifying, "To h—— with rehearsals."

Because of this attitude I made a drastic decision; I dropped him from the play. For now his behavior was undefendable. His messages dramatized his flagrant disregard for our need, evoked among the children the sentiment of his unworthiness; for he was destroying their tradition of cooperative conduct and threatening them with failure. I realized also that Hal was too sure of the adult. He depended so upon my understanding that he smugly anticipated sweet forgiveness the minute he arrived on the big day like a prima donna to save the show. With the egotistical pampering of his current mood he was abusing our relationship; he was pitting me against myself in the duality of my role, that is, he was playing my humaneness against my crucial need of him in the theater situation. And realistically it seemed certain that I could make no changes at this late hour, there were enough problems already. Hal meant to have his fun; we would pay the piper meanwhile and later everyone, but especially the loving adult, would relent to shower praises on a stage star no longer a recalcitrant boy.

I could have commanded his presence. He would have come in a truculent mood, all the more for his guilt in the matter, but soon he would have recaptured the old spirit, grateful for my having pulled in his reins. Normally this is what I would have done. But the boy was going out into the world. No loving adult awaited him to check similar emotional indulgences blinding him to duty. It was now my duty to be hard and cruel, to approximate the aloof impersonality of any future stranger in a situation of employer or dependent upon Hal. It were best that he should learn the price of disloyalty and irresponsibility at the hands of his loving leader, not only as a preventative in relation to a job, but also as an experience in personal relations which ruled limitations to the abuse of friendship. Any person who has experienced the thralls of a production will know the punishment this director took at the time—slicing roles, recasting them, realining actors, calling extra divisional rehearsals besides the regular ones—in order to send Hal out into the world with a last indelible lesson about personal behavior and its consequences.

Hal came running soon enough, brokenhearted, ready to work. It was too late. Another boy was in his major role; others were gallantly coping with his smaller ones. He pleaded . . . he would be humiliated if after two years in the group he did not now appear in the most important public event of all. As artist, how much I wanted to recapitulate, for no one would do as well as Hal! As person cherished by the boy, softened by his tears, how much I wanted to relent! We talked it over, and Hal understood and accepted my action on his score. He understood, too, that change does not stand still but involves with its momentum the basic feelings of other people, that therefore I could not undo the new arrangement without injustice to his fellows who took up his job when he was failing us. He offered a solution which I could accept with a minor yielding on my part and with happiness to him. One little role which he did beautifully would be his; as amends for everything Hal would be Johnny-on-the-spot for any of the sundry labors still necessary for a finished play. Hal was himself again!

Concisely, the job of the director as artist-therapist is first to do, then to undo much of his own work: that is, to purposely build up the cult of theater, making a sanctuary out of its house; then to remove stone after stone of its sacerdotal edifice to let in the air from the outside world, and to gradually open up exits into this world of reality. Thus, if the priest of Thespis should be tempted to overlook human problems in a too *esoteric* consecration to his mistress Theater, or if the harassed adult should be tempted to make things easy and smooth-flowing, then his obverse role must remind him that the whole of the theater is for nought if not for the preparation for living and that the ritual of life is noisy, *esoteric*; troubling, and cathartic in the way theater itself was in its beginning. In Part Two the artist-therapist pursues this dual job more fully than in these early chapters, building a system of his manipulations and devices to put theater truly to work to prepare troubled children for the major "production"—life.

THAT'S THE GROUP THEATER

Group song by one of the boys to "Happy Days Are Here Again."

Back and forth the boys are hurrying—
Late again the girls are scurrying—
Our director, how she's worrying—
That's the Group Theater.

Give me a drag on that cigarette—
Aw heck! The makeup's still too wet—
Say, aren't you all ready yet?
That's the Group Theater.

At last the curtain's going up—
It all comes from our own workshop—
It may be a HIT, it may be a FLOP—
BUT THAT'S THE GROUP THEATER.

PART TWO

7

Problems and Techniques

Introduction

Though the individual child may need to be treated on the basis of specific problems, what is generally good, in the same way as fresh air and nourishment, may prove often to be the whole cure or if not is the preparatory ground for more personalized attention. To be patient with one child, impatient, stern, or indifferent with other children for therapeutic reasons, yet to convey despite contradictions in treatment one's intention of wisdom and justice, the adult must first establish the general well-being on grounds of general interests and needs. A foundation for mutual interests exists in the shared opportunity to participate in theater. But a disquieting interest in each child is *himself* in his basic ego preoccupation due to one or many reasons of insecurity, and this divides rather than unites the children. Every child is a brooding Hamlet differing in his special inadequacy but alike in the conflict characteristic of the delinquent personality. He is in the poignant toils of a question he cannot settle for himself—"To be or not to be," that is, should he listen to his needs—echoed by the adult—to "belong" and to be "somebody" or not, so uncertain is he of himself and everything and everybody. To belong or to be worthy of affection and praise, and to be somebody, not only to earn approval but to obey the natural instinct for growth—the being active to a purpose, satisfying the restless body and appeasing meaningfully the restive mind—are tempting states could one believe them worthwhile or have faith that one could bring them about.

One can imagine the doubts in the hearts of the ungifted child, the backward one, the youth with a speech or body defect, the child habitually escaping to his own surer world of fantasy, the child enslaved to compulsive behavior or tied up in emotional knots, the boy or girl aware of educational lacks. While techniques building individual and permanent faith work their slow course, the adult creates the environmental climate tending to the general sense of security and unity. Something flows from him to the children, reaching their hearts, revolutionizing their outlook, proving beyond doubt that *he belongs to them.*

As the theater I deal with is no new form, so the approach to the child for the general good is new only as the old is new when it is remembered after having been forgotten. Children are people. What adults working with children tend to forget is the memory of themselves as children or groping *young people* striving confusedly to meet the requirements and standards of the world of *older people.* What may be forgotten is the guiding wisdom in the adage "Know thyself" by which cleavages are avoided in human relations, definitely the cleavage of righteousness between adults and children. "Know thyself" leads logically to respect for others, *even* delinquent children. Respect for the child then is a paramount attitude behind techniques; it determines the proportionate assumption of powers, rights, and responsibilities of the adult and the proportionate yielding of rights and freedoms to children. The attitude has guided me in the assumption of responsibility for the child's future; that is, it has forced me, despite the urgency of any immediate demands of my job with theater, to ever see the child as the coming man or woman enacting a role beyond the present time on a vaster stage, and with better skill, and with some measure of human happiness.

So the reminder of early actions, reactions, needs, desires, joys, frustrations, sensitivities, hopes has guided the control of my adult temptation to authoritativeness as well as the control over any adult weakness I might have to identify, at the expense of lasting good to the child, with his emotions. It has guided the control of personal bias, for naturally some children are apt to call forth a more personal response than others and the control is necessary for establishing in the ugliest, most uncouth, most ignorant or most inadequate child the feeling of sharing equally the good will, interest and affection of the adult person. It has poised the delicate balance between natural personal warmth and the detachment essential to unconfused and unconfusing leadership.

Adult as Instrument in Pointing the Social Direction

An effective sense of security does not come to children by the adult's merely shedding "sunshine and sweetness." Neither does respect in the mere social sense make a positive impact on the psyche. It is necessary that the grown-up should belong to the children by means of integral services, the uppermost being his proving himself worthy of trust. Children must believe in him before he can lead them into believing in themselves, and this is the respect he must show them that he deals with them like people who cannot be bluffed. The first *authentic* unity in the environment will come about only when the group, together, focuses its attention upon its leader in the first real agreement about anything, to say, "He's aces," or "He's the cat's pajamas" or plainly "He's okay." Finding the adult—finding *an* adult—dependable and worthy is the beginning of disconfusion in an important area. Later the trickery he plays by substituting demanding work for glamor will be appreciated in the light of the balancing impact his total behavior has made on the child's original uncertainties and cynicism.

For a while then I must speak of the director's first and permanent function in the environment, or the use of himself as an aware and conscientious instrument carving out, against the delinquent's stony skepticism, the social steps and directions the latter is expected to walk in. It is a first technique, in fact, that by the use of himself in a consistent pattern the adult shall represent the *living* and *workable* truth of the goodness and rightness of the social standards he and the rest of the world propound. I would say that the child's relaxation from ego preoccupation parallels his belief in the adult as someone worthy to listen to and to emulate. Social agreement and social attitude will follow upon the grown-up's *consistent* proof that he is rational—aware of what he is doing and saying and why—and sincere and dependable in human relations; that his all-over portrait shows him to be what by the attitude of his teachings he pretends to be.

It would seem unnecessary to state this emphatically, but adults seldom realize how minutely children weigh and evaluate them.

Morever, the director has the far-reaching duty to lead the children over the boundary of theater into life. If he hasn't the habit of remembering this duty he will be too often, under the exigencies of theater, the overtemperamental person—not too unlike neurotic parents—or he will rest satisfied with the proper attention to things theatrical apart from life.

For example, honesty, neatness, and responsibility are standards of our society. The theater process, in the rehearsal of even a single scene or in the construction of but a single prop, imposes these standards by the ultimata of experiences which lead either to success or to failure. A word left out or thoughtlessly substituted may change entirely the author's intention; more personally, it may lead to shame-faced chaos from confusion over the wrong cue. In the prop a nail placed instead of a screw by a lazy boy, a carelessly measured supporting block, a spilling not wiped up, a too hastily knotted rope or one not checked for safety—these may bring not only misery from destruction and failure, but danger to life. Thus truly honesty, neatness, responsibility are standards the theater teaches—but does not necessarily *perpetuate!* But between theater and the world outside its walls stands the adult representative of both worlds. His pattern determines whether a code of feeling and behavior shall apply for temporary purposes to their private cosmos or shall become habitual for the totality of actual living. He must avoid the acceptance by children of a code of behavior special to their privately cherished domain. Since he is in the position of examplar this is bound to happen if he does not play the evangelist with a social vision beyond the stage curtains, constantly expressing with attitudes, with actions, and with dedication his own social qualifications. What will then be done under theater will link to a growing ideology concerned with real living; its list will read respect for others, respect for the written and spoken word, an honest day's work, left-hand awareness of what the right hand is doing, etc. These will not be precepts remembered as phrases but attitudes learned from the adult example.

(1) As specialist of the theater the director will not be concerned with tricks of elocution. Sincerity in the acting will be his goal and this will come about from his own sincere example of seeking to understand the play's words, facts, people, ideas in relationship to each other; or by the example of his own concentration on doing an honest job with the play—with the attitude less of a theater director than a person responsible, in the absence of the author, to defend the latter's work against spoilage. Thus will he establish the *spirit* of the activity

as intrinsically human or inclusive of commitments which decent people must fulfill toward others, or in behalf of what is precious to others.

(2) As leader of the group the director will initiate ways for the children to follow him in the expression of social feeling. From his respectful and protective attitude toward anticipated audiences the children will prepare for their public as for guests to be pleased rather than applauding agents coming to satisfy children's vanity. Good diction will have the social purpose of kindness to people in far seats, as will the stage positions be planned in consideration of everyone's seeing well. Responsibility will extend to the auditorium and outside the auditorium, taking cognizance of people, *other* people. The auditorium will be kept clean and safe from fire hazard. Ushers will be hosts tendering every courtesy and care for guests. Or for other examples—programs will acknowledge any outside assistance rendered the group; social niceties will be expressed, as in the tendering of personal invitations to the play to cottage parents, teachers, or social workers; occasionally the date for a play will be set to make possible the presence of real parents; other groups or children will be invited to perform under the same program, as for instance the choral group. There is no denying that some of these things would happen of themselves by some child's great desire or unusual sensitivity. But such nicety may have personal motives behind it not intrinsically social in nature. It is for the adult, by his own leading concentration on people's feelings and needs, to motivate a similar and habitual concentration in the children so it becomes a dynamic force lifting theater engrossment out of its potential specialized snobbery into community identification.

(3) What are the words and tones the director uses? There are overtones and undertones to the most casual order or request we give a child. Let us not fool ourselves, we always give away our true attitude—by a nuance, or unwittingly by a word left out or added, or by a *certain* word whose synonym might send the listener into an altogether different channel of feeling. For example, it is natural for the director to be annoyed if some members of the expectant audience come half hour too early, then impatient under the wait, interfere with the last-minute inspection of the stage or players by questions or other acts of curiosity. In exasperation the adult may say, "*They're* very annoying. *Tell* them to *get out* of here." or "*It's* very annoying. *Ask* them to *leave* . . ." The latter carries out a social attitude of forbearance and courtesy. The former gives authority to

feelings the children already have and are ready to act upon; it is a spur to hostility, arrogance, and very near violence!

(4) "Sweat, labor, work—this is a man's occupation," says a character in one of Krembourg's poem-plays. The habit of work and pleasure in work are anticipated goals in the theater project. Here the director's employing himself as a worker is important in the child-adult relationship; the adult is not asking something he is not himself doing. He may not say "Do this" or even "Do this this way"; he must himself symbolize labor. But with all the incentives he must give to children he cannot consistently labor with rapture and so enrapture them *unless* his own incentive is *great enough*.

The high, wide and handsome art vision I have spoken of elsewhere will be an essential means by which the adult engages himself, even before the children, to goals worth his ceaseless self-investment; for his first duty is to make possible his own sustained interest, as artist, in the project the group is entering upon through his inspiration. He must be inspired or his self-giving will not endure, his inventiveness will lack a prod; his labors and his talk about the day's work will lack the authentic signs of personal engrossment necessary for carrying children along with him into a sustained interest and a progressive self-giving. The project must be rich enough to carry the adult on a soaring wave of creativity, for he must dramatize in himself, to children looking to "be shown," the adult person as all-sincere, all-knowing, all-skillful, resourceful, and a happy devotee of stick-to-itive labor. The director must be endlessly active, enthusiastic; he must be human—capable of despair, having troubles, longing for success to his efforts, getting tired, exulting in results. Only an authentic interest in the project can invest the training he gives with therapeutic value, for he must never be a teacher but a partner in a labor of love. As such he is one with the children in their common humanity of striving; he is superior only as an adult should be, in experience, knowledge and responsibility as leader.

Especially in early stages of a child's efforts the director's hand must physically participate in every child's work. The adult's taking over of the brush or tool from the child's hand, his own back bent over, his face professionally engrossed with the problem, his sharing search for the solution, his magical touch undoing a seeming failure—from this wrapt devotion to the work the child absorbs a feeling of devotion to himself who knows so little, who hasn't tried hard enough, and has probably been troublesome besides. Work and aims and progress are so tied together with a new sensation of human warmth and the same sense of "belonging" and getting on to being "somebody" that a concept of work as pleasure deposes the earlier attitude of work as hardship. There awakens a need to return good for good and effort for effort to the tireless adult who examplifies in himself an equation between work and love, and standards of work, leading to success. A new emotional attitude awakens towards whole-way accomplishment—if a thing is worth one's attention at all. A project not too interesting to the director, as adult, could not possibly dramatize the meaningfulness of standards to hold the attention and the longing of unhabituated children. It is the picture of the adult straining after the ideal—in behalf of *their* project and always patient and encouraging by the side—which endears standards to them. One not only works for theater, one's first love; one works more carefully, more patiently, in emulation of theater's personal representative revealed by his efforts as sincere, having a common humanity and worthy of following in his path.

In parentheses, the director must keep by him a sense of humor; he must watch himself lest the zealot of the theater should forget he is playing a role for the purpose of being a better therapist. The child's new-found pleasure in work makes work itself a new toy, and the first effect on a child's success in work is to bolster up his ego. He feels important, useful—and so to his mind capable beyond all bounds. And one day just before a production date the whole business shows signs of collapse because one or two work-drunk children have decided to go out on their own, add some little gadget, change something here or there. Usually the culprit is the child who has gone the furthest in adjustment, on whose stability one most depends. A "brilliant" idea assails him and from the tragi-comedy which ensues the adult is likely to doubt his own sowing whether he isn't turning out schizoids instead of normal children. (See page 79 for Irving's grotesque lighting equipment.) It is only that the child has arrived definitely at a taste for work and this development has travelled quicker than his emotional rise from the infantile level. But the desire to surprise the director with an original contraption, the need to privately try out a new idea, the engrossment with what he really believes will be a contribution; these are progressive symptoms despite their peculiar quirks. Blame the example of the adult as a symbol of labor, of high standards, of originality, of the experimental attitude, of consecration. Simple childish projects could not have widened the horizon of apperception by which ideas are stimulated and the will to stand on one's own feet encouraged. The director will have to remember the distance is not so great between a child's experimenting with a crazy idea, even though *wilfully* and at a temporary cost to the entire group, and eventual experimenting *willingly* with the sane idea of growing up.

In resume, what does the adult accomplish when he considers himself as the initial tool, used with consistency, for paving an examplary path leading into social living? He establishes a social norm of conduct; through his example good manners, poise, courtesy, consideration, cleanliness become the personal expression of good feeling, good thinking, and therefore good living. He inspires the desire for the creating of beauty and by his own example as an ardent and tireless worker leads the children to recognize the law of the ideal which exacts in any effort undertaken complete giving from the person, that is, honesty of mind, hand, and heart. He dissipates the concept of easy and selfish pleasure to be gained from theater, implanting the meaningfulness of standards as the realistic means for getting from work richer and more enduring satisfactions. And last, his planning from one play to another for richer and more intensive creativity exposes uneducated children to the need for books and the three R's as necessary adjuncts to successful work. An educative and cultural process begins. The use of art books, dictionaries, encyclopedias, the search for play material and the ways and means of production; the handling of tools, typewriters, and measuring devices; acquaintanceship with paints and other materials; questions, discussions, application of knowledge, intellectual exercise stimulated, the rim of the world enlargened—all this is possible because the adult does not play down theater to the level of uneducated, inadequate children, but by his example says to them, "What I am you can be; What I can do, you too can do."

Adult Function Upon Children—Acceptance and Demand

A trying symptom of maturation is the disproportion between the enthusiasm the child feels for the new world in which he is thriving and his emotional ability to move in this world in freedom and in responsibility. Before a pendulum swings into a steady stance it goes from one extreme to other; so the delinquent child in his new state of well-being does not yet know license from freedom, which demands not only the assumption of responsibility but the acceptance of limitations and consequences; by his newly acquired vision *he* believes he is right when in the desire to stand on his own feet he goes pell-mell and headlong into a fervent aggressiveness of self-expression.

It is now the adult's function to set down controls on the child. He must become the limiting person, aim to forge, by every possible device, awakened positive attitudes into the steel of habitual patterns. Every wrong gesture, every show of useless and careless work (different from inadequate work due to personal problems or lack of skill) that is, what the child has willingly undertaken and his behavior concerning it must be noticed and he taken to account for it. He must be made aware of his deeds related to his intentions. Once he has chosen a job it must be understood that he has taken on an obligation from which there is no turning. Nor is this a contradiction of the normal adult attitude of not exacting the impossible but only what is possible for each child according to his knowledge, intelligence, experience, and development. In this vein, with firm good nature the adult must insist that the job be carried through, as planned and as promised.

But especially where a child has *willfully* undertaken a piece of work beyond his measure should he continue with it to its logical conclusion. (Often a quick adaptation on the part of the others will be necessary to substitute for work so experimented with and necessary for the production; for the group this is maturing in itself, for it calls for reactivity to situation, resourcefulness and the readiness to assume responsibility unfulfilled by others.) The director must distinguish between hostile wilfullness and the arrived at stage of progressive–destructive wilfulness. For a child can only recognize the discrepancy between his ambition and his preparation for fulfilling it by the results staring him in the face. Often laughter is a good medicine where the extreme absurdity of his failure helps the child laugh at himself so that he *desires* to return to learning step by step, or to follow a simpler plan which he discarded in his ego exaltation, and he *wills* a control on himself related to reality.

Irving's grotesque lighting equipment exemplifies this. For a bit of color witchery in the coming play we needed a stand about four feet high with a movable reflector like a turning head. We had the makings for the head and also the gelatin slides, and no anxiety because Irving took on the job. He was by this time a good artisan. Top and strip and footlights we owned were due mainly to his industry since he had become interested in the electrical work needed for our stage. These properties showed not only progress in substantial equipment but personality development in the boy; he had at last be-

On the floor, table and chair unit—prop for puppet play Treasure Island.

Posters for the coming show.

Top to bottom: Harry's proscenium plague. Model state to scale of actual state with complete lighting system and set for scene in Rope*—cooperative job of unskilled with skilled children in brother leadership. Blueprint and design for french window for Alfred Krembourg's* Lima Beans *made by Irving introduced to a new interest. Also costume illustration for same by Sylvia. Example of constructive relationship built in special boy-girl sessions of members from all-boy and all-girl groups. Suggestions for various sets.*

Corner of our workshop. Notice posters made for various needs of production; also wallpaper on tables, designed and hand stenciled for special occasion of staff play, Chekov's The Boor. *Play was staged, lighted, and crewed by the Group Theater, proud to be helpful to the staff performers.*

The Hawthorne Group Theatre Audience

come part of the group working amiably with other children; he had lost much of his old-man quality, much of his stubbornness and jealousy, and he was in fact a leader.

The stand was to be simply a four-foot wooden rod on a base, center-drilled for the wire to pass through. It had to be strong to support the weight of the reflector with its turning device. We were in a hurry; we needed time for color experimentation. But Irving had suddenly a creative brainstorm! A day or so later I found the length of wood discarded only partially hole-drilled. Somewhere he had gotten himself an iron three-foot rod. On his table were innumerable, intricate working drawings—I had taught him to do this—of a contraption which looked like the taut beads of a rosary topped by a rotund eradiating jewel.

I said, "But this isn't practical. The rod is short. How will you stand it up? Where will you rest the reflector? On what will you screw in its turning device?"

Irving, bristling, "I have to do it this way. I can't help it. I have a wonderful idea."

"Do you really know what you're doing?"

"I wouldn't start it if I didn't. And I *know* we need this in a hurry."

Of course our talks were not so brief. But Irving continued doggedly cutting, drilling, and polishing innumerable small wooden rings of varying dimensions. I recognized the symptoms of the progressive-destructive period. And in his determination to stand on his own feet the old stubbornness was again rearing its head! He would not converse; I did the lengthy talking; but just once he pleaded with a return of his developed boyishness, would I *please*, *please* let him go on with his "wonderful idea." One day he had strung some twenty-odd rings on the iron rod well fitted into a base. The group gaped at this phenomenon. Someone laughed. Irving turned on him in a stew of shamefaced defensiveness mixed with wilful despair. For above the iron length the rings, strung merely on the electric wire, buckled! The reflector was still not on; but now reality seeped into his rational mind so long beclouded with the intoxicating urge for originality. He began to falter in his engrossment, redoing his contraption for long minutes, then ignoring it for longer intervals. At last he gravitated to other work tables and threw himself with studied interest into another job.

I insisted, "What about the stand, Irving? We're waiting."

Irving: "I'll finish it. I'm thinking out something."

I: "By doing something else? You know you're holding us back?"

Irving: "Well, the boys are laughing at me. I'm not going to make it if they laugh." Suddenly came a torrent of words, and he found a way out. "Anyway, I was experimenting."

I: "You haven't finished your experiment, then."

Irving: With a show of temper, "If they're so smart let someone else make it."

I: "I'm afraid *you* will have to, Irving; go back to your job and finish what you began. By tomorrow I want to see that reflector on. You wouldn't make the stand our way, you *must finish* it *your* way."

Toward closing time the next day Irving gave a shout—"It's finished!" He carried the lamp tenderly—in both arms as though holding a baby—to the stage for its practical debut. The group rushed excitedly into the auditorium, waited with poised attention while its creator made preparations for demonstrating its beautiful powers. And indeed for one wonderful moment it shot a beauteous crimson light on the assembled set! The children cried hurrahs; Irving was in his heaven. He changed the gelatin, turned the reflector head impishly upon us, out front. We were all bathed in a golden flood. But he wanted to enjoy the full glory, be among us. He took his jealous hand off his creation, began to walk off the stage. There was a sputter, the light winked out; in the flash we saw the reflector head nod, then teeter over its loosely strung neck. Like a dead thing, but worse because not in one part and noisily, the "wonderful idea" collapsed! House lights went on, there was a run to investigate. A wooden ring rolled one way, a large screw eye the other. The silence was broken by laughter, a crescendo of rollicking, tear-streaming laughter!

It sounded like good fun; it was painful. Then the three-week struggle in Irving was eased. He laughed, too. Then he grinned, put out his hand for a shake, and said, "You win, teacher. It was a screwy idea. Don't worry, *your* way'll only take a day. Tomorrow I'll do it over again."

Actually the child failing in responsibility and the child wilfully assuming responsibility beyond his powers, both suffer anguish under the situation, especially on the score of having gone beyond the point where they can themselves yield or turn back or acknowledge fault or failure. In the turmoil of emotion they stir up in themselves they long for the guiding and even stern correction from the leader. In fact, it is expected from the adult that he should not let them get away with nonsense. Also it is the truest kind of respect he can pay them. For acceptance by itself is a wishy-washy attitude, whereas *demand* is a challenge saying, "Be grown-up as you pretend to be or follow the steps I teach you by which you may indeed become grown up."

Acceptance and demand are of course opposites; nevertheless they do not confuse the child, for they are realistically attuned to his needs—the assurance of love and the assurance of guidance by limitation. Even in the beginning under the full blast of acceptance some demanding is made, but so softly as not to be recognized and not to be called by its name. There comes the time when the adult must no longer conceal its presence.

When the taste for work has been built up and the child is relaxed and secure with the adult, when some learning has taken place and the ego has had satisfactions, then is the time to begin a campaign whose movement of expectancy from the child is cumulative. The more a child proves himself capable of doing, planning, assuming responsibility, the happier he feels in his surroundings and in his achievements, the more exacting may be the adult's love demand that he live up to better and finer performance and behavior. The culmination of demand is the final expectation that the child will assume leadership responsibility with regard to the traditions of work, cooperation, and social conduct becoming a member of the group. As leader he will be expected like any senior in a family, to help in the guidance of new comers, to share with them his knowledge and skills with the same forbearance and patience with which he has himself been treated and taught. The aim is to develop individuality within the confines of social limitation; that is, to allow the child to develop his native powers and capacities; and to train him to use his individuality constructively and happily within the social scene.

Demand does not diminish the love tie between children and the adult. As their ego ideal justified by the authority of theater he *emphasizes* by this attitude his true acceptance of children as fellow beings and fellow workers who could not possibly wish to remain debtor-infants forever.

Free Expression the Technique of Mercy—Easing the Psyche

The play must go on! This is the basis on which Demand is made and which as an ideal the children undersign. By it the group never fails; by it the individual outdoes himself. But in some cases for months, beneath the tranquil sea of activity, there are children like undertows or crosscurrents in their troubled patterns and others remaining absolutely untouched, becalmed aloof spots in the midst of industry and fellowship. The usual procedures will not establish a relationship or encourage participation with the group. If a child has not been reached, or not been *completely* reached by the adult, Demand definitely may not be used for it will stir up active hostility or drive the child out of the environment. Instead there must be something benign and permissive, and not too encroaching, in the adult attitude to create an abiding quietude in the psyche—similar perhaps to the inactive well-being of convalescence which prepares a patient gently for more bestirring days.

The child is allowed his period of Free Expression—which has nothing to do with throwing objects at furniture or people. Free Expression means simply that the environment, despite production busy-ness, is not permitted to be oppressive or confining to these children; they are allowed time off for the spirit to integrate. Though I am stressing the special use of this technique for special cases, all children are in need of this period occasionally; and so its duration may be five minutes or five months. As enjoyed by the child free expression may signify a short breathing spell in the midst of labors, a relapse in progress like Hal's, a creative exaltation like Irving's, a psychic illness, a special adjustment period necessary to some children. This period has the quality of special giving by the adult and the rest of the group (children enjoying it are quite aware of the burden it puts on others) and has the following results.

The child has proof of respect for his private needs. Unchallenged moodiness cannot long withstand indifference nor remain aloof from the surrounding to-do of activity. The free or solitary period may be the wholesome means, in the case of the talented child, to rediscover himself after a failure or after exacting duties. A child may need a short holiday after exhausting all-giving to a production. Undue stress is lifted from the child by nature withdrawn or shy and trying desperately to thaw out; the activity about him, and he unmolested, provides him with vicarious participation while he collects his energies for venturing forth actively. The unreachable child softens up, meanwhile providing the director with the chance to observe him; the mere fact of the adult's letting him alone, that is, of not impinging upon him too violently acts as a sanction for his presence, so beginning the love tie necessary for reaching him.

Minor situations are of short duration. A child may stop work and sit down to dream, idle over a book, or watch another at work; he may claim a headache or show distraction. The causes may be the need for attention, disappointment in accomplishment, or profound stirrings of guilt, loneliness, and personal anxiety. When the child is not disturbing to others the free expression period, if only as the sanction of the understanding adult, will soon resolve his mood and his idleness into a return to work. Free expression asks for wisdom on the part of the director, when to whisper with a boy about his state, when to advise him, when to ignore him. On the other hand, a boy will one day shirk his work and begin to paint a Mother's Day card, or to carve the Ten Commandments on a plaque as a gift to the rabbi or minister. The director being human may feel annoyed. His time and energy are being wasted and the expression of love is for someone else. But the feeling for the carving or the painting comes from this environment—as well as the confidence that one can paint or carve! Some months ago the boy lived on the narcissistic level of expecting all good things from others! Some months ago he had no skills! He had neither an active love capacity nor the power of creativity for translating such a feeling! Decidedly this is a development similar to the progressive-destructive period—infantile in the thoughtless neglect of immediate duty, but mature in the urge to work out the inspiration for a love deed or an all-giving to someone out of affection. It is wise for the director to be more than permissive, to actually help the child with such a project. Not to do so is to be inconsistent as a social person, for the child is stepping over the boundary of theater by the lessons taught him in the theater. However, it is real for such a child to recognize limitations; demand should be put on him—to make him aware of the infantile aspect of his behavior—by some arrangement which permits his working on the private project on the basis of his fulfilling his group responsibility.

Major situations call for more complex handling and may endure for several weeks or for many months. Paul and Ben are examples of boys, one apparently dull and the other an "intellectual," brought by the privilege of free expression into health development—the former out of a schizoid pattern and the latter out of a superiority complex. I introduce the two children together because of the dramatic contrast of their makeup and of the problems they presented. Ben grew only partially on free expression; Paul's growth from an unreachable child into a healthy youngster came exclusively out of the laissez-faire period.

Ben was a shy boy, but he stated with a rehearsed boldness that he had no interest in the Group except as a means of using me for help in the writing of a play. Between blushes and stammerings he conveyed to me his belief that he could become another Odets; also that I would have to accept him on his own terms. He wasn't being granted; he was assuming free expression as his prerogative, his attitude saying, "The world owes me everything. I owe it nothing." But his self-confidence about writing was a challenge! I disregarded my usual procedure, recognizing that acceptance of this boy with the immediate grant of free expression would have to include a sterner component—demand. He would have the use of me to the fullest development of his talent, but also he would begin to pay immediately. By demand he would begin to "work for the world," though apparently outside of the group of cooperating children and seemingly a privileged person. I presented the price—for my private help in special hours he would have to do the following: do his pre-lesson writing in the heart of the group as a member of the Group Theater, write the play *for* the group and therefore set a date for its finish to give time for rehearsals and scenic building for a Halloween production; use the theme appropriate for such a holiday; create roles to include as many of his fellows as possible short of ruining the plot and the structure of the play; eventually interest the children by reading aloud his finished scenes and by welcoming discussion and criticism—my argument was the importance of arousing and sustaining the interest of those who later would be working for his play; promise to take a role himself—I argued that the author feels the central role better than anyone else.

And—I intimated physical duties, too, like sweeping around his work table and later taking a hand in the construction of his sets. But Ben did not write immediately. He was not at home with the boys; in a torturous way he alternated his behavior between shy aloofness and strutting, talking big and waxing worldly wise. But as he pretended to be writing I gave him his private lessons, took him to the library, and taught him how to look for his subject material. Then one day I used demand by inference. I refused to keep an appointment with him for our private session. That afternoon, in Group, Ben did some wrapt writing. Thus it went on for six weeks during which he half idled and half assumed his commitments. The first act was finally written and read aloud, and rewritten. Ben had taken criticism from the boys! He also had had the taste of companionship on the basis of a common interest. He shed some of his ego preoccupation; he was less shy and less spectacular; in fact, he was becoming a Group Theater boy. The feeling that the progress of his play mattered to so many people warmed what was lonely in him. His writing became technically better; but more than this, it began to have an inspired quality. Actually Ben had a literary gift! The free expression gave him the opportunity to experiment with it as well as to achieve an acceptance relationship within the group.

How different Paul who sat for weeks untouched, disinterested, becalmed! Why he came day after day was hard to say. However, paints and crayons attracted him, I saw, by his brief attempts to work with them. Because of this I tried to motivate him, asking would he like to design a set for Ben's play. I see his face vividly. He just barely changes his expression, which seems to say, maybe, he might try. There follow days when Paul sits over the paper as in a trance, immobile, eyes inward turned—or on a vision, it is hard to determine. Then abruptly he draws. It looks like creative preoccupation in the rhythm of seeing inwardly first, then fructifying. But day after day without discernible change in the done-over drawings the subject is *death*. Truly Ben's play has Satan in it, the River Styx and a child on All Halloween Eve stolen to the nether regions. But Paul's sketches show a cemetery on each side of a dividing road, and always there are crosses to mark the graves. My attitude is that of a professional producer—why a cemetery for a play not requiring one, would he like to read the description of the scene in the script? I also appraise the merit of his drawing. I go slowly with this boy, then one evening show surprise about the crosses since he is Jewish. A new cemetery appears and behold! there is one lone star there. Paul tells me, "My mother lies here."

From then on I push at Paul, I drag him from his inner preoccupations to reality. "Paul, what do you think of this?" "Paul, will you mix the paints?" "Paul, if you want to be a scenic artist you should know something about lighting—ought we to have a purple light here, or would green be better?" Little by little the boy is pulled into discussion. He has to answer. Occasionally he shows a biting wit, sometimes he joins in laughter. But abruptly one day he gives up his job, although he has at last a sketch within the frame of reality. He has decided to write a play for the Group; he can write a better one than Ben's!

Paul had not the mentality to write a play; still, this was the first expression of a positive interest to come from him. In some mysterious way the impact of his surroundings had pricked his ego to vie with the most sensitive and intellectual child in his proximity. If he could write, what rich material would he disclose related to his macabre drawings! What seethings within him sought expression which later I might turn over to the psychiatrist? Besides, sheer of destruction, I would let him try anything to thaw him out. An odd thing happened. Frozenly aloof from other boys, Paul was close with one dullard with whom he often engaged in conspiratorial whisperings. It was now their joint desire to collaborate on the promised play; now also, this partner was to enjoy free expression. Both dark, stunted boys took on an air of pompous importance—in fact, Paul emanated a vitalized quality as though he had found a purpose in life. At their isolated table they wrote endlessly, constantly consulting each other and showing signs of hyperexcitement. They would not show me their writing until it was finished, but I wasn't to worry. *Their* play was going to be a *real* one about *real* people; *they* didn't have to imagine things like Ben because coming from the same neighborhood in Brooklyn they had *seen plenty* and had *done things* themselves. The weeks passed—their effort was represented by reams of scribbled paper crumpled up, tossed away, rewritten. But Paul looked human! His eyes had the steady glow of living embers; they no longer signalled icy or overwrought emotion.

Then the genius mood began to work itself out. The two commenced to idle. No more whisperings, no more writing; they began to hover curiously over other children's projects. Paul said, "H—I'm no playwright! Let me finish the designs for Ben's play. Honest, I'm going to work this time." This was something from a child who had sat for some four weeks in idle somnolence, had taken another two months for pretending a participation without learning and without results. And Paul did design and later execute two sets of the five needed for Ben's play! In a year he was the busy man all over the place, with a springy walk and a possessive-protective attitude toward the properties of our shop. In the second year the boy was working feverishly in multiple fields, outstandingly as an actor and as a master electrician.

Free expression, in an environment elastic enough to permit it, unfolded Paul from his dark preoccupations, gave him interests and incentives to bestir himself who was an escapee from life. Demand that he behave and do like the other children would have driven him out of the environment to which by some instinct he had been attracted. How he would have fared without the impacting theater atmosphere and without the specially patient treatment is a subject for speculation. For in the cottage, in the classroom, there is not the ever-present current of energy from vital activity to shock awake a child despite himself—listening to the radio or making beds in the one or doings sums in the other can hardly have such dynamic, subtly indirect power. Even acceptance had to be indirect, treading lightly, speaking not too clearly nor too warmly, but remaining close like a fire on the hearth awaiting his outstretched hand—without the technique of free expression neither the cottage parent nor the teacher were prepared, despite kindly intentions, to leave Paul to himself long enough for his self-integration.

Every Scrap of Paper Tells a Tale

I learned something from Paul. Naturally I wanted to know what he was writing about. Since he showed me nothing I made a practice of uncrumpling his papers when all the children had gone. There it was—repetition ad nauseum, the story not now of cemeteries but of life ugly and disillusioned; and life was real and of the lower depths. The effect was that of a repeated cinema short around a fixed idea. Money exchanged hands for the delivery of a girl to a house. Whether in imagination or in memory of terrible experience, these two boys were pimping! The social worker (I reported this) said it was imagination. I spoke to the boys; their verbal exposition of life as they knew it amplified the vivid detail of the writing (boys have often told me with a humorous awe that the really bad things they did had not brought them to court, but some minor infraction). Whether it was imagined or real material doesn't matter. That which had been troubling them had been worked out of the system. Ever after, I made the habit to read every scrap of paper left on tables or tossed away. I learned from Paul that these were the unguarded revelations of the thoughts, feelings, and doings of disturbed children, that these compulsive expressions of inner life, if understood by me, would help infinitely in the weighing of what to do for and with such and such a child.

Demand by Physical Discipline

Physical punishment is a dangerous weapon too easily used by adults themselves inadequate, insecure, or hostile. Only where love is the foundation of the adult-child relationship may a blow be given and only if the cause warrants such extreme behavior that the shock of being struck by a person known to be sincere and friendly will act like a catharsis. Paul was now under the technique of demand; he was a leader; he was happy in his enjoyment of status within and outside the Group. But he used a shrewd bit of business against me when jealous of my attention to newcomers. Remembering how he had gained my first devotion, he would, at the height of our greatest effort when time was short and our nerves taut, stop in his role of actor or electrician, and effect his original pattern of unhearing and unseeing rigidity. This would happen just before a production date when all the children were outdoing themselves. Particularly because Paul was a leader such unseeming behavior upset them; the impulse was to handle him among themselves, but they waited instead to see what I would do.

Since my voice did not reach his ears, nor reasoning his mind because of his compulsion to possess my exclusive devotion, what was there to do as adult leader, but to use physical means! Twice he had had the upper hand; my appeals were exactly what he wanted—work stopped, all attention centered on him, and he poignantly but satisfactorily the core of my universe. I made a decision to use physical punishment if he behaved that way again. The next time, with what calm deliberation I could muster, I struck him with the back of my hand across his face. It was a stinging slap, which brought tears to his eyes. But it worked! Because the boy knew it was not enmity which struck him but outraged affection disappointed in him, and seeing through him! He apologized, nor did he resort to his trick again.

We had a private talk in which Paul recognized his conflict between continuing in the direction of maturity and reverting to his infantile position under free expression. The slap was a shock treatment necessary at this stage. It brought the boy permanently into reality; actually it was a needed adjunct to the earlier special love period, for observing Paul then I became convinced that much of his becalmed pattern was an act pretty much on the border of consciousness of what he was doing.

I am convinced, too, that modern squeamishness of physical punishment (I used it but four times in five years) is sentimentalism, pity the poor child, etc., and not true leadership. A child must learn his life's lessons from the person he looks up to. When no other method works, demand by physical means is indicated; some children under certain circumstances react positively and permanently to this shock treatment administered by the beloved and loving person. In this case Paul had to learn (as did Hal by another way) that love requires a return in kind, that it is stern as well as understanding, that it may not be outraged with impunity. Unfortunately, physical punishment has the harsh connotation of brutality. But it can be a love expression of sincere anxiety over the child misbehaving himself. As such it dramatizes the child's affront to mature standards.

The Social Person—Individuality and Conformity

Free expression has its dangers. If not used with temperance, the effect on the child will be a pampering of an awakened individuality swimming voluptuously on the crest of special privilege. The ego will be inflated by its power to hold in obeisance a busy adult and his own peers unusually patient with him. This is a technique of forced nursing and it is well to remember that patients under long tending are apt to become demanding and self-centered, what the delinquent in most cases already is abundantly. The hygienic aspect of this granted period is the child's security in the affection and respect of a strange adult, or his security in a world no longer hostile and awakening in him positive feelings. However, I have indicated in the cases of Ben and Paul how necessary it is to make efforts to tie the child realistically to the concrete problems of the whole group, to send him into coactive experience even while free expression is pressing out personal deviations. The goal must be—"You are loved and you are able to love. You are finding life good. You are discovering you are an interesting fellow who can do interesting things. But to merit love, to continue to love, to discover more about yourself, you must participate, give of yourself, become one of the fellows." Demand steals in softly in this period in the guise of encouragement which is really expectation.

Acceptance has its dangers; even though the mass of children works together from the beginning with less privilege and with more giving, the adult attitude centers pointedly around the individual. The temporary results from both techniques are good. Gradually individuality becomes positive. "I am somebody," feels the child in his innards, and "I belong." His opinions counting, his work growing, he sings at his labors. He is happy, but his new being has a quality of intoxication—"Behold. See me! I am surpassing myself!" is an overtone of his pattern within the group and abroad. He is wider awake, enthusiastic, outgoing, becoming socially aware and filled with the sense of power. He has been encouraged to speak out, to be original and enterprising with little curb to personal expressiveness provided it has some element of constructivity. Even demand has had the attitudinal quality of concern only for the child—that *he* or *she* might be happy, learn, grow, work out ideas, get praise, enjoy status! Therapeutically this has been good, realistically not so good.

To go out into the world, know his place, get along, hold a job, he must also know how and when *not to do* and *not to speak*. Individuality needs also to learn conformity to make really the social person. The social person needs to own that aspect of social intelligence which tells how to behave with superiors, which indicates when obedience is called for or when initiative may *not* be taken. The theater child must be taught conformity or the awareness of time, place and situation which demands that individuality put a controlling leash on self-expression.

This is easily taught because it fits in with the highest need of a good production. After the experimental stages of the play, when in the professional language everything is "set," the director takes over as a *professional martinet*. Actors on the stage, men at stations with the scenery or with the lights, the director out front in a darkened auditorium, his wish is *law;* his orders or criticisms *commands*. No discussions; answers to his questions must be brief and quick; directions must be followed without protest or explanation. A child sent backstage with the director's request must be respected and the request fulfilled promptly. No matter how far gone any child is in his role of crewman or actor, no matter what the cost this may mean in replacements, no child can remain in his job if he cannot conform to what the director calls the "emergency period." It is expected that everyone will yield up his personality out of deference to the total situation. This personality-submerging technique applies even sooner in the workshop where stock is taken of the progress made in the essentials for the play, and the "busy season" is on for finishing up all work. From then on no changes may be made, no personal opinions honored, no personal vagary permitted. Theater is not at this time an environment of acceptance. It is a factory where all hands work as one under orders from the director, a hard boss who wants a good day's work done. This discipling is of course related to the length of time a child has been in the Group, or to his development and the adult's right of expectation from him. We may say that this is demand according to the outside world's expectation from its workers most of the time.

Resourcefulness: *Idols made from cast-off piano legs for scene in desecrated Temple reconquered by the Maccabees—for the play;* The Banner of the Jew, *specially written to give birthright heroes to racially insecure children. Also; drum made for* Sitting Bull, *an Indian play; chosen for a holiday from more serious play material but yielding constructive experience in the feeling; customs; etc.; of another people.*

High Standard a Preparation for Living Fully

It may be argued that exact lighting or perfect acting or the best construction work need not be the standards for a children's theater. Certainly delinquent children get easy praise for even slight achievement. Sentimental praise like this is damning; it does not prepare them to face a world which will not reward shoddy workmanship, nor pay for pretense; nor is the delinquent so unknowing of the world and himself that he enjoys easily garnered approval. Moreover youth wants the thrill of overcoming obstacles. He revels in the sense of fitness and full-grownness which is his even in the *attempt* to overcome obstacles. Skill and subject matter control, conquest over stubborn materials, the struggle of the unschooled mind to visualize a plan or make a contribution to glamorous theater are experiences emotionally thrilling, similar to Jack's climbing the beanstalk, an insignificant youth hoping to kill the giant. When attainment is too easy the thrill departs, interest wanes. "Kid stuff," says the child, which means anybody can do it; for the delinquent has the psychology of the "bigshot," the fellow who covers up inadequacies with the pretense of being extra adequate. But this is his strongest weakness, the clue to how to make him truly adequate, or the ground on which to combine his living on an exciting plane with the realistic opportunity to rid himself of his false front. The high standard of achievement makes possible a cathartic struggle in which, wrestling with obstacles thereby discovering genuine values, he wrestles with himself until he achieves personal genuineness.

When in spite of deficiencies, lapses, and inner disturbances he enraptures an audience with the almost perfect beauty of a well-done play this imperfect child feels beautiful himself. No one but himself can give him the shining eyes, the straightened body carriage which are the emanations of *self-approval* measured by the man-sized effort he put into the accomplishing of a man-sized job.

The paradox of the high standard—the emphasis on perfected workmanship measured by the mature concepts of soundness, truth, unity of purpose—is that the child's consecration to ideals leads him closer to real life. It prepares the engrossed and activated child for existence in the competitive outside world by letting him put himself through the ringer of an exalting *self-competition*. If the goal of theater is really the child, then the goal of production must be perfection, for in the search for it lies the spiritual experience which prompts the child to "perfect" himself. Each successive play production should by its stiffer problems and goals make applause harder to win so that its winning is the real climax or culminating curtain of an actually lived out drama in which each child has played daily the role of protaganist. There is no fear that any child will suffer from being a perfectionist. The environment is too human, the art process too experimental, experiment too close to the quality of real living in the breathless watching over results, in the hair's-breadth differentiation between defeat and relative success. The heart and eye poised over professional perfection become intrinsically human, not only because catharsis mellows, but because it is shared with others "in the same boat." The higher the goal of production, the more it calls for all-giving, the closer out of necessity stand all the children in togetherness, helpfulness, common humanity.

For firsthand, they learn in the struggle for achieving standards that self-expression to be fruitful has to lean heavily on the fruitfulness of others as on their interest, encouragement, and forbearance of mistakes. The about face of the director during the emergency period would seem unacceptably authoritative did not cooperativeness become a rule of activity by its patent proofs that one does better and gains more well-being by it. Cooperativeness is not something which can be taught but only learned when something tremendous is at stake. Small indifferent ventures do not necessitate the girding of loins, the anxious following of a rainbow, the shoulder to shoulder march toward a goal, the united heartbeat over trouble, the circle of hands helping against defeat.

Cooperativeness is the affirmation of conformity. The knowledge of when to act givingly in self-expression and when not to act givingly, or when to give by not acting outwardly, is the fulcrum of balanced personality. The standard of perfection establishes the balance because its presentation of stern reality gives the child the learning opportunity to make demands on himself from the observable necessity of the total situation. With so much at stake, himself inseparable from the rest, he desires simultaneously his own enlargement and the perfection of the totality of work and of children; self-interest teaches him self-restraint.

The high standard aims at the future. The child will have to work, will need to know how to spend leisure time to invest his humble life with some dignity. He needs a preparation for warding off a return to corner and poolroom activity. The high standard stresses self-competition, that is, a regard for oneself as a total person for whom happiness lies in a keen curiosity about life and in the effort to know more, do better, relate better to circumstances and people and to new ideas. The self-competition of the high standard aims at effacing the envious, uncreative live-up-to-the-Joneses pattern of life the children are heir to.

For the child's workaday life it brings home the truth that in the world of work every man has a full job to perform, though sometimes a humble one, which is part of a bigger plan; that his share in the plan is limited (the high standard teaches limitations as well as extensions) to his own capacity; that if work is to be not slavery but freedom, in himself lies this freedom to make himself more valuable in the scheme of things by volitional exertion toward self-improvement.

For his private life, it prepares him to be an interesting, self-confident person. He discovers he is capable in many constructive ways; he has interests that prove pleasurable and profitable to his self-respect. He knows what to do with time because he knows what to do with his hands and with his mind. In the future he can join clubs which will welcome him with open arms, for he knows how to build, paint, converse, act, be intelligent about books and about the theater. He can lead others in the fulfillment of difficult plans. He has posture, appearance, good speech—social assets. Or he can relax at home with books, which have become meaningful companions. I do not pretend that the creative life as a permanent concept reaches all children profoundly. But merely as a carryover in the child starting anew, the memory of proven abilities and endeared interests still fresh will tend to fortify him in the difficult period when he must face the full blast of the world and perhaps need a special courage from self-confidence to say no to old pals waiting to pull him down again.

And last, as there can be no catharsis in a light comedy, so there can be none in this theater activity without hard-to-attain goals to intensify life, to epitomize what it actually is, real and earnest with its pleasures and joys having to be labored for and not always completely won. Children, like the rest of us, do not learn the truths of life by precepts but only by translation in terms of self from deep experience. What a child translates from his accumulated experience from many productions—his trials, errors, and human impacts; his swim and rise and fall in varied rhythms of emotion, serene or indifferent, exalted or low; his awareness feasted on so much learned, above all about humans as all subject like himself to law not written in penal books; in the final achievement, his union with others in the selfless joy of success; and in the aftermath his standing alone, having learned in this that each must stand alone, to appraise himself and to regird his loins for better effort for truer personal success—what the child translates from this is that life erstwhile hostile and confusing is merely strict to one and all alike, yet quite wonderful and rewarding if one meets her on her own universal terms instead of wilfully pitting against her on private terms.

The results of long-term molding by the high standard can be seen in the social portraits presented by Ben and by Max in their first year in the world. I doubt if Ben on his return home would have been gotten by the corner gang. He was not a follower and believed too much in himself as a writer. But he had it in him to become a jobless library bum, scribbling but never really writing, warming the reading-room chairs, smugly cynical of a society which had frustrated his dreams. I have no intention to insist that only theater had to be the medicine for a good many boys and girls; but for Ben I do insist even though at the school he was active also in the newspaper club. For I treated Ben's writing as seriously as though he *were* Odets coming to me for, and capable of accepting, professional criticism. This discipline of perfection immobilized his pretentions both about writing and about the world's debt to him; it was a mark of respect to him and a challenge to real work. And in the same group the same expectation of perfection in other labors and in his human relationships immobilized his snobbery and made him face himself as a total person. Two things Ben took with him to start life afresh: a desire for a job, that is, an attitude toward work as a means of self-sustenance and self-respect; a knowledge of dramaturgy (he wrote three splendid plays); and an attitude toward his writing as something related to real living, sustained effort, and continued education. This was before Pearl Harbor. When I saw him in the city (he very proudly treated me to coffee in a cafeteria) he had a humble daytime job, but had had two promotions and was attending high school evenings with a plan for college. He was supporting his family and had taken under his special care a younger brother, who was "going a little wild." And in what time he had left he was working on a novel!

Max had been a newsy and a petty thief. In the Group Theater he had become my righthand man and a good actor. On parole he took a job as soda jerk. But also he won a scholarship in one of the largest YMHA chapters in Manhattan in its school of acting. A year later a greater honor was bestowed on him. A leader was needed for a junior group of boys, and Max was appointed for the job! And later on a visit to me Max came to teach his teacher! He brought for me several political pamphlets. And here I must report that after this visit I was rejected by the boy as the older generation always is, temporarily, at some time by the newer. For Max was carrying a banner, in his heart burned a cause greater than theater; and I who had stimulated his intellectuality and planted the seeds for impassioned feeling, for curiosity and for courage, now seemed to have none of these myself. I became another grown-up who "just couldn't understand" when I pleaded, not against his passionate ism, but that he wait until he was of age to involve himself politically. But he was *youth*; in my anxiety over his getting into trouble, I forgot his was the period of ecstacy, the time for embracing causes, the windmill age of vision for a better world. I had sent him out into the world sure of himself, a social man. His way of being a social man was to immediately do something about the bad things in this world. For three years I had been his ideal person. Now another had become the ideal person! I should say Max was doing all right for a boy with his ardent nature! But this, too, he outgrew.

Help for the Defective, the Dull, the Untalented

I receive a Christmas card from Harry which says "God Bless You." I receive one from Paul which has an original poem ending with the sentiment "For you made of me a Man." Hal is discussed at the teachers' table; a teacher new at the school, and knowing nothing about the boy's two-year connection with the Group Theater, has just returned from Syracuse University where he had taken several of our children to participate in the nationwide contest in commercial subjects. This teacher speaks with awe—"Here was Hal in a crowd of college boys. What poise! *He* was telling *them* all they didn't know about acting, playwriting, staging, and many other subjects. I was flabbergasted! He had a better vocabulary than these college boys. They sat and listened to him. He was criticizing a movie we all went to. They still don't know the bright chap didn't come from a swanky private school."

Three boys—a stutterer, a dullard, and the third showing no apparent abilities, only that he was trying hard to be tough as they make them, but not succeeding. These, like Ben, could have been helped nowhere else as in the theater. Harry blessed me because his stuttering no longer made him incommunicado with his fellows, because no matter what happens in all the rest of his life he will always have the encouraging memory of having won the prize for speech in the graduation exercises of the academic school.

Paul we know very well by now. Before induction into the army from a southern city, he had been earning his livelihood there for two years as an all-around stage man in a small community theater—and this means construction, lights, crew work, janitoring, and stepping into a part without notice when emergencies arise. Hal, with whom I fought through a searing struggle in his conflict to be or not to be the boy he was intended to be, sensitive, beauty-loving, refined, and was won away from compensatory rowdyism through his engrossment with acting, before induction into service worked in the office of the rubber administrator of the War Production Board. Can one believe from his letter to me that such social judgment could possibly come from a child whose case worker said I was wasting my time with an "unreachable boy"? I quote—" . . . technically I work for Jeffers but actually I am in with Col. Bradley Dewey the Deputy Rubber Director who actually does the dirty work. *There* is a living definition of Americanism. A man who wants no publicity, a man who ruins his health in his all-out contribution to the war effort, a man who handles the critical section of the country's rubber situation with such diplomacy, patriotism and intelligence that I am more than a little awed with respect. He is a towering man with beautiful white hair and a booming voice . . . he'll not tolerate one of the many firm representatives who come to Washington out of selfish motives, but let someone express genuine concern . . . or offer informative suggestions . . . and then you see my definition of an American. Quite a man, Dewey." Mr. Dewey, have you ever in all your career had a finer, more sincere tribute offered you? Did you guess that the slender, soft-voiced youth, quick to obey your orders, ofttimes making humorous errors in spelling, too, had some three years ago been a budding enemy of the people?

Hal came to say good-bye to me; he was now one of Uncle Sam's boys. Like Max he, too, carried a pamphlet. But Colonel Dewey had become *his* ideal person. Hal was interested in Americanism. The pamphlet was a critique on Thomas Jefferson! Had I seen Kingsley's play, *The Patriots?* He, Hal, had been disappointed in it; he didn't agree with the interpretation; he had been doing a lot of reading about early Americans. And before me lies his first letter from his base in California. "My battery is the A group eligible for Officers' Training School. . . . The disheartening part is that though I have the march orders down to a tee, and handle the men well and can feel they respect me, lacking the necessary schooling I will have to instead take the eight weeks extensive radio operator course . . . No, this isn't the old Hal talking, I am not even remotely bitter. I have no one but myself to blame and if it was physically possible I'd kick myself where it would do most good. I am trying hard and if I make the grade I go to advanced school in Los Angeles and get a rating as Staff Sergeant which isn't bad for an eighteen year old soldier. . . ."

Let us examine the human status of these three boys before they found the many-sided, engrossing, and receptive environment of theater to welcome them in their troubled condition. Two of them. Harry and Hal, were unreachable by their caseworkers. To other adults Harry's stuttering was unbearable and they could not be bothered with him, while Hal's smiling mockery lurking behind shadowed eyes was an offense to adult inadequacy—or egotism—which? As to Paul, what could bring him out of his withdrawn state into the living world, and who could deal with eyes frozen and ears deaf to request or to command? The psychiatrist? But what can be done with a patient whose intelligence and will to be helped remain becalmed behind an icy barrier of indifference?

We may ask: Did the stutterer stutter because he stuttered or because the reactivity of people to his defect intensified it so that the difficulty with vocal expression was now a piled-up *result* of cruelty, inhibition, frustration, loneliness, lack of ego-satisfying and ego-building activity? We may ask about Hal: Was that mockery in his eyes vicious or was it a defense against further disillusionment; were not the satanic glint and the excessive effort to be tough of the same protective coat worn precisely because the boy *was reachable* but sought safety in camouflage against newer hurts? And of Paul we may ask: Was he dull because of a finding made through an intelligence quotient; was he dull for all time or because emotional and mental reactivity to outer life had not been stimulated by strong enough forces able to counteract the absorption of his inner energies by exciting fantasies, part memory and part make-believe?

Especially these types of children should be a challenge to the director. All of them need acceptance and all need ego-awakening activity. Unlike the talented, such children have no fighting belief in themselves, no anchorage to a stubborn self-esteem on some ground to give life zest and purpose even in the midst of chaos. By talented I mean the known or observable capacity of a child, especially when he is aware of it and fighting passionately for its recognition. I maintain, however, that delinquency except in the moron is an expression of greater than normal vitality; hence most children have beneath their layers of deficiency, defectiveness, indifference, banality, or dullness unplumbed potentials for the ascent into constructive living, that is, potentials for normal emotional capacity, capabilities, even real talent. The great need for such children is to be anchored to a fresh vision of themselves as persons in one way or another individually remarkable. The adult must find the way to ensconce them in a new human role so attractive yet sustainable that they will strive to perpetuate it. Inspired interests, manipulated work experience, opportunity for self-discovery, incentive for striving and climbing—a child becomes reachable the moment he cherishes existence for his right to pat himself on his own back. Existence became sweet to Harry, for example, when he found contrary to his lifetime rejection that we were all appreciative of his witty turn of mind; to Paul when we attitudinally told him he was valuable to us even while still indulging in his wakeful sleep; to Hal when we treated him like a nice boy and consecrated the time of several rehearsals—and the efforts of the other children—to the development of his part as though it were special. From then on the delinquent vitality—including neurotic trends—began slowly to stop short of rejecting goals, were they overt, guarded, or entirely introverted. To conclude, the therapy of theater lies in the inclusiveness of all children as though a theater production did not at all depend upon specialized knowledge or ability but upon the discovery of these assets where they are not supposed to exist.

Problem of Awareness—The Interview

In general all problems tend to occur and all techniques are apt to be employed simultaneously within the group, but not uniformly, because no two children are ever on the same plane of personal progress. What is uniform, like an army's having by a certain time to reach a named destination, is the expectation of progress for the *whole* group in the fulfillment of the production plan. Ideally, it is expected even by the child himself that the buildup of his personality will parallel the forward movement of the art process, for he is aware of the relationship between his participating performance and his attitudes and behavior.

But development itself often wears horns on its head. The

maturing delinquent, if I may say it this way, passes through a new adolescent period. He is dependable, happy, makes big strides in his work, his responsibilities, his relationship; then unaccountably he has a setback, he has a seizure of up-and-down rhythms which last for many weeks. Awareness has come to him! Awareness uniting his subjective with the objective world. He becomes introspective. Awareness whispers disproportionate facts to him about himself. He has taken on most earnestly the "cause," the ideal, or the goal; he wants to outdo himself; he is irked by limitation; he sees incomplete fulfillment as the result of personal fault. He expresses this either in unexpected truculence, moodiness, or loss of interest, or in words of despondency—"What's the use . . . I'm just no good." Inevitably—and through the years every child has arrived at this climax—there comes a day when in a kind of stubborn defiance, a self-punishing mechanism, he wants to quit. When pressed for the reason the answer is always the equivalent to "I'm no good, I'm only spoiling things for you." In fact, he has been the cause of irritation, loss of time and work, weakened morale in the others—the latter because the stage of self-rebuke, negativeness, and threats of withdrawal arrives when the child has become more or less of a leader.

But he is not now a delinquent child! He is a growing person. Everyman faltering on the upward climb! It is simply that the swing from rationalization, which habitually blamed the world for what he was, is now in its naturally extreme opposite point of the arc, where he places severe judgment upon himself. He is timid. He is fearful of not ever making his goal. His tenancy in the art process and the proofs of his own mastery have pieced together for him his once disjointed universe; and now that he sees it whole and including him, at the slightest failure he feels unworthy; more than this he dreads he will lose his heaven, and so in his growing pain he maneuvers the free gesture of giving it up of his own accord.

This is the time the adult must specially motivate, encourage, praise the child, reason with him, build up in him a counter self-illumination for dissipating the darkening shadows. He may never be too busy to see the child in privacy, for the *interview* seemingly casual is a restatement of acceptance and respect, two needs the child has in this period. The interview becomes, too, the hour of guidance. Of his own accord, usually, the child asks, "May I see you *alone*." Sometimes two in the same predicament ask together, meaning the three of us will be "alone."

I never anticipated the profound meaningfulness of a private talk apart from the noisesome atmosphere of the shop seething beneath its cordial air with too much variation in personality. What a marked effect upon the troubled boy it is to be quietly in the same place, which, silenced of the life of other children and of the sound of tools, emanates gently an unexpected and peaceful austerity! Things which are part of, or completed, dreams stand about or lie on tables, floor, or "horses." Things which perhaps ten minutes ago he touched with tender or reckless or indifferent hands face him with detached, albeit benign, impersonal judgment—things created, by the reflecting mirror of theater, censoring or praising the creator! Props, frames, partly finished furniture, here perhaps a Roman arch, there the walls of a cabin for a play by Eugene O'Neill, a tree beginning to bear its appliquéd foliage, a curtain halfway stenciled with bluebirds, curling roses more grandiose than in nature for Pierrette, a "sculptured" bust of Caesar done in paints, posters, electrical units, the puppet ship for *Treasure Island;* and reclining, standing, and sitting, puppet people, impassive appraisers from their distant world, and more and more.

These separately, whether in light or in shadow, take on a holiness as objects sanctified by tender memory. To the chld who was part of their making some few minutes ago, ages seem to have passed and with them the goodness of life. A quiet emotion gathers in him compounded of gratitude, humility, and reconsecration! I have seen it happen over and over again, the moment of ingrown solitude followed by the swift illumination of the whole being, and then this glow breaking into a self-conscious attempt at casual speech. "Gee! We've done a lot of work!" says the boy, or "Gosh! We're not so bad." The voice has a hushed quality. Soon he is moving about examining the work of his fellows. He stops before an outstanding piece and says, "Jake is doing all right; he's doing better and better." He laughs reminiscently. "Remember what trouble we had with him?"

We– he says we, not I or you or objectively the Group, but intimately in identification with the whole—*we*. But it is hard for him to stop before his own work. He hangs away, but how can he keep from it? Mixed emotions play in his face, then it brightens. "It doesn't look so bad! Why did I think . . . but . . . !" He turns with a grateful accusation, "You did something to it . . . I'm sure it didn't stand up like this—that's why I was disgusted." The adult answers, "Yes, I did, right under your nose while you were moping.

Look!" It is probable that the director simply pulls away a sliver of wood and the project sags, or corners gape, or canvas wrinkles. The boy is overcome. "Is that all there was wrong with it, such a little thing? I can paste that wood in or maybe nail it. Then *why* did I go haywire over it?" Says the director, "It was a very little thing except that you made it big by refusing to listen. You wanted it perfect, but you wanted it in a hurry. . ." Contritely speaks the boy, "*That's* the trouble with me . . . such a little thing and I was ready to throw it all up." The real interview begins. (Interview with Milton, p. 265.)

It is unique on several counts. The boy no longer hides behind words; he seems to understand himself. He traces back from the work situation to the facets of his current and past behavior. He pours out like a confessional his conflicts, fears, and hopes. He digs honestly—though he may still confuse issues—into himself to pin down exact feelings and thoughts. In the attempt to evaluate his progress he brings in the material of his delinquent history, *though the adult has never even by attitude suggested a knowledge of it.* One feels the child is groping his way into the future. And beautifully the cleansing outpour has dignity, for despite his ordeal the boy respects his listener by his self-conscious care in the choice of words. "I used to do things . . . you'll understand what I mean . . . to other boys . . . ." It is so simple an understatement; but the child knows the adult has understood the whole story. What a travel from a theater prop which would not stand up to an unbidden confession of secret private behavior!

Two things are indicated: the theater experience has taught the boy the interdependence of all things—behavior, performance, relationship, well-being; the theater leader is an adult to trust, a friend who will not treat lightly nor take advantage of self-revelation. Yet the same child in this sensitized period shies away from his caseworker's calling a spade a spade. "You shouldn't speak to *me* about this," I have often said. "Why don't you see your caseworker?" In one answer or another the response has been the equivalent of "I don't like the way he speaks to me." Yet this boy may still be vulgar-mouthed when on a rampage or when off-guard with his pals. But theater has refined his sensibilities. He cherishes the interview with the director because communion is dignified by tact; language is human, not clinical; attitude is personally warm, not professionally detached. The director does not usurp the place of the specialized worker, but as a personification of adult wisdom, understanding, and helpfulness he alone, though mincing no words, has the power to help the child through this growing-pains period. The interview comes logically from an inner need born of the living situation known to the adult who is not an official confessor but is a fellow initiate in the referential frame.

Related Facts—Choice of Serious Drama as Play Material

In a subtle fashion a fertile seed for child-adult relationship is sown when the child is introduced to *dramatic* play material. For in the course of rehearsing a close-to-life play the adult makes his reputation as one who knows life—the children having touched life poignantly, if sordidly, believe adults are either hypocrites or innocents. The adult by his mere functioning as director, asking pertinent questions, pointing out facets, or examining character behavior in a scene, stands out as one who cannot be fooled—he knows what makes people tick, a dynamic challenge to children adept at rationalizing self-conduct and successful in pulling the wool over adult eyes. One would expect for this reason that they would seek to escape the theater. But no, this search for the secret of behavior has satisfactions; it is a grown-up game played in equality with a grown-up; the conflicted delinquent, perhaps not knowingly, wants to understand himself; the curious adolescent seeks answers from the vicarious living through the people in the play.

The reading and rehearsing of a serious play removes the delinquent's habitual notion of adult unfairness in judging him. For the professional attitude in studying a play for production is that of a detached artist earnestly searching for truth, pondering words, directions, and descriptions for unbiased understanding of cause and effect of character and situation. Thus, the director does not *judge* character! And since he does not blame bad people in the play then surely he does not condemn "bad" boys and girls! More than that, he personifies a singular kind of love, different from the entangling, demanding, or punishing emotion known to them by the same name. As he stands before them he reveals a person in love with theater, with words, ideas, with the ticking in people, even with an author not personally known but merely for the artistry he has wrought. By translation he loves children—and without strings attached. Thus they sit up literally charged with new life before this new portrait of an adult who, they have decided, is not stern like certain parents, other people or upholders of law; yet not mushy and sentimental like others they have known. This special adult is both hard and soft; he is not a hypocrite, nor an innocent; he cannot be fooled, yet in spite of this is sympathetic toward them.

But they sense, as the work goes on, that he has a social bias, that he manages to *impress* his social preference. Delicately, he never digs into their past; nevertheless through art he makes his commentary on behavior. No, he judges not, he loves; but where he stands, and hopes the children will stand, he reveals by his unconscionable use of voice or verbal or facial expression—in the act of combing the script for its message, in his special engrossment with certain scenes, in his directorial emphasis on values found or values to be sought. In each child a new personal drama, unlike any he has lived, begins.

Act One—Scene One

The knot: the child, an entrancing activity, an attractive adult; and both, representatives of two antagonistic worlds here together on a common ground.

Other Scenes Unfolding

The child in a dual role: the "delinquent" on the "other side of the fence" struggling against the adult, cynically appraising the adversary and his world which he offers to share with the child; the "moral" child stimultaneously on the "same side of the fence," in a partnership with the adult—as a fellow artist more than going along with director and author, actively *living out;* under the catalytic impact of repeated rehearsing of the play material, its *human* and *social values* as though believing in them unconditionally.

Act Two

Time and the tides of experience; the child-adult amity growing and the latter losing his role of protagonist; instead at his side stands the child thrusting against a new adversary—*himself*—in the aware struggle of his positive and negative natures.

The struggle continuing: the love principle active between child and adult; attitudes, ideology, standards in common; the child looks upon the adult as ideal person and consciously aims to be like him.

The drama does not end here for it hasn't the logical movement of a threater piece, having more than one climax and falling back to more than one anticlimax; nor is the psychological action as simple as here indicated. We have simply followed it along a general course to see how play material having potentials for revealing the adult and bringing child and adult close to each other serves as a technique for hastening the delinquent's cathartic struggle in which awareness has to be an active element.

Serious dramas or true-to-life plays are mentally hygienic for other reasons. A basic one is the depth and variation of emotion called forth in the enactors. Besides shocking the child into awareness, this offers him a stirring chance to live as richly as he did amid the early excitements of his delinquent activity, so easing his nostalgic longings for the past. For drama reaches into the viscera, digs tunnels into the heart, and sends the mind seeking cause and effect about people and their mysterious relativity to aspects of existence. Drama satisfies adolescent curiosity and the adolescent needs to be in the swing of life.

Not so light comedy which for mature people has the ingredients of subtlety or irony or sophistication above the heads of children, for whom there are only farces which are more or less slapstick, noisy in rehearsals and in production. Farce gives the pleasure-seeking audience belly laughs, but what price the effort of adjusting the delinquent to let him repeat daily in rehearsals the undisciplined slapstick pattern of his own behavior? Besides, farce does not allow for the exercise in voice control, body control, phsycial decorum necessary to untamed children who will be given or *not* given their fresh start in life by the first impression they make on people.

Serious plays need not be devoid of gaiety. Between the sighs of earnest living there are moments for laughter which the director sincerely works for with his cast. Similarly, music and dance and every glamorous trick of theater belong more intrinsically to drama than to farce. Simply, they are not externally superimposed but derive from the natural movements of life in the play. Drama is a wedge into awareness since it is built on character, not situation; and on true emotion, not surface action. As actor a child identifies with the emotion of his role for the sake of an authentic performance; but rehearsals make him conscious of a totality of "living" people related to "living" causes and effects, stirring him to moral judgment for or even against his own character role. The plot of a serious play resembles life, and so the child instinctively makes comparisons with his own experiences and his own behavior; as lacking in ideational capacity as a child may be he becomes analytical and introspective. Dramatic material portrays through its plots life as struggle and through its characters some aspect of personal conflict resolved by catharsis, by which the child is encouraged in his own personal struggles. And because the economy of dramaturgy permits no confusion, confusion in the child over the contariness of existence disappears; for clearly etched in numerous plots are truths and simplifications which impact upon him as bright discoveries of hope for his future. His spirit is lifted as he learns that though good and bad in character are opposites like black and white, everyone has both colors in him; that human behavior is a rhythmic ebb and flow sometimes as near to black as he has been, but always as near to white as one *conscientiously makes an effort to be*.

Drama synthesizes life; by force of thinking about the make-believe people, studying them to interpret them, digging deeply within to emote for them to give them reality, living through them until there is no distinction between the fictitious and the real, the child comes to the mentally hygienic conclusion that he and all man are one, that he like all men has no reason for guilt or the feeling of rejection, that within *him* as within his new fellows of the world lies the power, if he but has the will, to use his failure as the start for his success.

Non-orthodox Casting for Roles

Whenever I have cast a play in a professional manner, that is, according to type, it was a proof that I was tired and making it easier for myself. There is therapy in casting a child in a part according to his needs, objective or subjective. It isn't possible to do this in any one play for all the children, but one can do this in every play for as large a number as one can handle in this special way. A knowledge of the child will dictate the casting. He may benefit from a role identifying him with his own behavior or with personality differing from him. If shy, diffident, fearful, an outstanding role may be good for him;

if boisterous, aggressive, uncontrolled, a quiet part of endurance and suffering may be good in one case while in another a characterization similar to himself may by art's reflecting mirror help him recognize his own pattern. In behalf of this special casting I have permitted myself to even rewrite Shakespeare! For scripts must be rewritten—parts lengthened or strengthened, softened, sharpened, simplified, or made complex to fit objective needs, or needs determined upon by the director from his observation of the child. For casting to a subjective need a role may not have to be tampered with; for here a child recognizes himself and wants the part to relive a situation or to atone for a secret guilt. An example is Nathan, who asked for the part of a pickpocket in *Fingers;* a play in which a boys' club is organized to rehabilitate the "bad" boys of the neighborhood. Nathan said, "Fingers, that's me. I was sent here for everything under the sun but the real thing I used to do. I used to pick pockets, but I got away with it."

Casting may be made on a physical basis in the attempt to eradicate *first* the *effect* of emotional disturbance and behavior, which so marks a child that it is an obstacle to progress. Changing the physical symptoms or giving the child a new physical personality can start off a hygienic movement in the psyche. If Sylvia protrudes her stomach and lolls her head as though she lacks a spine it is obvious she will benefit from the role of a sedate, poised, aristocratic girl or woman. For even if Sylvia wants to face her problem and change herself, her movement, voice, and general appearance mark her as a corner girl. One day, on a home visit, if due to months of rehearsing parts which have given her a backbone and an awareness of herself, she can walk down Fourteenth Street without being accosted, Sylvia will have started a new role in life. The habitual rationalization that her sexual delinquency is not her fault will have lost its forceful point that "they start up with me, I can't help it." This will be the beginning of Sylvia's facing cause and effect of her own desires and action. If Harry stutters it is obvious that keeping him out of a play will not teach him to speak, nor build up his ego. But neither may he be burdened with long speeches—difficult for a boy with his handicap, therefore destructive to his ego status as well as to the general morale. Harry needs a role of continuous speech participation in brief periods for exercise in uninhibited communication. For his sake, the dialogue of other actors is lengthened; that is, they are given added questions, exclamations, phrases, or sentences with which to interrupt him, thus changing his long speeches to a conversational give-

and-take, easy to carry and easier to listen to.

Ben has a soft voice; his movement is too refined for a boy—a bad combination, together with his writing interest, for companionable acceptance by peers. It is easier to fit Sylvia into the part of a lady than Ben into a really masculine role which he needs. The next best is to give him a character part calling for some coarseness, and in rehearsals to work on him for a raucous voice and exaggerated stance or any trick which may seem to develop the stage character while really developing him.

This kind of casting may not be arbitrary. Children have a jealous egotism which must be handled judiciously, all the more that it is often based on sound judgment. For subjective reasons, when a new play is read children relegate to themselves the parts they want; but objectively they align the rest of the cast with a fine regard for talent, potentiality, suitability. Fortunately, the ideal person has the confidence of the group. He is known to differ with them only when his purpose goes beyond theater for some special benefit to them. He always gives his reasons and they are worthy reasons; and the children, partners to the "master artist," knowing the extra burden assumed by such casting, yield, for if he can make the sacrifice so can they. Most times the reason is given directly to the child who is to receive the part. When the choice seems incongruous, however, a few words in confidence to one or two will result in the choice as the ardent desire of the group.

The director simply says, "Mary looks the part; but it would do Mildred so much good to be a princess. She's sad, it would brighten her, she'd feel as though she were somebody fine and good; she really is and we have a chance now to make her sure of it." The group talks it over in whispers, feeling fine and good, too, to be agents of happiness; they begin to find royal merits in Mildred—"She has a sweet voice, it will be clearer when she gets sure of herself," and "Watch her when she comes in, she holds her head high like a princess, etc." There is some jealousy of course, but the director finds a way to glamorize other parts; he points out their strategic position in the play, their special difficulty requiring intelligence or ability, or the specific good they will do the participants. Mildred becomes Princess Elizabeth in a youthful escapade. Who is Mildred? A withdrawn child (mother in an asylum, father has forced himself on her), pretty, delicate, guilt-driven, with a rigid body and a colorless voice. The honor brings the first youthful smile ever seen on her pale face. Later we seek constantly in her role for places for laughter and

Mildred develops a tinkling joyous laugh which all the children love. Rehearsals go on. Relaxation of spirit and of body, poise, confidence. Mildred *is* a princess! "What is this change in Mildred!" everyone asks.

In the same play Bernice has the role of a termagant. Bernice is stodgie, oversized, clumsy, excessively shy and self-negating. She is offered the part and almost faints with dread of participating. She cries, "But I can't do it. I'm afraid." "Believe me you can do it, and beautifully with this cane in your hand," I say, relating some stage story proving a similar fear in a well-known actress. The group stands by, pleads with her, encourages her, practically bullies her into the role! The children understand the goal—Bernice is to be habituated to self-assertion. A cane in the hand gives confidence very much like a cigarette when one faces an ordeal—this is negative help. But a cane to lift and shake at people, a cane to thump! thump! and thump! almost holes into the floor, that is a *positive* entrance into aggressiveness; with it come muscles singing self-confidence, a backbone strong and assertive, a voice thunderous unlike the mousesqueak native to the girl. After the play—behold! Bernice active in discussion, Bernice at ease with boys, and Bernice depending neither on cane nor supporting cast as piano soloist in the school concert!

Sometimes the director may not publicly admit the true reason for a casting and must find instead a theater reason. An example is the casting of a liar as the liar of the play. The hope here is, since the boy refuses to recognize his pattern, perhaps the logical consequences of the enacted plot will force him to recognize it. In this case Alex accepted the role enthusiastically but after three rehearsals came to me with, "You're not fooling me; you gave me this on purpose; I'm not going to do it." He continued in the role because he had no way out against my answer. "You're quite right," I said. "I hoped you'd find out through the story how people feel toward a liar, how he never fools them, how he is always mistrusted. If you give up the part you'll miss the chance to learn much for your own good. Besides, the boys will understand *why* you're giving it up." "But they're laughing at me already!" "So they are. The manly thing is to stick it out, have your last fling at lying, do so fine a job that your characterization will help other boys. Meanwhile, watch yourself when you're tempted to exaggerate the truth."

This method of choosing the Dramatis Personae for the play apparently contradicts the principle of the high standard, and the children at first protest this paradox in a director who enthuses over a fine art production, then makes it difficult to attain by overlooking the fact that some of them are less gifted than others or have not the personality fitted to portray required roles. On the surface this is a rational protest expressed as anxiety for the fate of the play and for the reputation of the Group. But it speaks loudest where ego preoccupation is in strong conflict with one's nobler yielding to unusual casting for the sake of one's fellows. For despite the stilling of active jealousy, out of sheer ego necessity every child wants the lead part; it is a way of attaining special importance, position, and praise. And what feeling lies behind the rational front is validated in the child's conscience by the reverberations of our culture, an element of which is the noisome publicity inculcated about stellar humans as specially exalted, adored, and approved of people above all the rest of this earthy world. Movie minded, the children cherish stardom. Troubled, egocentric, longing for status, they suffer star hunger. Twenty boys and girls want—nay, need to be stars—and all at the same time while only Mildred can get the princess's part and only two or three others can get similarly juicy roles!

My selling answer to "logical" protest as to egotistical clamor has always been couched in professional language as follows: in a great production, no *performer* stands out from among the rest, although from the story we recognize the central figure around whom the author has written his play for the purpose of proving something. The director is at fault when he centers attention on one person, for he doesn't give the others the chance to be equally good. In a play which stirs deeply (examples discussed) every one in the cast, no matter how tiny the bit, is unforgettable as an important link in the chain of events if he contributes sincerely to the total effect worked for. And last, good directors do not cast to type because good actors are developed only through the variety of the parts they are permitted to play.

After which *their* "good" director has always proceeded to prove this as if with a professional troupe. Art and therapy unite here. As an artist, the director pays precise attention to the unfolding efforts of the individual actor and actress. As therapist his artistic zeal is doubled so that the child may get from his acting experience that which he abundantly needs. Where does art stop and therapy begin when the adult says to Mildred, "*Now* you have it, that *lovely* quality in your voice!" or when he asks Alex, "How does this man feel secretly, deep inside himself, when he finds out that his lie spoiled his friend's life . . . and what *in him* causes his lying all the time?'' Neither Mildred nor Alex are aware of art versus therapy. They merely have a sense of well-being; Mildred because her heart is lighter, Alex because there is more open relationship between him and his fellows respectfully watching his work in rehearsals.

The play grows. Each child feels himself more a person. Or each child feels himself more an artist. They are one and the same thing. It takes hard work to become a princess! It takes mature courage to do an honest job with a displeasing role which exposes one! As growing people the children attain the attitude of professionalism, watch each other, encourage, criticize in the creative zeal to perfect the play. As growing artists happy in the good work they are doing, they attain the attitude of fraternity, observe and exult in the changes in each other, encourage and criticize with the anxiety of friends, become ''My brother's keeper.'' Casting to the child's needs does not prevent a production of high merit. It instigates it by its basic attitude of concern for and faith in every single child, which attitude has the contageous power of sweeping the mass into a similar feeling one for the other and all for the vast undertaking they have in common. The love principle as the atmosphere of environment truly exists; and has it not been said that love can move mountains?

Contrariwise Professional Rehearsals—Lines Never Studied by Rote

A special synonym for the word *professional* may be the word *meaningful*. Children want to feel one really means business; one isn't playing down to them; one isn't pretending. When the director originally said (and what he says is amazingly remembered and carried by one group generation to another until it is tradition), ''We are going to build a theater,'' implicit in this was the promise that ''We are going to do mature things the way they are done in a professional theater.'' This promise was the lure for getting down to work; its keeping is the child's spiritual leaven for carrying on and on. Furthermore, what does professional mean if not the exercise of certain attitudes and behavior toward one's work and one's fellow workers by which work is enhanced, the pleasure of work is increased, and a decent relationship among people with mutual interests is perpetuated?

Generally people do not rehearse children in a professional or meaningful way. The usual method is to have them study their lines, so many by a given day; to tell them where to stand and when to sit, even the exact moment for twinkling an eyelash; to teach them to gesticulate and to use the voice from out a limited and limiting bag of elocutionary tricks. The result is either a floundering performance or one of stilted perfection with the child's natural humanity of emotion and intelligence overstarched and pressed out into the stiff substance of cardboard superficiality. By this method the frightened child suffers to the last; the child who doesn't need self-confidence struts the boards more exhibitive than ever; jealousies over roles remain, for the limelight falls, and by the indulgence of the adult, upon those whose nature it is already to lushly bask in it. And can there be an enrichment of the total person where child participation derives not from the education of the senses and the growth of emotion and of the mind but from unintelligent, if pleasant, obedience to directions which seldom penetrate below the thin surface of externalized play presentation?

The above description may seem harsh in the light of many fine results by children in play-producing under the supervision of their sincere and hardworking teachers. Such results are due often to the choice of specially gifted children both for acting and for the construction of scenery. Furthermore, "normal" children have a resilient way of building upward from the most indifferent experiences and often furnish for themselves the constructive paraphernalia of the spirit overlooked by the adult leadership. They are generally disciplined students at ease with words and ideas whom the studying of lines by rote, if the practice does not enrich them, cannot permanently harm. But for delinquent and neurotic children, wasting any of the values of theater capable of awakening or developing them as artists—therefore as people—is a misuse of the children themselves. An equation exists between the activation of senses, emotions, and mind, and the growth of attitudes which may be called, exchangeably, social or professional.

In the professional rehearsal not a line is ever studied. Lines are remembered because ideas are understood, meaning becomes one's own, the actor ticks with the play character. This is the core of rehearsal—to be intelligent about the total process of re-creating an author's meaning and dramatization of life. Participants do not stick away into their memories unmasticated words and phrases to squeeze them forth sputteringly during rehearsals and then glibly on the great date, hearts despite assurance anxious, and bodies weighted down with stage panic. What stupid enterprise, a theatrical venture which would add to the original insecurity of the delinquent and the neurotic child the added anxiety of failure on the social scene through a word disappeared in a vacuum!

The goal of rehearsals should not be the finished play, but the play polished, perfected, enlarged artistically as the *result* of children gaining in security, poise, the sense of positive being. Poise, security, positive being are variations of the same thing, the integration of personality inwardly vitalized and outwardly effective. Rehearsal periods, then, must be periods of mental and emotional nourishment; they must aim at the inner child, at the union of his evasive or dormant or hostile inwardness with the surrounding outer world on whose behalf speaks the author of the play through the medium of words, plot, characterization. It must not be forgotten that the confused and troubled child is especially curious about the world to which he does not wholly belong; hence any meaty play is an excursion in search of knowledge, truth, the resolution of doubts and guilts.

On this excursion the child is attitudinally open to identification with all that is outside himself *if* the outsideness makes meaning, *if* he actively participates in it, investing at least a part of himself which will forever belong to it. Is the truth not always pretty, are there truths self-contradictory, is life not too consistent, must one face and accept these truths? The play can be for the child a probing ground provided that he is not an automaton pulled by strings, provided he is in reality an *actor;* one *activated* to probe intelligently, one actively engaged in every aspect of his being, one *actuated cumulatively;* by the light of understanding and refreshed feeling, to transmit to others through his enactment of a role feelings and thoughts become his own—at least for the period, believed to be his own.

None of this can be accomplished under the straightjacket stricture of lines studied apart from the living body and breath of the play, resulting in stage work made *subservient* to belabored vocal expression. For mind is not called into related functioning, nor is the spirit permitted rapture; and lacking is the experiential impact upon the psyche which translates itself into a corporeal urge for expression of *vitalized* and *conscious* inner life (sincere and intrinsic acting).

Words as the tools of attitudes, feelings, thoughts, and as the means for capturing the too easily escaping essence of new ideas belong to quite another method of rehearsal which permits talking about them, questioning them, doubting them, in short relating them to the totality of the play. Unschooled children, if you please, *analyze* the play material in the manner of veteran troopers. *Discussion* is the first step in the undertaking of a play and continues as the catylist for intelligent and wholehearted participation in the so difficult and demanding undertaking, an *honestly* produced play. (Discussion generally a preparation for mature living. See pp. 187-204.)

Discussion's first virtue is that it allows children who have failed in school to believe in their own mental capacity. The second virtue is that it teaches them how to study, that is, how to read and how to relate, therefore retain, the facts and meaning of their reading. And the third is discussion's chief attribute, honesty, as the attitude of probing which leads to personal honesty or the habit of self-probing. Last, discussion creates the democratic environment in which the Bens and the Pauls contribute to each other their thinking and feeling, learning with steady progress the essence of good manners or the art of composed and respectful listening as well as speaking in conversation.

"You dope," Ben may still say, "that's not what it means." And Paul may answer. "It does so, Mr. Webster agrees with *me*; I looked it up, smarty-pants." The invectives are provocatives to the thrashing out of the problem; they are the wings of exhuberant challenge one gives to the other in the cause of truth; they are not an expression of hostility but of goodwill. For immediately the two, waited upon by the intellectual curiosity of the others, thumb the fat dictionary in search of the word. Both read aloud, Paul with good-natured triumph, Ben with dawning insight. But Ben, a bookish boy, reads to the end. He finds a variation, a subtlety in *Webster's* which reinstates temporarily his fought-for point of view. He grins, scratches his head, and concedes, "Language is a tricky business"; and Paul echoes ruefully, "I'll say so." Someone playfully shouts, "Let's throw away that word, there are plenty others"; upon which Paul glares a pretended murder, from some depth acquires a resounding vigor and challenges, "What are we waiting for? Let's see which meaning the author meant. . . . He says here, . . . and in the next scene he uses the word again." One word leads to the questioning of others and to the analysis of entire sentences considered, no longer as printed, but spoken language revealing—even in the attempt at concealing—the true nature of the hopes, fears, and intentions of potentially real people. Words, ideas, motives, situations, people—the interrelation and interdependence of these elements in the play startle the children, thrill them wide awake with the discovery of the meaningfulness and the relationship of all things. In the beginning there is the word, in the end there is aware, sentient life.

Discussion may not be conducted like a scientific conclave, however. These are restless children with quicksilver nerves and muscles physically aching for action, many of them by the inertia of the limited use of faculties or because of emotional disturbance incapable of formal or long-period mental application. Round-table sessions should be infrequent, oftener with progress; their main purpose is the flattery to the child as an accepted thinker. They serve, too, as experience in civilized conversation and in the control of youthful jumpiness. They formally introduce the ritual of the dictionary to instill the dictionary habit and the habitual recourse to books in general. They place the mantle of dignity upon the activity—it is wonderful how purposeful, how upright, how fraternal are the faces of the youngsters aware that the workshop has been turned into a greenroom, exactly as in a theater! Moreover, this sitting down to intellectual and bookish pursuits, I believe, gives a feeling of being right with themselves as though recapturing the opportunity to be successful at school.

Habitually discussion takes place actively during rehearsals. Related to what is being enacted at the moment, in the midst of the movement and the emoting, the stage is thrown open for probing. Sometimes an actor initiates the discussion with an "I don't know how to say this, what does it mean?" Or a protagonist may turn to another protesting, "I can't respond because the way you act isn't natural." Most often the director sees the ripe moment and stops the action with lead questions. Discussion may ensue between actor and adult, sometimes only between the actors involved in the scene, usually it becomes general.

Lead questions are the same questions used professionally for helping actors clear up confusion, for leading them into correct directions, or for inspiring the flight of imagination. Thus: What is his exact feeling? What words in the script reveal this, what words contradict this? What is there different in this character which makes him behave in a way other people would not in the same situation? Did anything like this ever happen to you? Recall, how did you feel, what did that feeling do to your knees, your posture, and your breathing? What did it make you want to do; did you act as you wanted to? If not, why not? What difference is there between your character and the one you are doing which makes you both behave differently?

Sometimes the questions are interspersed with stern directorial accusation, thus: "I do not believe you" (meaning the child is idling, not giving himself to his role); or "I am not convinced" (ditto and by inference introducing the future audience who will need to be convinced by a natural performance). A child may say, "That's right! Do you want to put your audience to sleep?" And another will come forward, "I think I know what's wrong, let me show him." He steps into the role giving something new to the scene. "Bad," "stupid," "dull" children observe closely, afraid to miss some slight nuance of the new interpretation! The faces of those not in the scene are something to study. They have the rapt, studious selfless look of scientists observing a phenomenon. Only after the last word or gesture of the scene do they become children again in their differentiated expressions of disagreement or approval. A new discussion is on. Voices may sound impassioned, even heated; but their ring is sincere with reasoned opinion and the impersonal quality of objective criticism. This is also true of the displaced actor explaining his own characterization.

The intelligent response to lead questions, the spontaneous stopping of child actors to question some aspect of the rehearsal in a studious attitude, the very capacity to criticize constructively are the results of word or meaning consciousness. It is the mature or professional way of preparing a play. The actor is under a self-discipline by which he controls his mind to function objectively; though immediately, in playing his role, he yields his emotions to subjective identification with the play characters. The child who gives way to another to "show" him does so because he knows what it is all about; he is aware of the creative process to which he and the others are contributants; he has no feeling of frustration, jealousy, or hurt vanity; understanding has made him secure! Having been inwardly vitalized, he welcomes criticism which will make him as outwardly effective as possible. He has the professional attitude largely developed because dialogue has not been artificially stressed apart from the play.

But, one may ask, how do children give an effective performance, free from word anxiety, if they do not study their lines? If rehearsals are held with scripts in hand is not physical expression limited, so inhibiting emotional and ideational expression? The answer is that honest or effective expression is merely the outward life of intrinsic feeling and clarity. It is necessary for this feeling and clarity to become positive before any true interpretation through the body and voice can evolve. Relaxation in experiencing the entire impact of the play material is paramount—for joy in the work, for investment in the work, for poise, and for security. Early rehearsals are therefore reading rehearsals. The enactment of scenes is made with the scripts in hand until the entire play—one act or three acts—has been worked over, tied together in all its parts, understood and possessed as personal experience. There comes a day when the director believes the children have the "feel" and the "know" of the play. Then he suggests, "Let us see how much we can do without the papers." True, there is a momentary panic. He persists, "Let's try anyhow. You will surprise yourselves to find how much you remember." And they do!

It happens of itself! The continuous *active* reading of the familiar content, with the free obedience of the body to the repeated emotional pattern and with vice versa the sharpening of the emotional pattern from cues given by the senses, makes acting not an imitation of life but a naturally flowing manifestation of immediate and personal living. Neither fear nor strain are present in the reading rehearsals since there is no adult pressure about learned lines. In discussion, words have been given their merited dignity and from understanding them has come the dramaturgic conception—the synthesis of emotional and ideological movements in the story, the relationship of character to character, of scene to scene, episode to episode. In rehearsals, words do not exist for themselves but only as the vocal portion of a complicated orchestration of the senses played by each actor sometimes together with and sometimes in counterpoint to other actors. Memory has no existence as a thing apart. Memory is repeated experience; it is the *whole* experience in which words fall naturally into their places inseparable from *action* and *reaction*. And so, when the scripts are put aside the words flow easily, spontaneously, though perhaps not with concrete exactitude—but one may depend upon memory's awareness to furnish fitting substitutes. The *essence* of the script remains whole, its movement logical, its structure firm. The children are overjoyed, awed by their own achievement. Page after page, without a thought to words, lines have sprung from them spontaneously, ecstatically, responsively, in the give-and-take of real blood-and-nerve living essentially one's own.

As a proof one needs only to listen to the voices of the participants, not artists but children supposed to be unyielding, incapable of identification and lacking the capacity for ideational conception. Voices gentle with love, dreamy with hope, gay with humor, hard with speculation, terse with command, quiet with dignity—voices *cor-*

rectly placed without elocutionary tricks, voices obedient to mood and to meaning and sensitive to audience well-being. In the crosscurrents of feeling and the crosscurrents of will one hears not words spoken by make-believe people in a prepared play but the essence of the human heart stirred to speech (each time more sincerely than in the previous rehearsal) by the spontaneous prick of mood and circumstance!

As always I speak of these methods and results on a long-term basis, not of one play production as doing miraculous therapy but many with experience continued and piling up, adding to the child's stature, investing him with the outsideness of which he must become a part, building him into this outsideness so he wills to be a part. A good job done does more than furnish the applauding tap on the back. *Self*-judgment and *self*-applause (with its concomitant *self*-censorship) are born of sweat and awareness. So the director, to sustain the desire of the children to grow up, does not in the later rehearsals play down to their foibles or their inabilities. When the scripts have been put aside, work on the play begins in earnest. Up to that point the goals were: knowing what it is all about; release from strain; identification with the life of the play; freedom of interpretation; well-being from togetherness and purposefulness. Up to that point the adult had used principally the technique of acceptance. For demand the group must have become a united body with a uniting consciousness of solidarity in both enterprise and common fate. A group is not stronger or brighter than its weakest or dullest child; but the dullest and the weakest, if no sign is made of their difference, get to believe that there is no difference and, so relaxed, do become stronger and brighter. Thus, in discussion and in direction, only the director is cognizant—for he manages differently with each child—that some are quicker of perception than others, that some grasp nuance sooner and some sooner comprehend totality; but every child is heir to the sum of the *mass* effort. Progress is made in rehearsals because this mass identification puts each child, troubled in his own way, at ease.

In the beginning there is nothing noble in the recognition of togetherness, for the togetherness is one of anonymity—look around, everybody lacks a head burried in a script, nobody is watching and apparently not listening, everybody is too busy manipulating his stage business despite eyes glued to the script! But noble is the emergence of individuality freed from fear, from self-consciousness, from inferiority! The script is a blanket covering defect; it is to some a crutch, to others an ostritch hole; and for the overactive the sheef of typewritten copy is a safety valve dissipating that restless energy ready to cause disturbance and bring censure on oneself. Little by little one gets hold of himself; one isn't afraid of the sound of his own voice or the rhythm of his own movement; one isn't so self-preoccupied, one is lost in the life of another (the play character) who takes precedence over self. And one day one feels he is a part of a tremendous thing, a *team;* pulling together, and *this* is a new kind of togetherness having nothing to do with scripts now torn and wrinkled and maybe a page or two gone. And when on another day the director says to put scripts aside one doesn't worry anymore about one's hands and feet and voice and eyes, especially eyes, because one looks straight out and ahead and doesn't need to try to hide what used to be there, self-pity or aggrandizement, torment, insecurity, etc.

Now the director demands the best that is in one. Acting is a trying art. It requires giving of oneself without stint. Interpretation of a role may be free up to a point, but afterwards there are techniques to consider for the working in of one's part fittingly and beautifully with the whole. Do a scene over and over again. Do it thinking of tables and chairs and walls, thinking of timing as though one were making music, remembering boys and girls also anxious over the same things, learning to listen as well as to speak—till one is weary and about to sigh. "Hold it," cries the director. "Now you have it at last, you did it beautifully!" and the group feels weariness drop, loves the caress of those words well earned!

The children decide: How happy we all look! How good it is to do a job well! We can do even better! Concentrate, cooperate, don't let a fellow flounder because he has a headache or is nervous, but whisper the concrete word he lacks or the word of encouragement he needs. Strange paradox! The director has said words are not important. But he helped us understand them! Did he mean words were not important out of the right time and right place? Now the time has come—we must pull our scenes together, we're separately good but don't click in the teamwork. Ah, cue words, a little word here, another there—interesting how certain groups of words seem to open up doors; no wonder Jack played down his scene and Ann sounded flat. Writing must be a ticklish business, bet that author sweated plenty . . . gosh, we're killing that scene . . . hurry, let's get together and straighten out the mess. So the exactitude of words arrives in its place and in its time when in the polishing end of production the group has become truly united by the influences streaming upon them from the maturing professionalism of their shared activity.

The example of adult zeal for creativity, the common aim for artistic results, have brought numerous appreciations to children turned creative proselytes. Some they can speak about with the excitement of discovery, others are more intangible. From the dramaturgy there is the respect for language and for the writer's craft; the increasing knowledge of human nature; the recognition of form; the finding of the principle of unity (the importance of any smallest element to the totality) as it works out, for examples, in the clue of a gesture or word to character or to situation, or in the building up of a mood from seemingly scattered action or nuance, or in the structure of the play itself piled up brick by brick and story upon story the removal of any part of which must topple the whole. From the attempts at breathling life into the printed pages there is the deepened sensitivity to human potentials; especially a new regard for the clean and healthy body as the instrument of the spirit, for well-being as also for the creating of beauty. And from the bare floor and back wall which together make a stage there is the awed awareness of space, an abstraction, a tiny portion of which, limited and limiting, may actually belong to one if he learns to control, design, use, relate it to all things about him. Every moment of effort teaches the limitation of all things and all behavior by ungainsaid rules of existence; and simultaneously every moment of effort shows how, within and essentially *because* of limiting boundaries one is granted two things not possible in a boundless void or in a world uninhabited by others; one, exciting challenges to the imagination and to the will to overcome obstacles; and two, the satisfactions from maturity in the application of will and imagination to every step of endeavor as a contributive portion to a larger-than-self human chain of accomplishments or events.

There have been learnings, experimentations, purposefulness, every opportunity to fulfill the heart's desire to be grown-up. Hard meaningful work has affected the narcissistic attitude, tempering it slowly to the constructive, the cooperative, the enlightened attitude of civilized selfishness which sees one's interests in relation to things, people, and situations. By the time children begin to perfect even their first play there has been a mellowing in the individual pattern of behavior and outlook. The demands of professional rehearsing have been living demands of which work was but one manifestation. For life has been lived wholly, its lessons learned from the almost hourly reflection of related events and behavior in their effect on the beloved work. Not quite philosophers about life in general children have approached that status in relation to their play. They have acquired the professional attitude whose ethic, the golden rule, like Topsy "just growed." From one awareness to another, from self-centeredness to identification, there it is; and the volitional struggle finally, in the example of the nailing down of recalcitrant words, is the outgrowth not only of need to do a good job but of matured awareness that doing a good job calls for something owed to coworkers, author, director, and future audience.

It has often happened on the day of days after the last curtain has bowed away the group of happy successful youngsters that adults have marveled with the unreasoned sentimentality some bestow on the underprivileged, "My! How much talent!" Nonsense! Four out of twenty *may* be talented and but one outstandingly so. *All* the children, even the psychopaths and the dullards, each in his own degree of growth of course, carry through intelligently, feelingly, and with creative effectiveness. Their performance as actors improves from play to play in parallel ratio with their improved performance as human beings.

It may be argued that the thespian improvement comes from the practice in stage techniques; the answer is, a child does not work well or cooperatively until there has been some personal adjustment; that even in the legitimate theater it is known that this or that actor or actress "will not give" of himself or herself "until they have lived deeply and truly." As a matter of fact so often the talented child presents the worst problems in group discipline, slowing up progress; his first reaction to the stage activity is ego inflation expressed in reasonableness toward the adult but aggression of superiority toward other children. Not "how much talent" should be remarked but how much all around development. How much rebirth in a lost or never-had youthful ecstasy in inclusive living; that is, in breathing and moving and standing up to meet a fresh world, in finding delight in the little things with the glow of the mystical discovery of their adding up to the complexity of big things! How much of work habits formed; how much recession of narcissism; how much humanizing through the enactment of other people's problems, heartaches, hopes; and all this, while impacting on other children and being impacted upon in a busy environment ruled by a date synonymous with a contract, a public promise, or a social obligation! What approximates superior artistry—and in all the years there has never been a production without that quality—is in reality a combination of security and growth which add up to *poise*.

About Practical Minutiae–Makeup a Satisfying Experience

The worker in this field will want to know about some of the practical minutiae pertaining to the finished play—for examples, makeup, costuming, the supposed-to-be last or dress rehearsal. I would state it as a therapeutic principle that one must so organize the activity as never to leave last-minute anxieties hanging over the Group. There are enough emergencies which cannot be foreseen—like lights not functioning either from natural causes, or from aggression or curiosity or even overzealousness on the part of a child. There are enough things which can only be done the last, last minute—like the final checkup on props, the dressing and makeup, the replacement of a child absent with sudden illness. The dress rehearsal—in which are coordinated dressing, makeup, lights, scenery, smooth timing, duties of ushers and man at the switchbox—should occur several days before the show date.

But long before that, finished scenery or even finished portions of it should be moved to the stage to become part of the rehearsal experience—to concentrate group awareness on the wholeness of the enterprise, as well as to inspire the individual with the show of his progress and the related importance of his contribution. This leads to greater cooperativeness towards co-workers and readiness for extra labors. Each appearance of a prop, a wall, a color, or space effected by these makes new demands on the children in added work and in adjustability. Thus, actors need to readjust stage business; the lighting crew needs to change or rearrange effects or equipment; builders may need to alter or discard work jealously cared for; painters may have to repaint or retouch the color on costumes and sets. But they *see* for themselves, in the growing totality on the stage, problems or inadequacies which are related. Criticizing the whole objectively they are self-critical objectively. The director does not urge improvement; the children prompt themselves. Costumes are part of the staging, even ordinary clothes if chosen specially to suit characterizations. To feel at home in them or to discover necessary changes children should don them as they are finished or gather together—not necessarily all the children at the same time—several times before the dress rehearsal. The accumulation of the scenery on the stage and the wearing of the special clothes, besides being practical, have something of the nature of high moments in which all glory in the contemplation of their handiwork, joyously viewing ahead the beautiful full finish of their plan.

Too often makeup is the last-minute task of the adult, which it ought not to be. This is a fascinating and to children a meaningful art. The thrill of changing one's face has kinship with more than the godlike power of original creation; it is the thrill of re-creating oneself, of achieving variety, interest, glamor, etc., a dubious but very human and, to these children, a gratifying ego satisfaction. In the plasticity, too, of the greasepaint sticks, the crayons, creams, and powders lies magic to be unloosed on the world by one's own hands. The makeup completes the theater cycle as proof positive that the youngsters are being taken seriously in what has become an avocation. Meantime, the art itself affords the disciplines of practice, patience, relativity to purpose and cleanliness, as much in the care and handling of materials as in the doing a neat facial job. It were simpler of course, for the director to do the faces of the assembled cast just before curtain rise on play nights, avoiding this special training in special sessions. But it would not be good therapy; here once again professionalism and therapy coincide. Makeup periods unite a uniquely pleasurable creativity with practice for the assuming of this responsibility on the evening of the great event. As a by-the-way they focus the child's attention on his own appearance related to standards of neatness, hair combing, pleasantness of expression, care of adolescent complexion—in the case of girls, to the refinement of flamboyant makeup or hairdos and even to beautification through "disinterested" analysis; also makeup sessions are good medicine as little vacations now and then from labors of too long duration threatening to go stale. (Simplified, comparative drawings of Sylvia's head showing variations in hairdo and makeup proved she had made herself ugly by exaggerating imperfect features with wrong facial ministration and haircomb.)

Such times the workshop undergoes a refreshing change as tables are cleared and put together to create a vast dressing room "of a real theater." Before each child on a white paper or cloth are assembled wipe-off rags, makeup kit, and mirror. There is pride in the kits and in the mirrors. The former the children know are an investment in part, and in part unaffordable materials the director asked as a gift from the makers. The boxes and packets and sticks have been divided and subdivided to give each child his own private sanitary equipment, and the sharing has been a joy. As for the latter, they have been made by some of the very same children about to use them. Even the simple mirrors have required special easels for their easy standing, removing, and storing. But the group pride goes out to the professional makeup mirrors; nor does jealousy exist about their use since logic decress temporary possession to those whose character portraits require more care or to those beyond first lessons practicing more complicated steps. This type mirror (one example of the largess of the theater activity in promoting realistic needs for things to be homemade) requires the skillful mounting in a deep frame having electric wiring and, within its depth, sockets for the rectangular aura of light to reflect a shadowless image.

Makeup lessons are progressive. Who today is not in the play as actor, due to shortage of roles or to other stage responsibilities, tomorrow will be and must be deprived neither of the fun nor the good which may come of the experience. First come the applications of creams, skin tones, facial lines, and the neat use of tools. Later are added age and race and character expression. This sounds academic, specialized, as though the children were being prepared falsely for a career. Actually, all is kept very simple with stress put on social im-

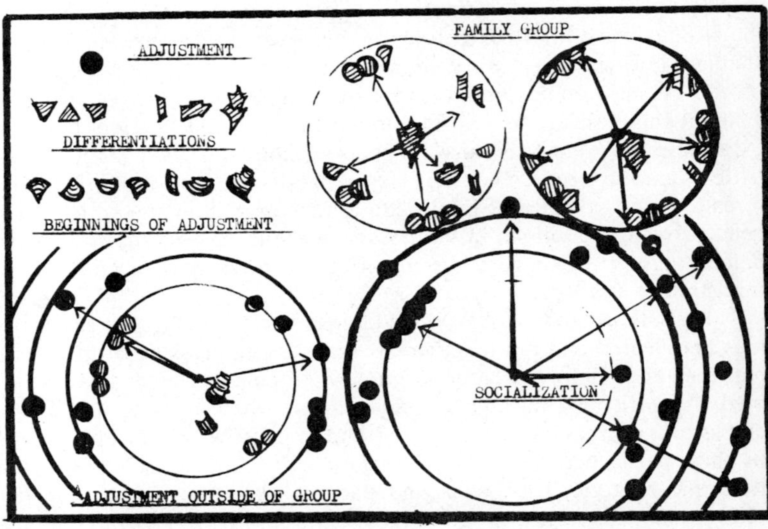

Symbol Portrait of Expectations in Individual Progress Through Theater

plication: from the use of picture material there is discussion on the likenesses of humanity, with the establishment of respect for its variations and the dissipation of racial defensiveness or prejudice the results of sadistic or comic indoctrination—like the nose of the Jew or the fighting jaw of the Irish; also, there is instigation to awareness of personal appearance with the stress on habits. Externally, of course, the lessons lead to the particular makeup needed for the current play and to the assistance those most proficient in the art will be able to render the group in the last tumultuous hour.

In that hour, again the workshop becomes a dressing room. Each at his table, costumed, deftly puts on his face. Among them the director keeps a studious vigil while also seeing committees reporting on completed tasks—essential minutiae or emergencies concerning stage, the house, programs, etc. Actors early finished help the less skilled with a dab of color here or a penciled line there. Each having done his best comes to the adult for a checkup and the final "perfect" touch. Professional or therapeutic? That swift knowing touch of the leader specialist, the combination of theater priest and ideal person, is to tense nerves a balm and encouragement, a restatement of faith in youth—for is *he* not sending them "out front," under the blessing of his hands, as a master his disciples or a parent his children?

Then: "We are ready; all out." Lights are dimmed in the shop. To the balcony for a restful moment wends the mummer's troupe. Actors, crewmen, sometimes even a home-grown author look down upon the curtain soon to rise upon them and their creation. "It may be a hit, it may be a flop" is a line from their own group song; it is natural to have some anxiety. But each knows the growth he has made away from his failings and the similar growth of his fellows. Fraternal admonitions are easily bandied around; if self-reliance has a touch of nerves it gains strength from total reliance on the group body. For example, there will be no prompter concealed strategically to help with lines—it would be a violation of the standard of art, and of training in self-responsibility—though a script will be handy in case of *absolute catastrophe*. But on the stage will move not only characters in a play but children with character each alert and ready to assist in the slightest adversity on the part of another. Solidarity binds them.

Tension is natural before a public appearance, especially when performance is tied up with rehabilitation. In these last minutes, then, the director calls a line rehearsal which is nothing more than an assuring cascade of sound, merely a swift and active tonic against restlessness or nerves. The moment is amiable, too, and closely knit under the relaxing treat to cigarettes from the adult's own pack (delinquent and neurotic youths are inveterate smokers). Almost the curling smoke is ritualistic, the ceremony of preparation for the Group to strengthen its united back for the business at hand, for the director to enact his last act of captaincy. "To your stations! Check lights, again check exits! Propertymen, crew, at the curtains, to the wings! Doormen, ushers, at your posts! Time . . . houselights on . . . actors to your places!" Hands go out . . . with ten or twenty or thirty theater people now, disciples about to show to the world their share of learning, artistry, responsibility, maturity, the "master" shakes in final blessing. "Good luck . . . good luck." The "leader" sending the children out on the high road will sit with the audience! Well do they know in this hour they must be on their own, men and women for the evening, after the weeks and even months of dependency; the tradition has been set that nothing less than sudden illness, earthquake, or fire in the world they now must run alone will bring the adult back stage while the play is going on!

8

More Problems and Techniques

Building Up the Family—Analysis of Human Material—Negative Significance of Positive Factors; Positive Significance of Negative Factors in Relationships

Up to this point I have tried to pin down methods and attitudes of the far-seeing director in pursuit of results tangibly effectual to all children in, so to speak, one "throw." Of necessity I have had to speak abundantly about the play-producing while conscious of the teetering danger of my seeming to fall into its total domain as though writing a specialist's book on production—so delicately strung is the bridge between its concrete reality as a work goal and its subtler reality as a humanizing force.

Were I to draw a diagram representing the results of a first play in terms of the human and the social child I would begin with a group of geometrical symbols: circles and squares, triangles, and other sharp or jagged figures denoting differentiation in troubled personality. A shape perfectly circled would stand for children definitely affected in the short time by the experience, perhaps because less sick than the others, or more resilient to influence, or even perhaps because circumstances have permitted intensive work with them; these would be in the minority. The jagged figures, though some might show the signs of curving, would represent the majority not entirely reached in the deep corners of the psyche. But close study would disclose all of these figures clustered in twos or more and all of the groupings gravitating toward an outer rim in contour a circle, the defining line still dim. This is the beginning of the corporate group: although identification is mainly confined to short circumferential distances, the linking into an embracing circle of friends and coworkers is beginning to take place; for already personal investment has been made in the mutual enterprise and various shades and degrees of the feeling of ownership and belonging have begun to show and to be felt. However, in the lonely naked stretch between rim and center still remain several isolationalist symbols—the very sick, the harder to reach, or perhaps the incapable of being helped. Were the diagram a moving picture, something interesting could be observed among these, too, an anguished effort despite earthboundedness to follow the others to the outer orbit.

Thus a series of drawings depicting adjustment progress play by play would show more and more circle symbols abounding and closing together as in a chain until sharp and strong would stand out the dark rim symbolic of the family group (even though a theater group), its unbroken line formed by the backs of the individual symbols. Later drawings would individualize, by markings or colors the individual figures, for true development will not in the cause of conformity flatten out the distinguishing variations of personality but will bring what is good into the light. And finally there would be a brand new series telling whether or not the work has been successful; here the group symbol would begin to lose its confining position, showing successful adjustment of the child in the distances he has traveled from the rim representing the group to ever wider rims, symbols of larger worlds fixed in reality. The first picture of this series would show the figures crossing over the group boundary into positive reactivity to teachers and academic work in the classrooms. The next circumference reached and hurdled would be the home cottage into which the child would bring to his cottage brothers a sharing of his enthusiasms and his rich learnings, and to his cottage parents an older son attitude expressed in the understanding of their aims and in helpfulness through mature leadership. In the end the original orbit of an apparently esoteric group would show as the mere core of many surrounding circles depicting increased socialization.

The determinants would be: the child's change of attitude to the laws of the community; his acceptance of other adults; the quality of his work performance in any part of the community under the impact of any adult whatsoever; his ability to get along with his peers; his foreward looking to the outside world with hopes, interests, and plans commensurate with his family background, history, and means.

In this last graphic depiction of children socialized through theater, the adjustment of any child would be verified by his capacity to perceive his theater activity as *no more* than a joyous, nourishing *temporary* experience of youth, a helpful stepping-stone to the path of responsible and satisfactory living in the permanent world. (The director will have failed if a single child leaves the Group not socially aware and socially expressive in behavior and outlook about the future; and the failure will have been criminal if in any child's bonnet there buzzes the fanciful bee of theater ambition to germinate a future postadjustment quarrel with actuality.

But . . . this child person or responsible, self-sustaining citizen will not have been built up without additional devices, methods, or environmental organization besides those already described. To understand this we must look at the group picture after a second or certainly a third play; for decidedly we have now the making of a cohesive group or family. Not the least of the intricate ties by which children are now consciously bound is the discovery each member has made of his own and his neighbor's duality. As in a dream they have seen themselves hitch their chariot to a star, then with seeming deliberateness, on the part of everyone at some time, cut the leashes and heckle the chariot destruction-bent. They have seen: themselves or their friends like untamed horses tearing in opposite directions, a prey to wilfulness and mood, stubbornness and perversity, and other frustrating manifestations; and yet unbelievably they have seen the chariot rolling on its chartered course! The beauty of the star was beheld, even touched; and out of it all came goodwill, a jealous love for what might have been destroyed, a discovery. For *who* lashed the recalcitrants, *who* continued against havoc, *who* yielded never to threat, *who* achieved the laurels of success finally? Even *themselves*–despite the sum of their vagaries, proving to be a *brand new totality* of goodness and strength and purpose never in existence before—themselves, the Group.

The discovery of duality is the beginning of the desire for adjustment; for now the child sees he is bad only as a lone creature and has infinite possibilities of goodness and constructiveness when he belongs with others in a giving and doing spirit. An intuition comes to him, however, that so much of his discovered goodness has been forced by mass pressure; that the Group has proven itself nobler than its parts at a sacrifice of its inherent potentials; that *he is* the Group as well as the obstacle in its brighter path, and so he owes a debt—to himself and the Group who are one—to curb the obstacle.

A new individual desire for worthiness now really cements the group, its output growing better, its united face acquiring a sobriety people marvel at. But the separate members despite better functioning on the surface remain still compounds of troubles and conflicts they *want* to but cannot resolve. The onlooker sees exhuberance, busy-ness, purpose, camaraderie—the elements of cohesion. The children know better that the group picture as a product of themselves is second rate. But this knowledge is not of the same substance that original guilt was made of. It is awareness shared under mutual tribulation balanced by mutual joy. Under praise they squirm a little, look into each other's eyes, withhold the telltale gleam of difficulties and discords endured. They no longer want to fool themselves *or* the world. And this is moral progress; the assortment of variegated personalities by the sharing of this secret becomes a family in spirit, for not only have its members nobility before the world, they have also the family skeleton to clear away. We have now children struggling, through their efforts to make the play, to remake themselves.

Up to this point of awareness cohesion has been attained mainly through general devices and techniques. Cohesion is fragile, superficial, like a pseudo-perfect painting whose glaze of neutral tone ties bad color and discordant value into a fictitious harmony. For the painter the problem is easy; he has but to learn the character and behavior of his pigments and to have the courage to destroy the old and make new paintings. The director-therapist has other problems. He cannot toss children aside for wrong tonality. He must keep them in the group picture. He must appreciate the *merit* of the superficial harmony, that it shows *progress* and was not wrought simply by his hand but rose upward from some deeper rooting in the children themselves out of beginning changes in character and behavior. He must pursue efforts to nurse this beginning healthfulness into sound and steady being whereby the wrong reds, violets, and yellows by further inner necessity right themselves, giving the group portrait its delayed actual harmony. For until each child is harmonious with himself he cannot habitually get along in true union with others.

From the very beginning until almost the end, to understandingly cope with these children in their inconsistencies, vacillations, outbursts, unpredictable withdrawals even from love, the adult must face certain facts. There will be days when, despite previous manifestations of orderliness in the psyche, the child will walk into the workshop or on the stage with spiritual dissociation. For he will not have come alone. With him will have entered his last night's terror dream, or the compulsion of his particular drive, or the anxiety over misconduct perpetrated elsewhere, or sexual restlessness, or the upset from a parental communication or visit, and so on.

By orderliness of the psyche I mean the toning down of the atypical traits he originally came with—stubbornness, stealing, arrogance, temper tantrums, impatience, fighting, demanding, hostility, withdrawal, incapacity for relationship, etc. On any day for many months the immediate trouble a child carries with him will bring to the fore the old symptoms, or if not, substitute symptoms of malaise. Naturally a child who has made real progress does not fall all the way back; for example, he does not suddenly steal again, but in his upset mood he deliberately hides another child's tool or materials so they may not be found.

Besides, for a long time *all* the children, despite their absorption in the common labor, retain the memory of unlicensed individuality. The welding process frets them with ambivalent feelings—on the one hand to give up the new found happiness; on the other to permit subjection to its travails, to its jarring and exposition of one's egocentric self and the yielding up of narcissistic preoccupation. I give this picture to show the differences in human values *despite* which an abounding likeness has risen to the top, a beginning of social living, a harmony strong enough to create a world of substance and dreams, so strong that a child under challenge refuses to let go of it.

I do not now remember the exact situation which called forth the following note to me. I could not have had the intention ascribed to me in the bitter tone of this boy; but I may well have suggested on his threat to leave the Group that it was perfectly acceptable to me (this boy was not of a group of seniors who had earned a rewarding trip to a New York theater and vaguely I remember his disturbance over this at the instigation of two other boys). The note expresses the ambivalent attitude of his new-found heaven, may give an idea of the importance of the creative approach the adult must have toward these children, for to have stood on my adult dignity resenting his tone was to have lost the opportunity to remold a vital child. The note read:

Dear Miss Avramo,

In as much as you want me out of the Group Theatre, to show you that I am not going to be forced out because you want to spite me by not taking me with the group, I am not quitting the Group Theatre. If you want me out you will have to throw me out, as I have a mind of my own and not like S——'s and H——'s. You see I didn't go to the Group Theatre to go to New York or any other place. So you are not worrying me by not taking me.

Very sincerely yours,
Bob K——

To the above facts must be added other data of differentiation among these children. In an age range of from thirteen to eighteen years, it will be unusual for any three children of even the same chronological age to function alike on the emotional and mental levels normally anticipated as correct for their years. It is as if emotional capacity, grade of mentality, and interests were qualities plucked willy-nilly from a grabbag and donned whether they became the wearer or not. The unnaturalness of an eighteen-year-old of brilliant mentality (or Max, *beyond* his age mentally, emotionally on a level below his age; or Ben, emotionally his age, intellectually several years older) behaving like a thirteen-year-old in his feeling reactions lies, however, in the mind of the annoyed adult; in the youth it is a natural result of his history and will be a problem no less to himself than to others. Within the large group he will find no segment to which he belongs for he will be too big and too mentally quick and so impatient with younger children on whose emotional level he will be; and with boys equally alert to ideational pursuits he will be a hindrance by his childish challenge to their annoyance and dislike. Or—a fifteen- or sixteen-year-old (Irving; and Milton before conversation in "Bad Boys and Girls.") will function at eighteen in his responsiveness to people and situations (the same assumption of adult prerogatives which got him into trouble originally, actually a spurious maturity reacting out of a love bias in certain directions with hasty, disproportionate hostility in opposite, opposing directions) but will be on the mental level of twelve, a standby for the director, one can see, but incapable of rational thinking in situations with other children made chiefly by his sentimental aggressiveness. Explanation of retarded education—even to not being able to read—or of emotional blocking to the necessary relaxation for rational processes, merely emphasizes the fact that he has no distinguishing age for sorting him out into a category of children with whom he surely will get along.

The population in this environment must be regarded as an adolescent population in which each individual has had unnatural growth in one or more directions and retarded growth in one or more directions. In the vertical plane we have a large family as of many brothers and cousins living together, we may say; but the family is abnormal having no defined horizontal planes, for its individuals in their own beings belong nowhere chronologically and everywhere at the same time. They will not in the normal fashion be moved to closeness with "siblings" near their age development, nor will they be moved to the normal camaraderie worship of younger for older "brothers."

I will say further that noticeably close relationships, in early days within the Group, bear watching as apt to be ties of psychic illness by which one child complements another in the fulfillment of a neurotic or a delinquent pattern. An example is the attraction between Paul and the boy joined in the pretense of writing a play but actually bound by the hypnotic compulsion to mull over their delectable—either fantasy or real experience—of pimping.

Or two youths will be inseparable, working well together, expressing toward each other a protectiveness and helpfulness in marked contrast to their indifference or hostility to other children. Their educational levels may differ, their ages be dissimilar, their range of interests may meet only here or there, their feeling capacity and intelligence may not be parallel; something strong unites them, absolutely not good for each other and leading to self-destruction. There is one exception; sometimes such relationship does connote the at last found friendship of two lonely, usually dull, boys denied by inadequacies of personality normal ego-satisfying contacts with other children. Overdependency in such case has its wholesome aspect in that two rejected children are in a genuine situation as receivers and givers of positive feeling.

Such unusual friendships are apt to reveal one excessively domineering and one subservient personality. Watch well and we find that one does the chores and the other swanks it and that protectiveness or cooperativeness or affection has a possessive element with periods of aggression. Such friendships may be no more than the pairing of the wilful and the easily willed bent upon fulfilling their psychic pattern. Frequently, however, there are telltale gestures and demeanors that reveal the relationship as homosexual, at least in tendency if not in consummation. Or watch other children when they manage to sidetrack the arrangement of their labors, catch a hastily whispered word or a hushed laughter, and one observes the ties based on the memories of delinquent participation in the past or on organized connivance, recalcitrance, or subterfuge in the present. Many months later, whether in general discussion or in the asked for interview, the children will themselves verify the above observations—of course, many, many months later when sobriety has become the pattern of living; when the past has been pushed away; when the prodding mentor raised by the vision of duality has started off the major catharsis tending to achieve in each child his sense of personal unity leading to the wholesome unity with other children.

Let us view again the early group picture. The shellac which binds it is psycho-therapeutic proof that the creative-environmental experience has loosened the chains, in varying degrees, from children enslaved to automatic behavior or to suspect relationships. Children feel deeply, even before they show any outward sign of it, the distinction between ego-satisfying and ego-aggrandizing absorption. Even when the problem of human material—how to deal with it, how plan for it—seems insurmountable and while the adult with tact and understatement attempts the separation of suspect unions or employs devices to the childrens' needs they themselves make movements in the direction of constructive relationship. Here is another perverse foundation upon which certain children gravitate toward each other. It isn't attraction, it isn't age level or emotional community or fundamental sharing of interests. It is a foundation of complex motivation. Lending a hand, doing a necessary work, absorbing oneself for an ego satisfaction which derives as much from pleasing the director and getting his approval as it does from being purposefully occupied—this artfully or may I say *craftily* covers an instinctive preoccupation with one's own position in the work situation. This self-preoccupation is on the social side but the rot within is anguish or uneasiness about one's deficiency (or a bias which covers deficiency); and so we have on the one hand an endemic passivity—not laziness nor dislike but passivity—toward many tasks and work participations, and on the other hand a spontaneous movement of volunteering which forms units of children about to share the same work experience.

Even children unwholesomely friendly and bidding together for the same job, under this spontaneous volunteering, do not find themselves segregated as desired. Others join them on the basis of a topsy-turvy common denominator, the similar sense of inadequacy brought to their awareness when the work plan demands at last the getting down to business to bring about results. Children realize sud-

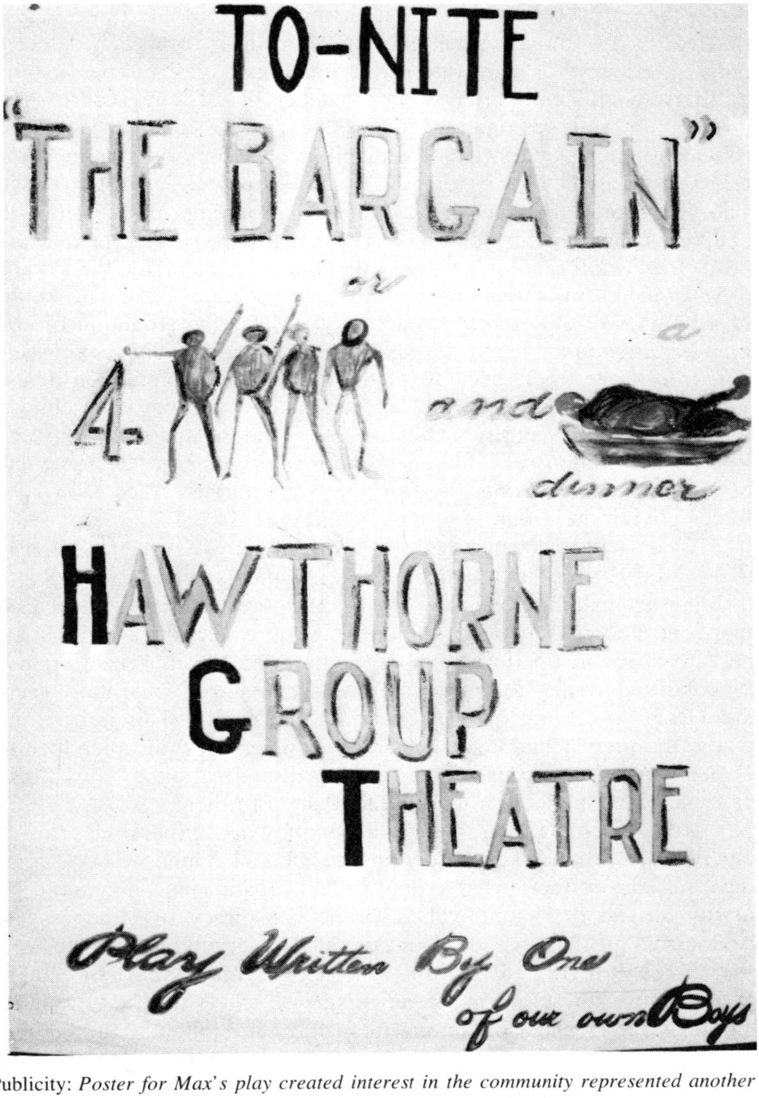

Publicity: *Poster for Max's play created interest in the community represented another project.*

denly their lack of needed skills, their wanting of the three R's; or they recall a traumatic experience of clumsiness or speech defect or other inferiority; or they rationalize emotional biases. The first impulse is to cradle themselves in whatever bit of sure security they possess, or have rationalized themselves in possessing, because of some particular superiority or pretention of superiority; or to volunteer participation where they will continue to feel secure. It can be said, therefore, that the first "healthy" groupings derive from the children's manipulation of the work plan for the self-protective purpose of *avoiding* activity which will *show one up* or for the purpose of *specializing* in activity which will sustain one's status. The joining of a number of children to do a similar task is the attraction of children having similar fears, needs, or biases, instinctively seeking support from each other, because of the usefulness or pretention of usefulness of their chosen work, against other work or other children threatening their security or status quo. And so, paradoxically, the first positive unions of children in the theater circle are confederacies built on negatives, since in fact they are unions of evasion. Odd forces govern the progress of these children!

When half a dozen boys offer with alacrity—even those known to be "lazy"—to haul lumber, omitting themselves from the more thrilling occupations, one may be sure they are nestling themselves in their one known superiority of brawn. The exception is a traumatic need to prove a superiority of brawn; here the task is seized upon as a public opportunity to prove manliness or disprove some more secret knowledge or feeling of inadequacy of that nature. This is true only where the preoccupation with manliness supersedes all other feelings of inadequacy or where there is no rationalization of superiority elsewhere. Let us look around the workshop further.

Here three or four boys with woodwork experience form a closed shop around a construction project. What unnecessary labors the "rascals" effect, what esoteric preoccupation and unnatural solidarity around their job, what a blithe conspiracy of blindness and deafness to all that goes on about them! It is largely an act of passive resistance uniting a group fearful of ideational or acting participation—these are not good mixers. Look at the first volunteer group of actors and find among them the vain children, the habitual shirkers of physical work, the good-looking ones. Case histories should disclose most of these as overloved children; they are the charmers who know best how to get around adults and whose major inadequacy is getting together in equality with peers. Some may have been in a school play at some time, but actually their union of preference is based less on interest than on the evasion of physical, especially dirtying, activity. They have a social bias against all work as beneath them; but also they lack minimum manual skills. See Ben at the writing table surrounded by the "intellectuals." These are the boys with the gift of gab. Perhaps one other child besides Ben has the claim to writing ability, but all together are united in a brotherhood of snobbery on the subject of the superiority of mental versus manual labor. Most of them are idlers living on the periphery of actual activity. They have charm, intelligence, and like Ben have no handiness in doing chores. Ben's play has furnished them the pretext for their choice of job. "We'll need more and more plays, we'll write them." But this, too, is work! Instead, ideas are endlessly verbalized, public attention is distracted by mental fireworks, and lo! the Group owns its own clique of the "intelligentsia."

Other isolationist unions have similar egocentric and evasive foundations. Yet are they all cases in the desert since no human movement may begin but it creates its own *tour de force*. Originating on grounds of one fiction or another, the various units gain reality and truthfulness under the momentum of experience forced upon their members by their self-made work—or living situations. For example, hauling lumber seems so humdrum, so mechanical a job unrelated to emotional living, aesthetics, ideas, other children, or other skills. What impact can it have on six boys so humbly engaged? What growth can it accomplish in each of them to make them feel happier, better men within themselves and in relation to each other? One must remember, "Sticks and stones . . . and power in everything." In the lumber there is a power!

For lumber is the raw goods of the theater, the *sine qua non*. It has sleeping in it, but to be touched into life, the dreams of beauty planned by these six along with the other children. And stage lumber four to ten inches narrow, ten to twenty feet long needs skill in handling or it will break or curl or warp.

Great is the responsibility! The six know they are preparing good or bad ground for the plan's fulfillment. The hands that lift the boards are gentle, sure. The attitude toward them is watchful, cherishing. Anger with a shirker or a funster is clean constructive anger, the protective anger of love for something larger than substance and larger than self. Sweat on shoulders is a proud sweat and the weight on muscles a tender burden. The movements of work become rhythms; bodies coordinate, selfless; all flesh and all spirit become one. Back and forth, intent, and purposeful, they move in pairs; or where the weight is cumbersome four spontaneously act together, or six if that is the need. No argument, just stepping in as in a dance. They initiate a technique—lift, on the shoulders, away we go, swing and take it easy, bend and careful, on the knees and down, careful, careful, edge on edge and here we go again. And one day song bursts forth from six throats—rhythm to help rhythm—but "We are six, strong and good," sing the hearts.

And the six good and strong men are risen in the world. They have status, usefulness, pride, satisfaction. With their union they have each singly acquired superiority in truth in place of that superiority which had falsely united them. They are skill-minded, risen above the show of raw brawn discovered to be wasteful of energy and destructive of substance. The emotional attitude toward materials, as toward other children, the workers on these materials, is expansive, colored by self-investment. Now, indeed, the six are educable. From their core of aware being they send out willing radii of confidence, curiosity, interest, fellowship—to the larger surrounding circle of environment. Still timid in most areas their attraction is logically toward the woodwork bench. Now for new skills, human impacts, learnings, and status growth; now for the ruler, the pencil, the compass, the saw; now for more and more intrinsic participation inside the "sound and the fury."

Similarly with Ben and his brain trust. The self-chosen encirclement soon seems imprisonment, its members fretting against the tides of aimless show binding them in vanity and idleness. The verbal vying with each other, however brilliant, becomes irksome; speech and opinion need anchorage to a concrete goal. Nor are the other children, now earnestly occupied, the enraptured audience they were at first. In fact they show impatience with the "showoffs," the "high hats," the "smart-alecks." Ben and his boys, unlike the six, are losing status, and so they have the need to account for themselves. They get down to work though still an isolated unit bound by their unfulfilled promises; but now the intention to prove superiority by deed is honest. Also Ben's progress with his play—he of course has been writing, out of a truer need and for other reasons we know—is a substantial stimulus. But were there no Ben in their circle, at least one child among them more imaginative, more vigorous—and earlier shamed than the others into producing work—would now fan the creative fire, shame intellectual pretentiousness into stick-to-itive effort. The director of course treats earnestly the "serious" intention of this settling group. It is not important whether usable plays will come of this; the "intellectuals," like the workers, are sweating.

The boys discover problems. Finding it harder to do than to talk about doing they are humbled, self-questioning; for they learn the difference between pretentiousness and performance, between the childishness of glib speech and the mature painstaking of fitting words to a sincere vision or purpose. Words used erstwhile for the evasion of work are cherished now for the pain as well as the pleasure they give to honest endeavor. Around the table boys are united by the knowledge of anguish and rapture all of them are experiencing in the struggle to pin down a feeling or a thought on paper. The printed word becomes hallowed as the symbol of an author's arrival at the pinnacle of *exact* thinking and *honest* feeling which by a stirring necessity is now their goal, too. Physically one writes alone the dream pushing into life from within. In the practice of the spirit everybody writes everybody's play. Because the investment, the ardor, the learning and the problems are the same; as is the leaning of the boys on each other for encouragement, criticism, practical help. This circle's charming collusion of bluff no longer exists; its united will is to work well. Its strutting superiority no longer exists; not only have effort and learning humbled the boys into authentic behavior—"be yourself," as the boys express it—but self-investment has brought them closer to the humbler children for whom they are writing (also, playwriting eases tensions; one writes out of oneself much that has been guarded within. See Chapter on Playwriting, page 204). Empty speech, mental gymnastics no longer exist; instead, earnest voices ask, "But what is your motivation?" or answer, "Listen, this is my objective."

However, this grouplet is far from crossing over its borders into the grime and muscle work of its artisan neighbors. Its spirit is ambivalent; for now without snobbery, on the evidence of what it is accomplishing, it assumes all the more its esoteric prerogative to be let alone, not to be "bothered with heavy work anybody can do"; but anticipating scenic projects for the needs of its plays its members respect and show curiosity about the plans, skills, and work of the others. Moreover, they have regained their status. The actors look up to them for the roles they are creating, the workers for the new jobs of work they are furnishing. There is no logical step to take from the writing table to the workbench. There is no common tool or material to arouse active interest in arts and crafts. Psychologically it is more natural for the artisans to turn to playwriting, as also to acting:

one, the vividness of the two activities inundates their existence despite withdrawal for reasons of inadequacy; two, the nature of their work forces them to make contact with manuscripts and stage; and three, as even the "workers" have a social bias about the superiority of certain types of human activity, it is a rise in the world and an honor to be able finally to engage in them. But the writers, ensconced in chairs of dignity, and with the approval of their peers, have less incentive than ever to lower their position to participate in, to them, humdrum and unglamorous work. What has been gained is that a number of idling, pretentious children are at work on something probably useful to the others; that among themselves they are living richly and genuinely in positive fellowship based on a common interest.

Related to the solving of other needs—and the fact that these boys will have to go to work in the outer world—they may not be left in this spurious position of isolated aristocracy. Some experience, some substantial thing must be found to enlist their interest in manual labor as no less glamorous and no more humdrum than their chosen task. This is necessary especially where the avoidance of work is due to lack of skills or inadequacy in doing things with the hands. Something must be given them to do which will have enough of the quality of romance to make dirty hands a matter of pride; something which serves as a natural bridge between the two worlds of activity. For this there is the typewriter, symbol of the white-collar worker, standing for soft hands and *class* superior to that which works in factories. Also it is a machine, attractive for this reason alone to children of our machine age.

The adult becomes a strategist. Oh, no! The typewriters may be used only for *important* work. What is important work? Not the plays being slowly written; only the needed manuscripts of the play already chosen, planned for, and perhaps, in its constructive needs, already under way. In short, only that is important which is the center of the whole Group preoccupation. Thwarted, each boy tries a strategem of his own; he remembers suddenly that he cannot type—and what is to become of his own play if he "wastes time on other scripts." But the suggestion about typing becomes a force; fingers ache for the machine; now arrangements can be made for doing one's own as well as the group work (the environment is elastic, it will be remembered).

But typewriters are not the clean, shiny perfections they appear. One needs to tinker over them, care for them, adjust slipping ribbons, prevent the keys from catching and clogging. The business isn't simple with carbons forgotten or facing in the wrong direction. And what about margins, and proper spacing, and unsmudged sheets? And the errors and corrections and a form to follow special to a play manuscript? Nor is one isolated with the troubles. There is public pressure; the scripts are wanted; the world seems concentrated on results in perfect, legible, and numbered pages on hand for scheduled rehearsal days. And worse than that, the director is adament about a rule for the typists—they must conquer the troubles of the machine themselves. They may help each other—but who has time? The director will instruct them what to do but will not do it for them—why? And one day the neatly fastened copies of the play are ready. Smiling, the "intellectuals" hand them out, hands grimed in the last excitement of finishing up, eyes shining with the satisfaction of a needed job done, pleasure received and given, and an awareness of adequacy never before experienced. Ben's words one night when he had succeeded with a perfect script well epitomize the boys' combustive awareness of themselves as persons before and after. He turned his blackened palms up with the amazement of one beholding a miracle. He said, "Look! Hands . . . hands have power. What power hands can have. . . . You sounded mad when you told me to fix the machine myself. I think I understand your reason now. . . . I'm not sure, was I afraid of being clumsy, or was I just lazy?"

Building Up the Individual—Importance of First Major Catharsis

There isn't space to follow the constructive development of other negatively founded groups. Rather, we had better observe from Ben's words a climactic moment in the development of the individual child, when at the peak of his first major catharsis he views the substantial evidence of new-found adequacy against the background of his inner biases and fears. But even Ben, with his capacity to express introspection, remains silent about the ultimate revelation the power in hands has made to him. Perhaps because, more than the reproach of laziness and sensitivity over clumsiness, his deeper trouble, the sense of inadequacy with peers, found him hardest pressed to admit relief from a pain too closely guarded. Ben failed to add what his bearing had said long before he had mastered his machine, "I am happy. With *my hands* during the weeks of sweeping the shop I have called forth from the boys their okay sign which was *their* comradely *hands* wacking me on the back.'' To each child in his own time and in his own way the job of work well done brings insight which shows him to himself related to the complete process of performance. For a flashing moment which he never forgets he is inspired to translate tangible substance into its intangible values. To Ben insight had to come only as it could to an aloof, anti work-biased, aspiring boy by his coming to grips with a romantically tangible obstacle and conquering it in a theatrical fashion—with, substitute for blood, sweat, and grime the intensified hero-feeling over perfectly typed pages, some of them the substance of authentic authorship and all of them the symbols of authentic adequacy in previously insecure areas.

I wish to stress this cathartic peak which I have observed over and over again—and worked for. It is a high moment necessary for the delinquent child to have graven on his spirit and the adult will have failed him if he hasn't led him to this pinnacle where like a flooding sunburst an illuminating awareness refreshes him with a new image of himself, that is, of his powers within himself. The radiation of hopeful joy which fills him is more than egotistical awareness, for he discerns an equation between his new stature and his own active part in it. He has, himself, made this satisfying stature. This is not the awareness of duality but that of freedom. A puppet released from its mastering strings, made conscious of ownership of its vital life, would by the first instinct of free existence radiate this clean joy. And hasn't the delinquent child been a victim puppet directed by merciless strings—but less fortunate, for being human he has suffered both guilt and retribution which the creature of rags and wood does not? Life has been messy, involved, a painful slavery; although the child by his active human mechanism seemed to have an active will in the matter of his behavior, he was an *automaton* moved to feel and act by energy touched off within himself but not generated by himself.

Then one day after certain experiences life is suddenly simplified. Ben sees himself an adequate fellow, not lazy, nor clumsy, nor disliked by other ''guys,'' and also writing his play—but no longer with the tearing, exaggerated compulsion about himself as a playwright. He has climbed his mountain and experienced revelation; and with his spirit whole he speaks universally, ''Hands . . . hands have power''; not *my* hands have power. But what he really avows so joyously is the doing and the well-being achieved as the result of energy he has himself generated. Symbolically he has had a hand in the growth of his stature; ergo, he has been freed to direct his energy in favor of the continuation of this growth in stature. No moment of awareness he will have again will be as emotionally shaking or as determining in the tide of his personal events as this first one in which he gets his initial affirmation of himself as a person. It is now he looks with askance on himself in the personality of the delinquent; it is his moment of first *unautomatic* consciousness of himself as a cause worthy of espousal. This is steps ahead of the blind attempts at worthiness on recognizing duality. Then he did not like himself; the inspiring cause was the beloved project. Now himself is the inspiring cause; he has found *himself* worth struggling for. In this moment of lucid "seeing" is born the responsible intention to come to grips with what is undesirable in himself. Parenthetically, it is now he publicly verbalizes the growing feeling he has had for the adult; he frankly calls him, "Friend!"

But the joy he experiences is unique on another count. The awareness that he is capable of joy is the ultimate freedom; for never in his emotional memory has he felt this alerting sense of harmony, this mood of personal innocence related to a sense of the probable innocence of the "hostile" world. It is not an accident that Ben writing his ordered play for Halloween develops within the atmosphere of witches and goblins a subjective fantasy in which the central figure, Ozzie, cries out tragically: "And against one's own will! But have I a will? I am that fly struggling in a web of evil, enmeshed . . . helpless . . . . Helpless—? Nay, I am not bound. My movements are free! But freedom is not mine unless courage is mine . . . . Freedom is courage! Nor am I a mannequin of sticks and ragged cloth . . . . I am a Man! I am capable of making decisions and acting on them . . . . By all that is good and holy, I swear I am making a decision now. I will fight the Master of Evil, Satan himself!" Ozzie the mannequin has made a decision, and Ozzie the man will act on it!

Heterogeneity—The Leveling Process—The Overlapping Device

It may be asked, why go through trying periods waiting for positive factors to emerge from negative ones? Why work with such large number of difficult children? Why not work with smaller separate groups on some arbitrary classification such as talent, median ability, or category of disturbance? The answer is that heterogeneity makes possible the development of homogeneity; that the theater environment has the potentials of a catalyst and as such ought to be exploited. Alone, talented and bright children would merely be encouraged in the development of abilities without regard to problems of personality, would be deprived of the situational experience necessary to adjustment for their individual thriving in the homogeneity of the family and the outside world. On the other hand, average and "dull" children would miss the stimuli for development which contact with intelligent and imaginative children could give them.

Nor do I mean that what goes into the melting pot shall come out of it boiled into uniform character. The very nature of threater precludes this. But into the pot—along with the sum of the skills, knowledge, aptitudes, etc., which perfect the common project—goes also, and vastly more important, the sum of all the emotional and mental variations of differentiated personality. What is hoped for from this pool of psychological ingredients is that each child will be able to get from it what he needs of the positive and necessary for vitalized growth into a social person. If the flame warming the kettle is the theater activity, what it cooks up by a process of forced yet gentle commingling is a dish whose separate materials are refurbished, spiced or mellowed by what they are able to absorb, contribute or throw off through contact with each other. I call the whole the leveling or humanizing or democratizing process.

I believe children suffer as much from the deficiencies which preclude full membership in their own youth world as they do from unhappy relationships within the home; for then they have closed to them their rightful place in their own cosmos. Adults, more or less, need to reinforce themselves daily for heterogeneous living. To children heterogeneity is natural as the instinct for testing, smelling, experimenting through the muscles and the senses. They are curious about each other. They want to do what the other does. They want to share their experience and they need the acclaim of their peers. Troubled children are fundamentally lonely children. They look wistfully over the fence which divides them from "good," "normal" children. They're only exaggerated patterns of normally growing children, but the exaggeration marks them and prevents their crossing or being invited over the fence. And they do not even belong with each other as *marked* children except that some common denominator in their highly individualized patterns gives them a basis for companionship with peers.

There is an instinctive need *not* to be different from other children, except for the desire of the ego to have just enough difference to win admiration. What is Ben's snobbishness if not a concentration on the latter, a whistling in the dark to cover wistfulness over a world to which he does not belong? Even among delinquents and neurotic children he is an outsider, a stranger in the volatile world of robust, energetic, easily mixing, devil-may-care youth. At first he feels left out even with Max, his intellectual equal, who by virtue of glandular overactivity has some of the characteristics of the others. What is the contempt the hail-fellow boys shower upon Ben's kind if not a cloak for insecurity and inadequacy in the quieter world of scholastic learning? There is in the bringing together these opposite elements under the theater roof the opportunity for children to enter, and so unite, both worlds into a new totality of youthful living. The immediate effect of this is its promise of happiness in undifferentiated camaraderie. Subjectively the child feels, I'm together with these others, I cannot be so different in quality, ability, mental, or physical qualification. Psychologically it bespeaks a denial of limitations; it frees from the loneliness inherent in too divergent or individualized personality; it satisfies curiosity, presents a ladder for earning status with peers.

For dramatic clarification I have stressed, above, two extreme categories of children—except for the intimation that Max fitted into both. There is a third or middle class, and of all three I will speak later on at length; even then classifications will be arbitrary for rarely can a child, as I have described the human material, fit snugly or completely into any one class. But I wish first to introduce the *overlapping device* or the technique for making heterogeneity truly effective as a leveling agent. It is, when the time is ripe for it, the quick seizure of opportunity to arrange children into working groups which will best benefit the individual in his emotional, psychological, and learning needs. It is the frank manipulation of the human material within the work situations—in his turn, the adult's arrangement of unions for positive purposes—and would fail were the children not prepared to obey his counsel as the summation of a sincere personal philosophy implanted through specific attitudes.

For example, his attitude of hope and anticipation about progress possible to all children makes him casual toward talent and ability per se, and enthusiastic about effort and growth as remarkable phenomena. Or he appreciates human differentiation—the unique merit of each child—for its blessing upon the total group in enriching its life and in contributing to its success, so emphasizing the rightness of having divergent character qualities, potentialities, knowledge, etc. His attitude of encouragement carries to outside interests the child may have, and shows under every condition of managing work or managing children. Except where individual vagary threatens the Group he treats it casually, always living his role of trusting leader. And always he acts the Pied Piper, playing his undaunted tune about good and beautiful work to be done by "capable" and "well meaning" children. As part of his philosophy he sometimes acts the martinet, because he is anxious about his flock. But above all he is an evangel proclaiming hopeful tidings, insisting with a voice of consecrated faith that children are more capable and more wonderful than they themselves know; that happy children are those who give themselves a chance to prove this. Thus the director amalgamates the heterogeneous group with an outlook upon life which has the hope of security in it: he helps to remove children's biases or evaluations tending to insecurity with each other; he introduces constructive values by which children may gauge, on new planes, their growth status among peers all of whom now are measured by the same rule.

It was chiefly leadership by these attitudes, highlighting the commendable aspects of the negative unions, which helped children upward despite negative purposes. By it Ben was led from a completely aloof behavior to move into the human tide, as similarly the lumber haulers were upwards led to interests they shied away from. Or put differently, the director's leadership over developments in the voluntary grouplets was mainly indirect leadership or the use of indirect motivation or psychological maneuvering (the typewriters) for attaining positive ends. Externally he was permissive about who would work with whom and seemed content to let children and work develop by a hit and miss process.

The point of demarcation is the child's ultimate moment of awareness, for now confidence in self and in the adult is at a white heat. Also, children observing the growth phenomena in each other are drawn close emotionally because of pride, gratitude, and the hope it holds for themselves; the fraternal family enjoys confidence in its members. All want to move forward and outwards. They are ready for any and all experimentations with work, other children and themselves. As personal counselor, as foreman of the theater shop, the director may now use *direct* motivation or the frank communication to children of what he desires from them. What he desires may be more learning, adult behavior, that a child try something he has no interest in, that he work with a child or children specifically chosen; in short, that in activity and in attitude he should *overlap* into untried domains for his own good, or for the good of others or for the needs of the project. The aim is the physical organization of the environment in such a way that children will rub shoulders with as many others as is possible in as great a variety of work situations as is possible, in order to get, from new interests and from specific contacts, observably needed benefits. The method is to gather about the workbenches, writers' and artists' tables, on the stage, at the bookshelves, on the discussion floor, all the children as though all or none were talented, bright, skilled, knowing. This cannot be done all at once, but children can be staggered into the varied activities so that every child will have had a hand in every kind of chore and art and skill in close relationship to children good for him; with the initiated ones taking under their wings those with less knowledge, ability, experience, etc.

In parentheses, I must distinguish between direct motivation and a technique used seldom which may be called frankly *mastership* or the adult's use of his position of authority. In specific cases observation of a child will realistically prompt immediate demand as a shock technique, all signs pointing to his unreachableness by slower, gentler methods. The pattern of such a child is either a cold aloofness or a testing of the strength of the adult. Without psychic preparation and without reasoning, the director gives him work to do, places him where he wants him. Perhaps, because it simplifies existence for certain types or they can yield only before authoritativeness, they progress best when affect is created through impersonal relationship, the courtesies from the work contact serving as the minimum acceptable dosage of personal infringement by the adult. This arrangement seems to grant the psyche a touch-go, contact-severance mechanism by which it preserves for itself emotional intactness, warding off the inevitable moment of yielding entirely to surrounding influences. Such children have the advantage over the others in the quicker learning of skills since neither time nor effort are expended on them for other development.

In terms of the necessary success "on the great night" teachers and certainly theater persons will cry "impossible" to the overlapping plan. Nevertheless because of the plan the Group has never had less than success. Overlapping divides responsibility between those who can and those who can't. In the skills and arts necessary for production this provides an effective balance between inefficiency and progress in industrial and creative output. But we are interested in the successful growth of children. Overlapping permits a balancing of personality or provides for a *planned propinquity* of children most likely, because of complementary qualifications, to benefit from each other in learning, human experience and the acquisition of status. To children growing less self-centered there is appeal in the practicality of the plan as formulated by an anxious foreman of their shop to get things done. To those who have learned how to work and to those who have yet to try certain skills it represents fairness in proportioning responsibility according to progress—and without threat to self-esteem. If Ben learns from Charles at his work bench and from Mike at the switchboard, about woodwork and fuses and wiring, both in the playwriting hour (for all children will be attempting to write plays) will be looking up to him for creative guidance.

However, it may happen that children will not always be rational about the personnel arrangement. Charles and Mike may be *humanly* good for Ben because their intelligence may equal his for a working basis while their manliness and happy-go-lucky quality may be aides to boyish development necessary for him. But Ben having his own inclinations may insist quite logically that Frank is as good a woodworker or that Paul is as good an electrician as the two boys chosen by the director. I have spoken of the environment as elastic; it is elastic only if the director is, so if he has the wit to bide his time he will not force the issue. Ben will have done well enough to want to work at two unknown skills. Ben on this day may not be amenable, but the tie between himself and his leader is stronger than is apparent. Awareness and love have developed empathy. The boy will not be at ease. He will be mulling over in his mind how the ideal person feels about being thwarted in a plan made unselfishly for his good. He will live over again his cathartic moment, remember his self-made vows and the purpose and quality of the adult intention. Perhaps in an hour, perhaps in a day or two he will find his way of his own accord to the place and the persons chosen for him.

Overlapping gives practice in democratic functioning, for it emphasizes the *whole* of a job as the result of the same spirit of cooperation on the part of coworkers but not necessarily the same kind of contribution. It vitalizes the slow, dull, unskilled, or unschooled child because it gives him something to do in a helping and learning opportunity touching upon the greater part of the job in the hands of one more capable or knowing in a brother-leader position. The arrangement is aboveboard since cooperation, learning, growth have become the living standards or ideals of the Group. All children in functioning thus together, within their limitations, gain the feeling of adequacy; the know-hows because of maturer responsibility; the do-not-know-hows because they are psychologically in the position of knowing how, since they do contribute something and do earn a share in the credit for the completed job.

This democratic functioning extends further to dissolve preconceived, absolute notions of superiority or inferiority. A dull or backward child in ideational, artistic, or artisan activity but adept in the humbler tasks of caring for materials, cleaning up, or keeping inventory may well be the foreman over a crew of "superior gentlemen" cognizant of their shortcomings in method or skill to do these necessary and indeed fundamental jobs on which rests the structure of the enterprise. In the all-over picture, which finds children active in several fields in reversed positions, no child is unknowing or inept, unneeded or inferior; for in some aspect of the complex theater environment he has his own superior niche which permits him, too, a brother-leader responsibility toward others. Every child is a master and every child a learner, both at least to the minimum degrees required by the ego for incentive to cooperate in its own reconstruction. So, there is released from child to child a humanizing attitude of respectful and encouraging forbearance toward ignorance, inability, and personal troubles as *relative* human failings remedied by patience and understanding on the one hand, and on the other by the willingness to accept help and to make efforts.

The results are warmth, camaraderie, progressive learning—and there is no demarkation between the learning to work or the learning to play or smile or quip or prank, or to help one's neighbor, or to conquer lack of confidence or self indulgence, etc. Above the noise of hammers and the swishing of paintbrushes and brooms, current in the heated communications on work matters, in corners, on the scaffolding, at the light boxes, a gathering spirit grows of usefulness, well-being, belonging. The placing of the sentient with the callow, the weak with the strong, the knowing with the unschooled, the incapable with the capable, the negating with the enthusiastic—wherever possible, the placing of personality with its needed complements in the work situation—enforces on the materials of playmaking a service more potent and enduring than seems in their mere physical use for immediate purposes. For tools, materials, books, manuscripts, and whatnot serve them as the stepping-stones from tactual and sensory experience to better climates in emotional and human experience. The general movement is toward secure rational being.

The overlapping seems to put into action a psychic weaving force which picks up stimuli like threads and shuttles them back and forth from child to child and from the individual to the aggragate and vice versa. As though the work directives were the warp and the movements of personality made the woof, the brand new cloth under manufacture is the closer knit Group, becoming one in purpose, industry, inspiration, fraternity. But a fabric is not stronger than its contributary parts. Across and in and out of the warp—the learning and the creating activity—there is a shunting of fresh and vital threads from the heterogeneous pool to weak places of the human material whose loose or ragged fibers or dull colors, by a sifting and intertwining operation, are caught up, strengthened, brightened or mellowed, re-created.

I cite the concept of weaving because *melting pot* may still suggest a result in uniformity. The aim of the director is that each child shall stand forth adjusted, an intrinsic entity, happy in the proof of his own powers and satisfied with having acquired the faculty of being the best of himself within the limitations of his being—and without inferiority. To continue—in the process, the intertwining threads cannot help but plunge deeply and surely into the intrinsic quality of individual being unlike anyone else's; so linking the psychic filaments or attributes of separate being; and forcing, by the refurbishing, an awareness of distinct, new, self-totality which makes each child proudly feel, "This is myself, I . . . " When at last the beauty and wholeness of the Group fabric is actual, its oneness like Joseph's coat of many colors has unity but not uniformity; its many parts have unique color or character or individuality. But a singular harmony governs all. It is the mellow, interwoven patina of shared human experience or the same binding mood of ultimate awareness of and pride in "belonging" together in a common humanity of basically similar hopes, quests and outlook upon life.

Overlapping individualizes the child through the very process which I seem, in contradiction, to call leveling. I have defined the individualized child above. I want to distinguish between the connotation of the word "limitations" in the phrase "the best of himself within the limitations of his being and without inferiority" and the use of the word elsewhere in my objective measurement of a child's capacity of the moment. The child individualizes when he *knows* what he can or cannot be or do; but what he knows from the accumulation of his experience may either confine him to limits narrowed by the dissolution of pretentiousness or may widen the scope of his powers freed from the oppression of inferiority or guilt or other limiting factors. In this sense limitation becomes known to him as a universal law governing all children, hence people, in varying degrees, but bringing along with curtailment compensations; so that a child knows where he stands and finds serenity and happiness, while before he suffered doubt and confusion.

It comes about that there is no contradiction between the director's evangelic leadership toward becoming greater than one is and the eventual reality which shows loss of some trait or bias or pretentious or unreal hope. There are no losses but negatives, and all gains are positive ones, for knowing at last what one can or cannot be or do is inclusive knowledge as much about relationship and living as it is about capabilities, interests, and learnings from work experience. The child is individualized because he is free, aware, responsible for himself.

This is the metamorphosis in the child: that before, his individualization as marked by the delinquent and troubled pattern, was anarchic in nature and in expression, and he moved lonely in a world of chaos; now his forces are gathered and active in a recognizable unity on a cleared road on which he moves with others befriended. The osmotic process of leveling has given him something, taken something, gradually bringing personality to its best possible expression on its own natural level. He has learned through his democratization that against certain unavoidable truths there are other truths that balance the scale of well-being for all: that people are not alike, not similarly endowed, not similarly acclaimed; that, however, a man useful according to his ability equals another according to his because it needs all levels of personal worth to run a nonchaotic world; that a man has dignity and equality in the world, when, accepting himself at his best, he fulfills his special responsibility. Individualization and democratization are one and the same thing really. The child feels larger having found himself, fearing no longer his differentiation from others; because he is tied to these others by the more important similarities of human feeling—the universals of hope, despair, joys, aspirations.

After a while Sidney* will say without reservation, "Boy! I'm getting along fine. I'm learning a lot. I'm not as good as Irving—I

*Sidney, pp. 26, 36, 62-63.

just haven't the same kind of hands. But nobody can keep this place like I can. Guess the Group couldn't get along without either of us." And he by capacity a porter and Irving* a born artisan, and Ben whom we may one day read, go off together with a roll of laughter like the Three Musketeers, bound by some intangible flow of sustenance they get from each other. Except for their mutual interests from the environment they are on different potential levels—of performance and of anticipations from life. But they are pals; and the echoing laughter of three so different boys comes as from one heart. True, Ben will be talking mostly about the new scene of his second play, and Irving will vie for attention to speak about his construction set; and only edgewise will Sidney get in something rueful or humorous about his chores. They will banter each other, commit a bit of slapstick; but also they will take each other seriously—and this is a far way from the early days of no meeting ground at all, and more recent days of joining together only for reasons of evasion. They will fortify each other with feeling as with practical advice—haven't the three a personal knowledge of the problems of writing, building, cleaning? But more beautiful still—will this be Ben the highbrow, the snob, taking seriously the punch criticism of a Sidney guy who speaks in blunt reaction, having no glibness of words and only a rudimentary intelligence, "Go on! Real people don't talk that way. It stinks."

But the starch in Ben's stiff-shirt intellectuality has been washed out; he is now a "boy." Not only will he be happy under the naked criticism, really a kind of flattery proving his acceptance by boys; he will heed it, respecting the opinion of a "simple guy." Much of his serenity will be due to Irving's influence, for it is he, belonging to neither extreme type, who has known how to translate the emotional and mental language of both boys into a common medium. Irving represents the third class of children in the heterogeneous mass. He has a direct function in the leveling process, for it is through his kind that the two extremes of personality get boyishly together.

Let us return to the top and bottom layers—arbitrary classifications, of necessity—of the Group Theater society. Ben, Max,† and Harry,†† are representative of a small upper class of unusually bright, sentient, gifted, withdrawn, or aloof—as the case may be—self-

*Irving, pp. 26, 34, 37, 77, 79, 83-4, 136.
†Max, pp. 52, 99-100, 136, 149.
††Harry, pp. 25, 34, 37, 100-103, 111.

superior or its concomitant—obverse self-depricating children. They live on imagination, ideas, real or rationalized ambitions. They are not easily identifiable as "bad boys." They emanate a quality of being "nice" boys; about them is an aura of refinement, of poise, even of integrity. They have awareness of the organized world and feel a deep sense of loss, for they consciously want to do things, fit in somewhere. The picture blurs sometimes, as Max who has superimposed on him an unreal toughness, who is a "fresh guy" with ready tears behind too hard eyes; as in Harry who is physically unkempt. All of them, despite having come afoul of the law, are "pure" children—Max pretending to be of the gutter and Ben and Harry actually not having been touched by it.

Sidney, Paul† and Joseph* belong to the class which may be described as casual, gutter-hardened, matter-of-fact, and underdeveloped or underpriviledged in natural endowments or the heritage of decent background. These live by their senses, are ambitionless in the social meaning, lack the power of perception for the necessary anxiety about their destiny. They are the youth who as men will fill the ranks of the slum proletariat if not the criminal class. They are apt to have a direct pattern of lawlessness, hooliganism, the immediate satisfaction of promptings undiverted by the neurotic conflicts of the upper class. They are the least educated in the school sense and not easily educatable. They are the men of muscle, the irrational haters of books, study, ideas, those symbols of a world to which they do not belong. One sees in them fearfully the future hired ones to break strikes, the followers of demogogues, the breeders of a low posterity.

Set the stage on which both classes may move toward each other and see what each can bring to the other. The upper class needs toughening in its emotional and physical fiber. Its children need vulgarizing or the ruffling of their too-smooth feathers; they need a comedown to easiness in devil-may-care attitudes, to fun-of-the-moment capacity, and to forthrightness in animal spirits. The bottom class needs sensitizing by exposure to interests, modes, and feelings different from, and inspiring beyond, any heretofore known to them. Its children need the atmosphere and goads for incentive to climb upward. The rejectors of as well as the rejected from schoolrooms, they require subtle influences to dissolve the hard crust over

†Paul, pp. 89-93, 100-103, 118, 137, 152.
*Joseph, pp. 25, 36, 62.

hearts and minds for the letting in of a change in sentiment toward the things of the mind and the spirit, until learning becomes a personal necessity and books and ideas assume at least an elementary meaningfulness. The upper class needs relief from introspection; the bottom has need of its development. Set the stage on which both types meet in a working alliance and immediately there is established from the necessary communication of shop the foundations for the communication of vital influences necessary to each class.

The vivid character of these two at opposite poles constitutes a balance of impacting power. We have the challenge of articulate, probing, sensitive youth to emotionally callous, mentally idle, sensual youth. We have the aura of attitudes: on the top, aloofness, engrossment, real or pseudo-superiority; on the bottom, hostility, inferiority, inaptitude, and some curiosity. But aloofness is a wistful emotion awaiting inroads upon it. And hostility softens with acceptance; the mere commingling in a partnership with "smart" boys for something so high-flown as an art project translates to the abject ego the feeling of acceptance in equality. However, challenge precludes the hope of immediate peace in an atmosphere volatilized by immoderate interaction from both sides passionately not seeing or feeling about things alike. They could not last together for mutual benefits without the influence of the middle-of-the-roaders from the in-between third class.

This middle class, to the bottom one, is also a status class relatively smart, schooled, skilled, but closer to itself in the knowable patterns of street talk and outlook; therefore its middle position of ease with upper and lower establishes the latter's acceptance in absolute measure; for it provides these children, by its overlapping in both directions, with the encouraging nod of intermediaries effecting valuable reconciliations. The chasm of obstructive feeling sinks away as over the bridge of common goals and labors a gradually classless society crosses back and forth with riches from opposite worlds. The tall talk of youth who walks in the clouds and the rough talk of youth earthbound, both level soon to a single language, its vocabulary moderated downwards and upwards. It is the remedial tongue of adolescent humanity, the common, understandable articulation of curiosity, awareness, elemental feeling, exchange of "culture." Literature, and Odets—Ben's playwright examplar—and the urges and moods of creativity, become the psychic property of youth who knew only Edward G. Robinson in a finished gangster role; the ninth inning and anguish over a disappointing game become the property—

and education in lighter ways and moods—of youth too tense and lofty for normal well-being.

Now let us meet more intimately the third group of children. It is a class less dramatic in its indication of troubled symptoms and individual potentials. It lacks the self-conviction of the others either in the quest for self-expression or in the justification of asocial behavior. Its personality may be called Philistine, for a shrewder social intelligence guides these children in concealing beneath a decorous, amenable manner their true state of feeling or intention. Aggression, demand, protest are held in bounds to be expressed under cover; knowing right from wrong, they play two sides, the public one of polite, rational exchange, and the private one of deception, trickery, etc. Perhaps this is because they haven't the outright claims against the world of the lower strata or the frustrations of the upper. Among them is average to superior intelligence; but no conscious aspirations move them though they have some constructive interests and generally some schooling. They are the first to achieve a reasoning, cooperative attitude—as a group—toward the work plan. When the others go haywire these, less ego-explosive, are the dependables, the backbone of the environment balancing the disturbing weights of top and bottom; they are soonest the mainstay when things go wrong, the minutemen preoccupied more with the "cause" than with themselves. Speaking the original language of the rougher element and understanding intuitively the other language, these average children become the practical leaders, the harmonizers or voices of fraternity and common sense. Irving, Hal,* Milton,† and Bob†† of the challenging letter belonged in this category until they became individualized.

I have emphasized this class's progress *as a group* because individual progress is apt to be more chaotic than in the other types. Right after the moment of high awareness, when the adult anticipates inspired performance, he is shocked to discover what seems like a setback. Negative patterns show up; not new ones but the old coming out of concealment. Is it the development of the superego, the desire for facing oneself to be above board? What is apparent at this time is that selfhood exists, that the discovery of powers, and the satisfactions from status, mobilize the child into fullest self-expression to *the*

*Hal, pp. 62, 64-66, 100-103.
†Milton, pp. 20, 21, 25, 37, 50, 52, 61, 136.
††Bob, p. 135.

forgetfulness of assiduously tended controls.

I believe this is what happens. The delinquent pattern of this middle group has less to do with psychic upheaval than with a tendency true to average people to follow the crowd. Given enough personal and background history for separation from the normal life of "good children," they have followed the crowd of "bad children," boys much more disturbed and antisocial than themselves. Boredom, purposelessness, the enticing mores of bolder youngsters, the fear of being different, desire for companionship, the instinct against loneliness, the need for approval by peers have made them follow an imitative pattern bolstered by just enough personal reason or need to give an intrinsic note to what is mainly the result of habituated expression. The getting along with adults, the amenability, and the facile transference to them show an area in the psyche not too scarred by hostility, capable of the exchange of approval and love. Some of the concealment of the negative pattern must be due to this. Much of it must have its roots in the psyche's compromise arrangement achieved in the past to balance what had become automatic behavior with the pangs of awareness from the pain or tears of parents, brothers, or sisters.

In the theater environment this same child finds purpose, loses boredom, discovers a mores of existence and a "parent" who doesn't call up guilt. Though here, too, he finds his old pal-type, the leadership comes from children closer to his natural character than those he has followed. Moreover, in this fresh world he is quickly acknowledged, for though it breathes by the inspiration of a few unusual children it builds its substance by the calmer labors, the average abilities, the rudimentary skills, and the cooperativeness of his own kind. The multiplied presence of his kind, the dependency upon them for the fulfillment of clever and imaginative plans, brings every child in this artisan class into a feeling of ascendancy. *He* is now the *crowd.* He has no need for aping others. The beguiling pattern of the rougher children loses attractiveness—in fact, in learning how to do things, even in soberizing, the latter hope now to emulate him! There is now the discovery of himself, the discovery of powers of imagination, of ideational and emotional capacities and sometimes talents which bring him actually instead of by identification into the status of superior children—it must be remembered the overlapping has given him a chance at everything.

With the result, unless he is truly mediocre, that he appears one day, his middle-of-the-road character gone! He has been in the presence of the "intellectuals" and "artists" in so many ways his exemplars; just when they are soberizing, coming down to earth, he becomes temperamental, gets fixed ideas (Irving's lamp), etc.: which behavior is partially the misguided aping of qualities he has observed in the leader class. But preponderantly these are the symptoms of forces gathered into individual and aware entity; they are the intoxication of the ego which has been jolted into an active will to express itself wholly; and so what was concealed comes forth aggressively together with what has been newly learned for self-expression. Therapeutically this is beneficial to all concerned. Out in the open to be worked through with the child come tempers, stubbornness, rationalizations, Philistine dishonesties—replacing surreptitious spites, stealthy connivances with peers, and the false sniveling obeisance to the adult. In these moments the adult has a hard time.

The child, weary with the effort of sustained goodness and freed from dependency by the evidence of his own rise, though loving the ideal person, temporarily rejects him. This may be for a moment ever so often like a reappearing rash or may continue like an unabating eruption in outbursts, pigheadedness, or moody uncooperativeness for a spell of weeks. But he is an aware person at this point, more guilty toward his new selfhood than toward the adult. He has the best ally in the world to assist the director in the establishment of equilibrium after the tumult, when his left hand will have discovered what his right hand had been doing—his individualizing, integrating ego.

Democratization, individualization—without pretense to the miraculous, I may say that the most potent accomplishment of the overlapping device is the dynamic reeducation of children by children who, under the vital challenges of creativity, become themselves creative forces impacting on each other. I have tried to follow the reeducational development in what seems two almost simultaneous movements—a horizontal one and a vertical one: the former, a rhythmical exchange action outwards and selfwards, a giving and taking to and from others' values leading to growth, or skill and learning values inseparable from psychological and human values; the latter a vacillating change action like that of an unsettled indicator on a meter, sliding up and down seeking its topmost level for rest. The exchange movement is a relating to people, new phenomena, ideas, the broadening world. The change movement is a relating of the awakened self to a slowly emerging superself, censorious (like old-fashioned conscience) and self-prodding, wavering less and less on the evidence of powers, capacities, pleasures from the new living and the higher standards, and settling when the newly formed self-image shows constancy.

I doubt if a new self-image could rise up before a child's consciousness, despite the love relationship with the adult, despite the work media through which is established this relationship, were he not commingling with peers in a heterogeneous group, making the extensive variety of exchanges possible only under heterogeneity. For the self-image is not the specialized extension of one's old self as a carpenter, a writer, a person of some special skill. It is a vision of all-around newness rooted only partially in what one has learned to do and mainly in what one has learned to feel. Reeducation is a matter of attitudes. The director may teach educational externals; he may inspire and set the example for fundamental intervals of feelings or attitudes. But without the variegated milieu of children acting upon each other he cannot perpetuate these attitudes, which can only take hold by contagion, by children seeing it happen to other children, by children voicing in their own idiom their enthusiasms, their new interests, and their new well-being. Indeed this contagion is the most potent commodity of exchange, not as obvious as fellowship or helpfulness or the concrete barter of knowledge or skills, but present as the life current which encourages, gives confidence, and charges and recharges the change indicator in its upward climb.

In the beginning I emphasized: (1) the importance of vitally engrossing activity to counteract the attractiveness of delinquent activity; and (2) the high standard of achievement for the conquering of obstacles to satisfy the need to be grown up. It may now be added that without the three types of children working together there could be no vitally engrossing activity on a high standard of achievement helping children to mature. There might be an activities program of a kind, but not wonderful enough to stir children out of themselves; for similar children would not have enough to exchange with each other to stimulate interaction making for change, and to awaken attitudes appreciative of change.

Obviously, just as ground explored for gold will give none unless the rough ore is hidden within, so environment, the creative process, techniques, and peer influence will net in personality growth no more richness than is innate in the basic quality of the child. The special concern, therefore, is with the lowest category of youngsters. But what do we anticipate for them? That for their happiness and well-being and for the good of society they shall feel humanly close to people, understand something of what is going on about them, have a desire for the basic schooling they rejected, attain the security which grows out of constructive fellowship and self-pride. To the extent that the director can employ his techniques to attain these ends he does so. In the overlapping, he bolsters up acceptance with every effort to let them discover in themselves swift substantial proof of having something to exchange with the others; to this end early participation is scaled to current capacity for performance; and no job is entered upon which does not hold implications of value both to the main enterprise and to ego satisfaction in terms of status, confidence, the promise of moving into more interesting and more intricate activity. But actually reeducation is by the other children. They spread the contagion of attitudes toward creativity; their enthusiasms are the exhalations and the deeds of an infectious love for books, words, beauty, work. They carry the barbarians along in the pursuit of ideas, in the forming of plans, the seeking of goals, the following an ideal.

Some of the latter, their depths plumbed, their basic quality surprisingly fine and reachable under new opportunities, rise forever out of their class (e.g., Paul). Most of them will never be seekers of knowledge nor worry about the fate of the world; they will not write me as did Max and Hal in almost identical words from their distant fighting fronts, "I have managed to read all of Ibsen, Steinbeck, Jack London and the Irish playwrights," speaking also of the "new world" they were glad to be fighting for. And one or two will be touched, only temporarily, returning to the gutter as the way of least resistance, lost human material too far gone for permanent adjustment. But almost all will have attained a feeling for, if not a concise understanding of, the function of ideas in our society; and in what humble station they may move they will retain always a nostolgic regard for people active mentally and creatively.

To this extent, that youthful experience brought them participation in creative activity and attained for them self-respect for some success in it, will they have been lifted psychologically from the slum proletariate mire of existence. They will have achieved some skills and will have learned how to read, write, and figure; for the contagion of attitudes toward lofty accomplishment, with the concomitant *must* of academic skills, will have brought about a practical interest in them and the need to learn them. (The next step after the halting practice of the three R's in the workshop is a wider awake application to classroom studies.) They will not be theatergoers or readers of editorial columns. But it is astounding to watch these erstwhile illiterates grow critical about movie shows, with a point of view about good and bad acting, and even about content; and to see develop, though not too profoundly, a curiosity about the doings of the world. This lowest strata of children attains poise, acquires the knowhow to get along in a sober civilized way. The barbarians are reeducated by the potent companionship with peers.

Exchange and Change for Aid With Obnoxious Traits or Symptoms

Youngsters slowly adjust their difficulties as the environment by the children's own exchanges and changes mellows, becomes ever more the living workground of a large artisan "family" happy in the shared and mutually upholding life of creativity. Children getting along well with themselves are living harmoniously together in work and in fun and in a new outlook. But certain obstructions in personality linger longer than others, such despised traits or symptoms of disturbance which impact as irritants upon the surrounding group causing hostile embroilments. I cannot presume the correct clinical explanations for the crybaby, the sickeningly ingratiating child, the youth who trembles before the virility of his fellows; it is enough for the director to recognize the disturbing factor of these patterns, as much upon other children compulsively goaded to intolerant reactivity as upon the "sinners" who by this latter fact alone rather perpetuate then eradicate their hard-to-live with traits. The child whose obnoxious behavior makes him, while others are enjoying close and constructive friendships, a failure among peers, resorts suicidally to his habitual mode of crying to or currying favor with the adult, or of showing a cowardly mien before muscular strength.

To help him adjust his position among peers the adults must be wise in the choice of the proper overlapping place, in the planning of where and with whom the child will work most engrossingly or where and with whom the human exchanges more than the work exchanges will tend toward a transference in child-to-child relationship—minimizing the need to run to the adult or, in the case of the coward, effecting a mitigation of the fear pattern. But first the director must establish an exchange with the child which is a permanent understanding of love-demand so that sternness or indifference or even harshness will be translated by the child as a kind of code message for guidance in beneficial behavior.

Briefly, the ingratiating child is hard to deal with; he bends his back too easily, he is so quickly on hand to be helpful. He is the temptation of Satan to bribe the busy director into forgetting his therapeutic mission. This child disturbs the fine balance of fairness with which the adult deals out acceptance equally to all children. On the other hand, the crybaby upsets the balance, not by offering the adult more than do the others, but by demanding more from him.

In the first case, the director must guard against accepting gratuitous activity in his behalf, insisting with schooled casualness or kindly aloofness on receiving only, and no more than, that performance which he asks from this child. By attitude the adult refuses the child's emotional entanglement with himself and establishes an expectation of the child's cooperative relationship with other children. The intention is to amalgamate the child with his surrounding environment of interdependent peers. In the overlapping he is best placed in propinquity with a leader type—unless his own abilities and qualities suggest the solution of giving him leader responsibility. The brother-leader he needs is one who can make constructive demands on him in terms of the mutual job; who is secure enough not to mind another fellow's hand in his work; who, having a goodly portion of creative egotism will not be swayed from his course, and by his ability and concern with what he is doing, will be able to encourage emulation.

The same treatment applies to the crybaby except that his propinquity mate needs to have the capacity for big-brother patience; for the crybaby makes the trouble he cries over, buzzing about other people's affairs, overcurious, and opinionated. The leader should be an older boy, sentient and intelligent enough to cooperate with the adult in helping the younger. The director, of course, will have a cold ear for the tale-telling of the crybaby. But his responsive formula, "Go back to your work and don't let the boys see you crying," despite its demand harshness will be sensed as a love intention of wiser and wider protectiveness than the immediate haven the child is asking for. In both the crybaby and the ingratiating child it is necessary to eradicate the vicarious parent image these children attempt to foist upon the director—in the first, of the archprotector, and in the second, of the adult needing protection. Practically, both patterns are attention-seeking devices. If in a small area of the environment these youngsters can have a start in winning *approval* attention from peers, with a progressive flow of positive feeling exchanges between them and other children, there will have been begun in them the movement of change—the release from compulsive entanglement with the adult and the establishment of a normal child-adult relationship.

As to the cowardly boy, let us observe Leo as an example. Although he comes each day exuberant and impatient for his work task or his acting role in the play he ends it in a morose mood; sometime in the latter part of the session he becomes abstracted, perverse, or recalcitrant. He uses the *loving* adult as he would his parent, for upon the director he thrusts the hostile pattern of his misery bred elsewhere in the shop. Periodically, too, he makes a stubborn request to leave the Group "forever." He gives no reason except the terse reiteration of desire to be on the farm where, parenthetically, one works a good deal in solitude and never after dusk when the theater group meets most often. His reason is nameless, for he will not call it fear, and fear is a sickness because he is a physical coward whom the boys have further undermined with ridicule. Corporeally fear stalks Leo, especially in the person of Joseph, who has been mentioned in these pages as sadistic and insecure with boys of better ability. Joseph has a low IQ: Leo is not too bright but brighter and has some scholastic achievement.

The two work the shop's distance apart but must naturally cross each other's path sometimes. Then Joseph's prizefighter build and bulldog features cast their shadow upon the slighter child. It isn't pleasant to behold the change in them but a minute ago, "normal" boys, for generally Joseph no longer teases boys or pushes them about. But Leo shows so obviously the uncontrolled symptoms of the cornered creature, he awakens in the other the dormant lust for violence. And by the stern standards of adolescence the latter isn't too wrong with the rest of the group, which feels more or less the same distaste for Leo's weakness. A sickness passes through the mass when Leo ducking Joseph's menacing arms becomes the target of his hate-energized hammer, so virulent is the hostility of the fighter for the boy afraid. The sickness of the group is the conflict between elemental fascination for this primordial show and humane anxiety, albeit tinged with contempt, for an endangered fellow. Thus, group sanity and group work are interlinked with the special problems of two sick personalities.

For the sake of peace and health in the environment and in behalf of the production at stake the director might dispense with the presence of one of these two boys. He may judge that Joseph should be the one since he is perhaps too far gone to be helped into permanent adjustment. But like a physician he may not give up his patients until everything has been tried. He remembers that Leo must learn to grit his teeth and to put up his fists in a world of men, just as he remembers that perhaps Joseph can be changed. Moreover, he reminds himself that Joseph is that needed element of heterogeneity immeasurably valuable to such as Leo. For without him the environment would be too unnaturally sheltered to prepare Leo to get along with the Josephs he is likely to meet one day on a job, in a subway rush, in the army, etc.—or the Johns whose respect he will have to win.

One doesn't need a clinical analysis to conclude from the simple outline of Leo's history that to free him from inadequacy with virile boys would be effecting his eventual freedom from other related symptoms of disturbance such as stubbornness, sulkiness, taciturnity, temper tantrums, infantile demand for attention, victimization by boys bordering on the sexual sphere. (Certainly other youths with a similar history of emigration from two such hyphenated cultures as Sephardic and Syrian to so different a culture as ours have adjusted better to the new climate. It may be that Leo came to these shores already troubled.) However, for practical therapy the clear symptom, his cowardice, relates to his incorrect and unhappy functioning among peers; and both facts, without a forced search into hidden mysteries of personality, point believably to causes closer to date—to wit, the uprooting of this child into a different civilization; the tearing conflicts born in him still living the Eastern life in his family circle; the difficulties that had naturally to arise in the life with boys in the school and in the streets, American boys spirited and overflowing with animal energy, not formally mannered, full of pranks and jibes and fisticuffs, and the Western bias about masculine behavior.

In contrast, Leo discloses to these boys an outlandish pattern of personality, the marks of his culture and training from a land and a household where this or that is deemed unseemly in a child; where children bow before adult dictum; where play is sober and contained or has the aura of tradition; where refinement inhibits "smart" talk and muscular outlet of energy. What if Leo went to an American school and learned our language? There was no one there to balance the scale for him between East and West, especially to educate the swift ease of the American way into his sinews and muscles and tongue. And children are cruel to the child who is too different. An olive-molded skin without ripple of muscle in limbs and gentle bovine eyes are difference enough to mark timidity and confusion with the wrong name until at last coward is correct for terror before strong boys (and general insecurity with peers).

The director has two psychological aids to support him in handling the situation. First, the necessity of theater, to which the children willingly bow, requires for the sake of its fulfillments civilized behavior—and to this argument that he has made the Group and the work suffer Joseph will apologetically yield. Second, despite compulsive patterns every child has taken to his heart consciously and gratefully the acceptance principle by which he himself has thrived and by which he has seen others thrive. Honesty about personal problems, with understanding helpfulness and not blame, has been the voice and the deed of this living principle; and traditionally this "family" has had its closet skeletons worked over and changed into successful and happy boys. Therefore the director may take this situation up privately and publicly.

In this case I opened wide the closed and guarded books which were Leo and Joseph. In privacy I named to the former the reason for his desire to leave the Group, and explained the meaning of coward as the opinion of his peers. Joseph was dealt with in public as a bully in no uncertain terms because it was important in the light of the emotional seesawing of the others that they know the feeling of the ideal person in this matter. Also I confided to them a psychological picture of causes and effects in the behavior of the alien boy. The effect of the conversations was catharsis, a clean sweeping of the spirits of both adversaries and of all the others; the two were prepared to accept what plan the director might have for better relationship; the group sympathy was swung to support Leo in his plight.

I planned an experiment which might bring them together instead of leaving them inimically apart. So, casually, despite the fact that we were very anxious to have a certain job finished, I opened the subject about fighting. "Men are supposed to become fast friends after a good fight, isn't that so? All right, here's your chance. Joseph, you've been aching to fly at Leo; we cannot afford the destruction you cause instead. Go ahead . . . Leo, stand in a fighting position; hold up your fists." Leo flushes red but rises slowly, still remembering our conversation. Joseph spits on his palms and pounds them one into the other significantly. A boy inquires do I really mean a fight. Yes . . . I mean a fight, a knock-out brawl if that is what Joseph wants . . . Leo will take it like a man. The boys, at first fearful, slowly, grasp my intention. They encourage the victim—one sets Leo's stance, another arranges the half-refusing arms, a third poses his back, etc. There is no blood lust in this whole scene unless in the little eyes in Joseph's already excited face. Leo, the center of a delicate solicitude, must feel like the historic goat tended and wreathed for slaughter. He searches my eyes, and I send him a message to be brave.

For Joseph this ritual takes too long. His pugnacity is dampened. He isn't the center of attention in this which is his forte. The "specialist" in him becomes annoyed with the imperfect tutoring given by the others. Some influence of the months of living in the Group stir in him now and mix with present sensations, and he kicks over a chair. He cries out: "H—— I can't fight a guy like that! And you guys are all wet, telling him to do this and that, as if you knew. . . . Some fighters in this crowd!" He towers over Leo: "Come on, you, I'll show you." He gives instructions, pulls at Leo's body and limbs with the impersonal giving over of the artist for his craft. He no longer has hatred, only impatience, for muscles slow to obey the requirements for fighting perfection. He hurls imprecations but not in bad humor. Leo has lost terror, but anxiety plays on his face until he achieves a better than failure rating from the other boy—or better still until he feels in his body the beautiful unaccustomed stretch and ache of physical power! Then cries the teacher, "Now punch me, up, this way! . . . Again, that didn't hurt, come on, come on, harder!" And finally—why expect the impossible from Joseph?—"Now I'm coming after you. You better punch hard because I'm going to lay you flat."

And then at long last there is Leo panting, hot, elated, wincing under the congratulatory back-poundings of his applauding fellows. There is Joseph, perspiring, with a wide benign grin, who says, "Go on, I didn't hurt him, ask him." He looks more like a paternal Caesar than a gladiator as he looks Leo over, then laughs out heartily: "He likes it. Look at him—he *likes* it." Sure enough, Leo has been caught—in the surge of his ego satisfaction projecting an inner vision of himself as a fighter—heedless of onlookers, pantomiming the steps, moves, and postures he has just learned! Bravos ring to the rafters.

I hoped it would be like this, but I had taken a chance. I had been sure of the other boys; in Joseph I had counted on the psychological effect of his seeing his quarry stand up to him for a beating like a "regular fellow." Also I had decided—and had prepared his cottage parents to accept it as the sign of progress—that a few bruises would do Leo good, in his relations with peers, as honorable decorations of courage publicly won. For the aftermath I had a plan of exchange in the work situation—this was the reason for my beginning speech about men becoming friends after a good fight. Now I was wondering how to choose the convincing words to gain acquiescence to my plan for their working in propinquity. But Joseph, too, had had satisfaction from the fighting bout. He had sublimated his need for violence; he had pulled his punches and had assumed the role of trainer; he had the goodwill of the boys for his decency. It was Joseph who did me a service, for he offered, "You know what? I could make him stand up against anybody if we had ten minutes together every day . . . (with a grin) boy; could I teach him! (ruefully), but if we would be seen doing it, it would be stopped, nobody would think we're up to any good."

Said I, "Maybe we can arrange it, here on the stage. It'll just be another Group Theater project. But we're behind schedule and we have lost time today. You're both behind in your work because of your quarrels. How about a fair exchange? Leo is good at woodwork; if he gets down to business he can do wonders with the troubles in both your projects. How about it—Joseph, you work with Leo and learn from him; then about ten minutes before closing, you, Leo, get up on the stage and learn something from Joseph?" Leo answers shyly, "Okay." and the other echoes loudly, "Okay. It's a deal." He jumps up—"H——! We have to shake on that." The handshake is a significant ritual in the Group; it connotes now the promise of the end of hostilities.

Did hostilities cease altogether between the two? Did Joseph abruptly stop playing the bully, or did Leo immediately lose his terrors? But what I had externally manipulated could be merely the opening up of a window to let in purer air, or the showing to Leo a hopeful vista of well-being among peers. The external climax of the situation had slowly to do its internal workings on both boys through the exchanges which would add up between them, beginning with the quite tangible and more or less superficial exchange of "skills."

The very immediate effect of the fight and the barter was a better climate for all. And the two boys had now a positive contact, the boxing lessons; and a rub-shoulders get-along-together contact in the work situation to become increasingly positive through shared experiences. The event had brought them status with a balance of position for maintaining self-esteem; the one was work master to a boy whom he had feared; the other as strong-arm teacher was "nobly" employing a decried capacity to help a fellow. There was another psychological balance. Joseph's pugnacity had roots in his feeling of inferiority, in the knowledge of his poor participation in the labors of the group. He loved the Group Theater and fretted against his own lack of skills and continuous failures. Leo's better artisanship promised him greater usefulness and higher credits. He could take learning from a boy whom he had held in contempt because this boy was now to be his creation, a being recreated by his efforts into a semblance of his own sensual self. Leo's compensation was similar; but added to it was the fact that by merely tussling with him Joseph was changing the public opinion about him; he could take bullying or teasing now that Joseph's training him seemed almost an act of love—wasn't he sharing his metier with him, taking pains for him?

The exchange, especially for Leo who had more potentials, led to receiving-and-giving rhythms in various areas, and finally to observable change—in Leo's relaxed, industrious person reaching gradually a position of leadership in the group; and in Joseph's better work contribution, within limits, and better still in his more civilized relations with people.

Change and Exchange by Indirection

The memory of Sim haunts me. I must give him separate pages as in our environment I had to give him a uniquely separate attention, since for almost half a year none of the techniques seemed helpful in his case. A stolid youth about sixteen with immobile, handsome features, he never smiled or recognized or showed human warmth; and verbal articulation consisted of "yes," "no," "I don't know," or terse variations of these. There seemed no human language, word, gesture, or attitude for reaching into him or for touching off a live response as with Paul. The latter had seemed to be alive in some dark secretive place. Sim seemed altogether to lack the vital spark. He had no anger, he had no joy; he gave outer obeyance in a passive-pacific mood like an automaton. Sometimes stubbornness without words flickered in his eyes; but resistance, too, was passive; he merely froze up. A boy described him once as a "blond zombie"—it was a good description. If Sim had ideas, if he agreed or disagreed with thoughts or plans voiced clamorously about him, I did not know for the better part of a year.

Sim had taken up carpentry in the school woodwork shop and

this is what he wanted to do in our midst. But he was indifferent to motivation. During free expression, while I was wondering what to do with him, he volunteered projects which seemed intended as contributions to the plan. He *seemed* to carry through, but successive pieces of work appeared to be in contest with previous ones as merely larger and better nests for accumulating thicker and longer spikes. Hammer, nails, and lumber held a complex fascination for him; he destroyed what he made by his fantastically indiscriminate, compulsive, and not-to-be-reasoned-with nail-hammering. I tried mastership (see p. 151), telling him what to do step by step, placing him with another child or a group of children. The result was the same despite his outward obedience; but now he injured the work of other children. They were nervous; they rejected him. The longest sentence he spoke at the time was, "I want to work alone," upon which a quick boy imitated him a la Greta Garbo, "I v-a-ant to be-e a-lawn. . ." For some reason he did not want to leave the Group. The psychiatrist explained the nail pattern as his individual way of expressing hostility.

Because of Sim we started a special project which I had to think up—a puppet show. A set of twenty-one puppets, a version of *Treasure Island* written by Nathan (see p. 214), three miniature sets, electrical equipment for lighting, a designed proscenium with a curtain system of ropes and pulleys, props—a lamp-post, tables, and chairs for the inn, a ship that sailed, a barrel to hide in, treasure bags, costumes, etc.—all revolved around a lad who couldn't and wouldn't work with other children and who contributed nothing to the plan nor to the sustained enthusiasm with which the other labored for many months afterward (this project was additional to the current preparations for already planned productions). All revolved around the eleven-foot marionette stage I thought up as a destructive-constructive vehicle for socializing Sim. It was large enough to need spikes not insignificantly small nails, and would need many of them; it had a meaningful relation, in the reverse, to the activity about him—practically, everybody was working for his project; it gave him opportunity for status growth for the same reason, and for the learning and obstacle conquering opportunities it held. This was overlapping on a grand scale, the universe changing its course to be noticed by the little man wanting only his pristine solitude.

I should not like to make a cost account for the materials Sim wasted before he had a presentable open platform on hinged legs—for easy storing—to which he had yet to add more wastage in time and material in order to append table sides meant to support the proscenium, light equipment, sets, etc. In his early attempts the nails were so numerously helter-skelter one saw only black beetles dotting the satiny cream of wood. There was no intelligence in his work; the boy was on a sensual holiday. The bang, bang of his hammer made the children jittery. Not only the noise, the recklessness and the stupidity annoyed the boys; they had an investment in the stage—the work they were preparing for it. They hovered around, pleaded, advised. For all the anxiety, the attention, the attempts to reason with him, the first platform was solid! Sim had either an emotional blocking to the plan or he could not visualize the plan of working puppets upward from beneath an open stage.

Two occurrences ameliorated the situation. In desperation several boys leaped upon his "table" and gave vent with their feet in retribution for his hammer poundings and his stubbornness. "We'll show you," they shouted. "First it has to be an open stage . . . open . . . o-p-e-n, do you hear? And second, we'll open it for you because—you dumbhead!, see these nails?—they've cracked the lumber, it won't stand up" And the legs buckled, the top splintered, the boys jumped to safety. Everybody laughed. Sim showed the first fleeting smile we had ever seen on his face. After that the boys appealed in a body, "Please, let him work in the hall. He works alone anyhow. He's too noisy, and if we don't hear him we'll not worry about how he's building this thing . . . please!"

The boys had taken a good deal for the sake of one boy. I had tried everything; why not this? Now Sim was really alone. Did he miss the fuss made over his job? Did the muffled sounds of activity from the other side of the wall make him *aware* of his isolation? Or did he miss something human which in these many weeks by the sheer poundage of impressions had made a dent on his shut-in being? If in the first week the lack of banging sounds outside our door was pleasant it caused no surprise. Sim was measuring lumber, to start all over again. In the second week this was still quite natural: Sim was sawing or planing various parts, on the corridor floor or on a "horse" he had made for himself for the purpose. The third week odd things began to happen. People passing him asked why he was working outside. There were moments of heard silence as though he were not working at all. The boys were aware of something unusual and would cock their ears, remark about it. Occasionally I went out to see and to casually instruct Sim. When the banging started again the rhythm was changed; it was less voluptuous, lacking its former staccato swiftness and endless duration of time. Sometimes Sim had to come into the shop for some necessary tool. He began to stop, as in passing, to look over some other boy's job, especially the work pertaining to the puppet project. A pleased boy would say something to him about it then ask how his stage was getting on. Terse conversations, but some exchange was taking place in the mood of coworkers. Then he made a habit of calling me out for instruction—especially for that related to the use of nails. One day I sent out Irving with him—to "show him where big ones and where little ones are best, and how to space them, etc." From then on Irving served as brother-leader. On another day the stage was brought into the shop and Sim became part of the group of fellow workers.

Exchange had taken place indirectly until Sim's acceptance of Irving, who also had been a work-by-myself boy. I would say that this indirect exchange due to Sim's negativeness had brought us something too—the beautiful project I had to think up, the rich experience the boys were having in creating its parts, even the aroused "family" feeling over his negativeness, which made every aspect of this project dearer, more worth protecting and working harder for. Exchange and change occur in devious ways, and for the children who are not ready or able themselves to get all the benefits there are children who are; the most negative situation has inherent in it a positive component eventually beneficial all around.

We can leave Sim now still taciturn but less silent, hammering nails more intelligently and with artisan purpose, occasionally smiling, conferring sometimes with coworkers on the problems of their joint project, slowly socializing under the influences of direct exchange and change like the others. And some months later, on play programs, we will even find his name among the painters, the electricians, even among the actors.

Conclusion—Leveling—Love the Equality of Inequality

In summing up the effectiveness of overlapping—for individualization through leveling—I find the phrase *love principle at work* as perhaps the best explanation of what takes place to help children find their natural level of being, happy in being just themselves without the sense of inferiority, genuinely appreciative of their fellows even those who have surpassed them. In the beginning their was love *from* the adult. Midway somewhere together with love for the work there was love *for* the adult. Little by little there rose to consciousness *self-love;* not in the egotistical sense but in the hygienic sense of loss of guilt, hopelessness, inadequacy, etc. But infiltrating these love streams, and flooding the atmosphere of environment finally, there was simply love like breathing, without the directives for, or from, or self, simply outgoing being or enlightened love—what Milton had termed "unselfish love."

Slowly individuals emerged from the mass. The delinquent face and voice and walk disappeared. Children appeared as persons, spoke and thought and felt in ways distinguishable from the speech, thought, and feeling of anyone else. Except that a synonymous humanity, a similar out going quality became an attribute of this emergence. In development most children surpassed themselves. A few who by objective judgment showed no marked growth nevertheless disclosed the signs of inner fortification. And some children, in the combination of personal adjustment and the revelation of unique ability, surpassed their fellows to such a dramatic degree as to win public acclaim. If these, true to human nature and despite the no-star system, became "stars" and swaggered a bit; or became "master" technicians and bossed it a bit; or posed for a while like Max, Ben, and Nathan in the heady excitement of successful authorship—it was all taken in due course without jealousy, without the old feeling of differentiation, with at the worst a shrug of the shoulders or a tolerant twinkle in humanly softened eyes.

I might make an equation: results in humanization are in equal ratio to the strength and number of love ties which the overlapping has been able to bring about in children disliking work, study, social existence, people, *themselves.* (I know that last word does not tally with the impression most people have of the delinquent, confusing the symptoms with their own absolute values; if he loves himself why can't he look the world straight in the eye; why is his look masked except when he is able to muster up a fighting expression; and why is a first symptom of adjustment an open look as though the face, like a window, were washed clean, the murk of the secretiveness erased?)

Love is a lacking ingredient in the delinquent personality, especially that constructive self-love on which is built growth and without which there is no possible interlinking of self with others in a normal love attitude of identification and of giving. In the beginning no child had use for another in the human sense. The only common feeling among all was disgust, unhappiness, the sense of inadequacy or inequality in relation to the organized world. The immediate mood was a disgruntlement with peers, not getting along. Delinquent and neurotic children are extremely cruel to each other. (This does not contradict the description of behavior to pals on pages 147-148, of delinquents on the loose joined by necessity and untouched by social influences.) They are cruel, not in thoughtlessness as normal children are, but to give pain, to cease being the classical goat for a nonce and to be fate or God or virtue over a more vulnerable creature. It is odd, but they do not hang together except at the moment when the common enemy, society, threatens. The code of the disinherited exists only for committing the asocial act and not telling, or for knowing who did and sealing one's lips. But very personal trials get no sympathy. And a child's differentiated character or unhealthy behavior unlike their own—like bed-wetting, anguish over ugliness, lying, fear, homosexuality, stuttering, slowness, ignorance, clumsiness, etc.—they seize upon with an uncanny synthesis and gleefully expose by innuendo, name-calling, taunting, and tattling, or by anonymous references on blackboards or passed-around notes.

Isn't cruelty of this kind a pitiful attempt at vindication—a minor-keyed conqueror's shout that others are out of shape, not oneself? Notwithstanding normally acceptable inequalities as humanly natural, troubled children have an exaggerated feeling about theirs, though they seem to belie this mood with compensatory attitudes and behavior. It is necessary to listen to the counterpoint tune, to the abiding mood of hopelessness and frustration, which accompanies any and all of the variations of unacceptable behavior of these children. To the raucous, or the adamant, or the muted song of "I can't," "I don't want to," "No!" "Give me," "I don't care," one can hear, if one wills, the plaintive and human obbligato, "I have been deprived . . . deprived of my birthright . . . deprived . . . deprived of my human equality, my equal heritage before men to express my being . . . *to be fully*—in a way possible to me alone—useful, loving, loved, in a purposeful existence . . . deprived . . . deprived . . . deprived." Hence the cruelty, especially to peers. It is the crying out, "You see . . . I am like everyone else or I wouldn't recognize these awful things as bad things. Really my inequalities, *my* differences from and with the world are by comparison such little faults."

To these children the theater experience gave back their birthright, that fundamental equality which is connoted in the concept that all men are born equal: intangibly, through the love attitude of the adult who took all children equally to the heart and gave all children a like opportunity to love; tangibly through practical ways by which all without exception led an equally useful and purposeful existence, grew and shared success side by side, had equal opportunity among peers to build up fellowship in mutual appreciation. The humorous riddle of which comes first, the egg or the hen, cannot be answered. Self-appreciation relaxes the psyche from tensions which emotionally block the ability, or the desire, to appreciate others. Appreciation from others relaxes the psyche from tensions which prevent a happy mood concerning oneself. Either way, to appreciate may be defined to love; that is, to put a high value on someone (or self) regarded rationally, with an accompanying feeling which is pliant, positive, ardent.

The integration of the various love streams or movements of appreciation—children for the adult, children for themselves, children for work and learning and growth, children for children—was mainly the work of the overlapping. I suppose *death* is called the great leveler because the lifeless are supine, without will or desire, uniformly equal in that final anonymity which a barrier curtain has shut down upon those whose impulse had been identity or fulfilled being. Troubled personality is bound somewhat like this in a half supine anonymity, and a half vitalization which agonizes in its plight. To complete the allegory, one may say that troubled children are those whom an overzealous henchman of the reaper has attempted to level before their time; and that numerous child Hamlets had been caught by a halfway curtain on a midground, Chaos, between full life and limbo; and had been automatized to a stilted rhythm of repititious seeking and rejecting escape from this fate. In the sense that *life* is called a leveler, the overlapping has succeeded in breaking this puppet rhythm. It unionized the timid love currents set up by the other techniques; gathered them together into a force so vital that the recharging of one protagonist brought courage, intuition, concerted will to all; and together they made the forward leap. The halfway curtain was an obstacle passed. And on the stage of life a vitalized mass went through an intricate and imperfect choreography until, habituated to the new way, finished performers assumed at ease the postures, movements, and moods of individual mold.

Do not the members of a family express fullest being or fullest giving to the whole, growing by this, when all are equally warmed, soothed, exhilarated by the love presence in their midst—regardless of individual divergence? So in the theater family. The overlapping made practicable the love principle, substantiated its existence as something happening, giving sensations, satisfying one's being—it was not merely the kindly fiction of adult philosophy. For overlapping began with collectivism, throwing children together in equal belonging in the environment—the deed, not merely the word of faith and hope of the adult. It comforted and inspired—again the deed and not the mere word about the basic equality to start over again, to prove useful, to be happy. It implanted a concept about human equality as the practice of a similarity of spirit acquirable by personal growth. It implanted the concept of personal growth as a progressive movement of growth-to-growth self-acquirable through effort. It gave proportionate position, instead of absolute, to such uncontrollable elements as similarity to others in personality, ability, aptitude—equalizing the unequal as the collective and equally essential parts of the (theater or any) group being. It made children discover themselves with satisfaction. Finally, it removed the obsession for self-justification because of the original sense of inequality before the world. Children moving in aware and acceptable identity had no longer the need for cruelty, jealousy, hostility, asocial compensations.

"I can," "I know," "I'm somebody," "I care" said the attitude of youth reborn. And "I own the future, the future is mine, the past is dead," said the voice, posture, nerves, sinews. "This is I," and "This is he" spoke the alert mien of children as fellow got together with fellow. And responsible, responsive children seeing what each had become above his original stature beheld each other with the creative rapture which they felt for their finished works—this, too, was the result of their togetherness! Together they had created, climbed herculean beanstalks to slay the giants Ignorance, Insecurity, etc.; but more wonderful, together they had observed the re-creation of every one of themselves; had in fact invested personally with action and with attitude to assist the re-creative process in their fellows. So having struggled side by side through both processes, the creative and re-creative, they could the more appreciate—themselves so vitally renascent—the success story of every pal and peer. Though the success stories were not quite similar and not all as grand, each had the knowledge of human equality in fundamental things having been like the others a protagonist against odds, successful in finding purpose, usefulness, and love.

In this kind of writing it is the vogue to eschew soulful words, leaving them to literature; but the story of the adjustment of the delinquent and the neurotic child is far from mundane to those who watch for and witness the joyous unfolding of personality with its embracing gesture toward life. The word I want to use in this adjustment portrait of the Group is the word "great" as we use it of distant figures who have climbed unprecedented human heights. Because each boy and girl looking upon the other did achieve for a suspended, not-to-be-forgotten moment, that rare greatness when one recognizes the universal in the particular inclusive of self; or when each child accepted the human worth of his neighbor, recognizing the human spirit above its representative substance and felt awed before its humblest emanation from his humblest fellow. From then on children measured the essence of the maker or doer in their midst above the limited results. This was love, and by it children helped others to extend these results; or where it was beyond the nature of a child to grow further, love made possible his acceptance of himself as he was as well as his appreciation of others as they were.

Thus as nearly as possible children arrived at the truly democratic spirit or the feeling through, to each other, with the creative attitude which spurning externals, revels in the promise of good and growth in others. And the brilliant, the not too bright, the self-discovered limited, and the potentially extended, walking each in his own dignity, in his very own quality, had the knowledge of differences but not the attitude; for this was loving knowledge respectful of the person for his humanness and for his essential merit related to the totality of their life together. Differently developed, they walked all the more in solidarity, each remembering the raw human material (like the discarded or old stuffs refurbished for production needs) and the growth from growth (like the project with its trials, experimentations, and triumphs) and finally the upstanding, dependable comrades (like the satisfactory lighting on the satisfactory stage set and the actors and crew a linking team), giving the sense of harmony and of all things being right with their world.

Children now appraised themselves and their fellows by the social standards of the adult world. The standards were their own, ingrown through environmental experience, born of the struggle to achieve cooperative works against obstacles, taken deeply to heart as the cause and effect of well-being. Thus, work—constructive activity—had a top place on the appraisal list. They honored each other as workers, or as talented people, or as peers making constructive efforts although not specially gifted. They honored each other gratefully for helpfulness, determination, unselfishness, courage, forethought, poise; for all the qualities which had made amiable their working and living together, or had glorified their trials, or had by deed, attitude, or achievement enlivened and sustained their new outlook on life. Nor were they righteous, nor did they judge by absolutes but humanly, by the measure of the related lessons they had themselves learned. They were strict with each other, but just and tolerant; and they faced themselves in the same mood. And since some are born to be leaders and others to herald them, the Group Theater now had heroes, home-grown.

Forgotten was the gang-leader prototype, or the publicized criminal, or their facsimiles of the silver screen once followed or identified with. Youth experientially, both the centers and the critics of growth processes, judged and acclaimed the outstanding ones among them with the ardor of an enlightened mass for those who epitomize in their being their own lofty needs and aspirations; or with the ardor of the average person for the superior, of the limited for the limitless. He who lacked the degrees of knowledge, kindness, courage, maturity, etc., which rated one as leader strained toward these qualities by followership and by identification. And now at last there was in the "family" the normal sibling attitude of comrade worship of the younger—the less developed—for the older members. Or, in the sense of the larger human family in the wider world, there was the appreciation of social individualized character as the norm to strive for. But so much awareness had the democratization wrought bringing all things and people into focus for appreciation that the child made hero by the majority was himself a hero-maker in an overlapping system of fluctuating majorities.

Paul became a hero. His was one of the best success stories; for in the memory of his peers he had been "queer" dreaming away his days in a trance but to waken to abnormal activity, intellectually pretentious; and after that to overzealous participation mainly through brawn which the boys had felt from his ready fists—overprotective of our goods—and which we all knew from the anguish over earlier projects almost smashed or disjointed because, like Lennie of *Mice and Men,* he did not know his strength. For the beginning periods the others had felt curiosity, sympathy through the adult example, and then annoyance and contempt. Afterwards, for the volatile activity of his muscles the boys had felt a mixture of dismay and of awe—what adolescent does not worship brawn as an attribute of manliness? But the threat to beloved works showed up brute strength as a weakness; and therein lies the secret of Paul's final acclaim. For the boys had seen his inept aimless fingers grow knowing and gentle; had seen his sinews learn to obey his developing artisan intelligence and his forthright devotion.

Paul becomes a hero as a worker. Who sweated over wires, burned himself on hot bulbs, made deft changes in equipment, manipulated his fingers into impossible places, crouching, crawling, climbing to achieve more than one dream of a lighting beauty? Paul, who had been clumsy, ignorant, self-preoccupied, brutal! Who single-handed held up a toppling scenic wall for nigh to sixty minutes, unbearably cramped, to save the actors on the other side heartbreaking, calamitous failure on the big night? And who on an another such night chinned up the straight wall of the proscenium to untangle the snared curtain ropes noticed by no one but by him awaiting his cue in the wings, and keeping his head, too, by adlibbing lines from his monkey retreat to delay his entrance? Paul, who had been unseeing, hotheaded, unresourceful! Who could forget the apt interpolation of those adlibbed lines which kept the meaning of the scene but added a laugh for the audience and extra time for him to boldly leap—and enter the stage absolutely in character? Thus amazingly Paul was discovered anew, having not only poise but the snap wit of a comedian. Paul became a hero as a person; not because he was strong, had achieved skills, or had become the Group's all-around man; but because he had used the skills and strength finally with courage, loyalty, insight, because he had become a giver as well as a doer. He had achieved a social individualized character and as such he represented hope to his fellows in an intimate, proven way, having started out with less than most of them and more grotesquely.

But to Paul, Harry became a hero, having conquered his poignant physical handicap, the stuttering, emerging to the glory of the Group—and to its greater appreciation of individual struggle, with its own satisfying role of helpfulness in the struggle—as its wittiest, most charming and intelligent speaker (see p. 251). And Max became a hero to both. In the ultimate phase of his acclaim Max represented Limitless Talent, the Unattainable where it seemed not naturally to exist—for Max was a superb actor, puppet manipulator, scenic painter and the author of a good play, *The Bargain*. (It will be remembered that Max received a scholarship in acting at the 92nd St. Y and was given a junior group to supervise.) But in the daily and more dramatic, because human, phase he symbolized revelation or self-discovery through interests, self-confidence, intellectual curiosity, and daring—having known no more than the others the fund of his talent except that he must try everything. He had been noisesome, aggressive, and annoying in the finding of himself. Thus he had been negatively outstanding. But in his finished totality he had reached into the hearts of his fellows as an example of the truly socialized being because more than anyone else he had become the Big Brother; assuming the responsibilities which the gifted must assume, siding and encouraging the less gifted, prodding them and sympathizing with them, explaining to them and teaching them with a kindly patience second only to the director's. Besides Max there were other developed artists, but he was the hero for the enthusiasms which he shared, for the unselfish push which he gave to his fellows.

Ben became a hero—though he never became an ace as an artisan. He was the Group's intellectual member although Harry and Max had keener minds than his. But Ben had the glamor of the intellectual personality, the sudden stray look indicative of his pursuit of an idea, the slowed-up voice in apparent obeyance to a concentrated listening to his inward thought. This is what had set him apart to begin with until the performance of writing his play under the eyes of all, and the result, integrated the opinion about him as someone different from the rest but "special." He was mind even though others expressed themselves more brilliantly. He offered a treat to children curious about phenomena—for they caught in him the machinery of mind perpetually at work (Max was too, like themselves, thinking in gusts and splurts noisily from any part of the body but the head; and Harry was just a little less like them disclosing the onslaught of thought in fits and starts on inspiration). Nor had anyone turned out a play as wide in scope as Ben's, as colorful and as deeply revealing the personal feeling most of them had about adjustment. Ben was imagination, he was the universal spokesman. To the dull, the unschooled, the mediocre, amazingly through him, the written word, the exalted thought, the turned phrase became something to hang on to, to ask for more. But not while he stood aloof presenting a picture of better-than-thou!

Contrasting scenes come to my mind: (1) Ben at his table like a composite island retreat in the midst of high seas—and by tacit agreement everybody ignoring his zone; and (2) weeks later the night he took the broom in hand to tardily fulfill this item of the bargain he had made with the adult. The boys watch him, sending signals to each other in the silent code of lifted eyebrows, expressive shoulder shrugs. They observe him—pale, self-conscious, awkward, moving with barely concealed hatred for the adult for what he believes is an indignity. Swish . . . swish . . . goes his broom (around his table only), in haphazard strokes bumping angrily against obstacles. A current of feeling passes through the others; contrapuntal thoughts seethe—Ben's unworded, those of the crowd whispered, then catcalled. "Well—well—Look who's with us!" "Come on, somebody, show him how to hold a broom!" "So he's off his high horse!" "Hey, watch out, you'll break up the place!" "Look, boys, he's going to dirty his hands—what do you know!" Ben's face breaks out in a sweat; he reddens, works more slowly and quietly, remakes his round with exaggerated painstaking, "Ah! That's more like it." Max strolls over. A long, painful silence. Max softens, "Say—that play you're writing—we might even help you; why don't you tell us about it?" Chorus of voices, "Yeah, why don't you?" The ice breaks. Words, challenges, answers, the first smiles, an easing up of tension on both sides—communication is a live wire sending back and forth living stimuli which predicate fellowship, respect. Ben has made his first gains as the "people's" playwright by showing himself as a worker in an environment of workers.

But humble children become Group heroes, too. There was Wandi, whose shortened name had the fitting and odd sound of a goblin character in a folk tale; except that he was big in a bony, horsey way. He stirred one poignantly with his mild manner, his push-away gesture of the hand which said he was not worth troubling over, he knew his limitations. His readiness to do chores, his humility, a sweetness which made even his slight stammer charming endeared him. He was like a child and had that appeal—in his earnest efforts to cooperate and to make good—to his superior socializing fellows. When Wandi became an actor they watched him solicitously. "How hard he tries, poor chap!" "Here, Wandi, let me show you how to do it!" He became a hero, this awkward, underpriviledged boy, as an actor—for keeping his head under circumstances which might have lost it for a professional. It was a question of a loin cloth. It had been wonderful with what detachment he and several others had allowed me to pin together their loin cloths in the dressing period before the play—besides Indian bands and feathers this was all they were wearing. I thought I had done the job carefully; but perhaps my handling the actors, because of the intimate nature of the job, had been overly careful. To the consternation of all of us, but not to the audience's, Wandi's cloth was slipping. A too-hasty crewman beckoned him that he was going to drop the curtain. Wandi, who had suffered the longest five minutes of his life surreptitiously managing his loin cloth, now became frantic over the outcome of the play. He knew he must prevent the dropping of that curtain!

He gave a stentorian "No" to the boy; turned to the feathered Chief with a "Big Chief . . . ugh!"; gesticulated with his free arm in the direction of the wing; and continued in the Indian rhythm of speech and with ritualistic movement, "Heap bad enemy out there- . . . . Rain god not listen to prayer unless I go see, send'um packing"; he turned, always in character, and made his exit. A fraction of a second went by before the Chief grasped the situation and uttered a belated "Ugh!" The drum beater took up the cue and beat out an unrehearsed tattoo to fit the stalking of an enemy—and to bide for time. The rest of the cast fell into the scheme, raised meaningful cries, went to look-see—and came back with Wandi, now snugly pinned up, and beshouted with trimphal whoops as a conqueror should be. The audience never knew all this had not been part of the plot. Nor did it know later why, when Wandi made his bow before the curtain, having to be pushed forward to do so, he was enthusiastically clapped and huzzaed by his co-workers with "Wandi! Wandi! Three cheers for Wandi!"

In similar ways from top to bottom every child had had his at least one outstanding moment of complete affirmation, when all sense of limitation vanished before the acclaim of his cronies for some action, quality, ability, or achievement special to himself and important to all. And this was good for future sustenance; for gradually "normal" adolescents began longingly to look over the walls of theater, warmed and prepared for the high adventure of real life. At this period awareness of self, one's fellows, and related facts were at their height. One day when we were straightening up, relaxed after a play of the night before I asked, "I wonder what you really got out of all that you have been doing!" I quote Irving because he had been of all the children the most inarticulate.

"Well—the Group Theater is not only for the correction of the boys—their behavior, that is, the creation of morals and giving them backbone and confidence; it is something to fall back on and not to be downhearted, and for the correction of the body and speech, and the experience not to say, 'I can't'; and to lose self-consciousness and nervousness through going on a stage before an audience. Also the stage work includes several trades which are of interest to the boys for now, and even for the future. Gee! I can't get over it—look at Harry—correcting his stuttering is the greatest marvel I yet have seen; and look at Bob—coming out and telling all the things he did for the last three years to get it off his conscience; and Milton—he was a poor foreigner lad who came over a few years ago and now he is reading and writing and he made his graduation after you wouldn't listen to his poetry unless he could write it, and he never held a tool in his hand in his life before and had the biggest thrill when he touched a saw the first time in the Group Theatre; and Sidney—what a great change there is in his features, his character in his face I mean, even though he still gets into trouble on the rest of the campus. And do you know—myself especially, I can't get over it! I'm not like I used to be. I conquered my biggest enemy, stubbornness, didn't I? Gee! I remember the first baton I cut, how I didn't follow the measure and it wouldn't go through the curtain hem and tore that good cloth—and now I feel I could hold down a job. And then the writers we turned out—it gets me, boys who couldn't write a letter trying to write plays, and some of them good ones, too. Gosh! If I go on I'll soon make up a book! And the best thing of all is how I feel—when I go home I'm sure I'm going to get along swell with my stepfather—I see it now, he wasn't so bad, it was I, because I was stubborn and interfering."

To which Milton added, "In plain words, the Group Theater taught us how to live in different ways—for now and for the future." At this point, were one to study the filled-in chart I described earlier one would see some half-dozen symbols rounding the firm circumference of the Theater circle and perhaps a similar number moving closer to join this chain. Outside of this orbit, like travelers following each other to reach an appointed goal, would be the symbols of Max, Irving, Ben, Paul, Milton, Sylvia, Harry, Hal; they would be moving toward and across the wider boundaries, sometimes almost together, in some cases lagging or getting ahead, going forward each in his individual stance, no two developments being exactly alike. And inside the family chain the symbols Sidney, Sim, and Joseph would be in halfway positions, leaving one uncertain about them—perhaps more time would tell how far they could go; but the symbol Oscar would be hovering too near the original center stopped by his obvious limitations from making the whole grade. At the same time in and around the center would be the jagged, sharp symbols of the newcomers to the environment. But for these the start has been made by the old-timers who will smooth the way with enthusiasms, traditions, and the big-brother and big-sister attitude. The environment will be mellower than for the original group, but only until the adjusted children leave for good and the preponderant number of children will be beginners having to build anew their own theater environment.

9

Subsidiary Techniques

Discussion as Medium for Self-Expression; Ego Construction; Social Education

Discussion, a potent factor in adjustment, merits special attention here; or my brief mention of its civilizing effect in the passage dealing with rehearsals may lead to its acceptance as a mere by-product of more important activity in which children seemed usually too busy to converse with constructive intention—to contribute something of their own minds and hearts, to arrive at decisions or to influence directly the growth processes of each other. I distinguish discussion or more or less formal conversation from talk, the normal spontaeous communication of people or children thrown together and bringing of course its own leveling benefits.

But when people talk, generally, thought merely skims the wavy surfaces of exposed and inconsistent emotional attitudes. Conversation lacks the disciplines of topic concentration intent on learning something new, understanding better, contributing and reevaluating opinion, and widening a point of view. The incapacity of most people to engage in discussion begins perhaps in the classroom where teachers ask questions, pupils answer briefly. Talk here is limited to what one has learned factually from the teacher or has had to study. This ritual leads to marks; it is not oriented to emotional and mental growth, for it offers no open ground for insight and rationale to be developed. It lacks discussion's freedom of expression—the exchange of ideas and opinions together with emotional attitudes, biases, and factual errors laid open to challenge; and its concomitant disciplines imposed simultaneously—the necessity to think through one's arguments, assuming responsibility for the expressed word, the self-control of courteous unemotional listening to opposition, the emotional courage to yield before proof or superior reasoning.

That most people are insecure under a sustained discussion, lacking the habit and therefore the capacity for this intellectual activity, may serve as an argument of skepticism or a why-bother whether unschooled children with problems enough attain a skill beyond the subjective need of average people. But in the Group Theater discussion was not a skill exercised for itself. It was deliberately initiated and encouraged as a vital medium for growth in the heterogeneous environment. We may call it a subsidiary technique used by the director for the mass overlapping of children in the mental area—not separable from the emotional area—for the rubbing of minds as of shoulders; for the encouragement of original and resourceful thinking; and mainly for the implanting of rationale as a habitual pattern of the psyche.

We must remember that insecure children are emotionally blocked from reasoning or being reasoned with; and as only the patient can clear up his conflicted life by accepting reasonably the facts and responsibilities of reality we must help him to learn how to reason—or to question himself, reevaluate his "opinions," widen his point of view, disentangle himself from emotionability. Did not the other techniques—and the entire creative process—tend to awaken security, awareness, and general reasonability discussion as a lone technique would be nonsense. But there is a power in words—as I have shown in the pages on rehearsals—which may not be minimized for the negative symbol which they serve to delinquent and neurotic children. To them verbal communication is a tool and a weapon of warped emotions; so that words, whether listened to or spoken, are never what they are but subjective distortions of intention and interpretation. The troubled child, lacking even the rudimentary discipline of the listen-and-answer experience of the classroom, does not hear with his mind but with emotional tentacles which always signal back to him negative messages. He "hears" in the simplest words, opposition, frustration, denial; he "converses" with rushing phrases, or if he is inarticulate with ejaculations, which are defensive-aggressive in mood. We say that he rationalizes, which means that he reacts with a twisted reasoning to serve his own purpose; he is impervious to the other side of anything; he lacks the discipline to listen slowly and to answer responsibly.

We know that young children pass through an imaginative period when they listen to adults with a subjective ear attuned to an inner reality alien from ours; they interpret our words and themselves speak with innocent disregard for factual truth or falsehood. Parents guide them gently out of this habit, so that normal adolescents know untruth or unreality or exaggeration when they tell or think these; and recognize their subtle differences in inception, purpose, and even in the inner sensations, from what they think or say purely from the imagination. The delinquent, too, has need for disregarding the true from the false. But he is not, because he does not feel so, innocent; nor is he imaginative in the joyous pursuit of a rich inner vision or experience. He automatically, and sometimes deliberately imagines what he hears and makes up what he says because he is inwardly burdened, out of self-defense. He needs guidance like the young child; training in calling things by their factual names, in differentiating fact from fancy, in assuming responsibility for the spoken and given word. For what we want of him is that one day he will engage in silent speech, in sober discussion with himself when listening and answering he will cogitate, come to conclusions, and make the decisions which the patient must make to be able to clear up his life.

The intelligent parent does not say to his offspring, "You are lying," but accepts the make-believe gravely in the mood of the child. He follows, however, with talk about surrounding things and teaches, This is a house, a block, a plan, a shape, etc. And he initiates doing something together paralleling his guidance with encouragement to the child to contribute to the plan, express his opinion, make his choice, etc. The doing of things and the parental permissiveness for self-expression with the rewarding sense of security and status growth are profoundly linked with the feeling quality of give-and-take spoken words. Much of security, reasonableness, and social attitude the child gets from communication—from the growing structure of language experience which permits him to hear, and respond in kind to, the constructive human message behind even the most mundane of words, giving words a significance beyond their practical use or definition. The tone of communication thus set early continues with peers and other people.

The values and tone of communication set for delinquent and neurotic children have not been ego constructive nor attuned to positive vibration. Thus, habitually they hear, not with their minds nor with easy hearts, but with the specialized reactivity of nervous systems frayed by the sounds or the impressed echoes of sounds carrying negative, punitive, complaining, and generally distorted messages. Discussion therefore—simple conversations at first, anchored to pertinent subjects with the adult and with each other—was initiated to educate them to a capacity for positive communication, or to reeducate them to this capacity since they had to unlearn a previous pattern. Paralleling its meaningfulness to the very young, discussion served to establish the attitudinal verbal link which makes complete the rest of experience—the doing of things with the parental blessing and guidance and with the rewarding sense of security and status acquisition. In the Group Theater children had a voice from the very beginning when obviously most were incapable of formulating plans, were not habituated to give a tolerant hearing to others, could not divorce self-interest from the substance of argument, and in many cases were so language poor in the academic sense as not to be able to follow the simplest topic.

But neither could they paint, build, act, write a good sentence, compute figures, fulfill commitments, or get along together. All growth waited upon the feeling quality, the constructive human message which had gradually to inundate freshly sensitized and relaxed nervous systems. In this we depart from the young-child analogy. Adolescents thrown together haphazardly with peers could not completely be granted the missed intermediary steps with a parent-adult. Intercommunication as a positive movement for the beginnings of confidence, status, and social attitude had to be engineered deliberately since they could only be gained, earned, and developed among and with the help of peers.

Because theater necessity demands thoughtful, sober, and realistic facing of what must be done, planned, and resolved, primary discussion originated from the problems at hand and from related living situations which needed settling. The immediate goal—for it would be easier and quicker for the director to hand down decisions and judgments—was the buildup of the ego, or its reorientation to a sense of worth and compatibility through "intellectual" participation. Expressing himself, the child would have the status feeling of being a contributant, a person with ideas or convictions, and in the heterogeneous environment one able to hold his own against better thinkers. Gradually real worth and real compatibility would grow by force of the disciplines inherent in discussion; and by the educative and reeducative power which lies in this kind of human exchange. For its ultimate goal discussion was to serve as a preparation for life beyond the adjustment period—through the acquisition of a body of ideas and of feeling reactions to concepts and facts which would motivate a propriatory curiosity about the world and sustain the travelers on difficult roads.

In the previous chapter I was too concerned with the all-over picture of overlapping to include a specific picture of the impacting power of discussion as a first aide in the leveling-individualizing or status-building by delimiting process. Let us see a very early moment in the Group, remembering the differentiated human material assembled—the differences in Intelligence Quotient, aspirations, personal equipment, and individual problems. Although there are many more participating, we'll follow a mere handful. A play has been chosen, has been read aloud, and now there are problems to face. In various tones and degrees of capacity the children are saying to each other the following:

We're going to produce a play. How? When? Who? With what? And who is to do what and when and why specifically? Gosh! A play between covers sounds easy! Who would have known all the things we have to worry about? We have to face it, boys, this is real and we have plenty of troubles. Gosh! Gee! and Heck! Nobody knows how to do anything (and each one to himself says—this is sure a show-one-upper . . . I don't know how . . . I don't know anything). Listen to this author; does he think we own the Roxy? He says here, "brilliant sunshine streaming in; and we don't even have a window on our stage!" The voices resound with enthusiasm, negation, doubt, reasoning, impulse, inspiration, rough talk, grunts, etc. It is the beginning of intercommunication in which each reveals something of his patterned tendency in facing problems, also a hint of proclivities, capacities, knowledge, or lack of it—and discovers children to themselves and to each other.

Among them are Timid, Arrogant, Know-all, and Know-nothing, the boy looked upon as a "sissy," the youth called "moron" etc. In the beginning Mr. Know-all and Mr. Arrogant do the loudest talking—but do not solve the problem. This is encouraging to Timid, who haltingly offers a suggestion. The contagion spreads to Know-nothing. He is hushed up but it doesn't matter. He has found his voice and will speak again—he had discovered he is not much more unknowing than the rest. In the to-do thought is mainly banter, scoffing, ego articulation; ideas are too vague or too self-consciously pretentious to pin down. There is little listening and much voicing. But the sense of purpose is there; also the discovery that no one has been too bright or too stupid. The "bright" boys have come down a peg; the less bright have climbed up a peg.

There are subsequent rounds, on the morrow and on succeeding days, and because a cooperative job must be chartered carefully children school themselves to give and follow thought. In the quieter air reason's labored breath is felt.

"But you said . . . it can't work, I'll prove it to you.

Don't you understand?

Just like the real weather it gets darker at the end.

Suppose we do it this way." And at the summit of surprise that this could be happening to him and to most of his fellows—Moron, or someone like him, exclaims: "Hm, do you smell what I smell—wood burning?!" Someone suggests a rereading of the script.

Suppose it is Harry a stutterer, a "sissy," a bookish boy who assumes the role of clarifier—reading a text, exploring meaning is "up his alley." He is carried away with enthusiasm. To prove certain requirements of the play he reads aloud, forgets to stutter, holds the others spellbound with the ring of his voice and the revelation of a witty and giving intelligence. The biased feeling about the "four-eyed bookworm" is shaken. The dislikers of those who are different respond to his quality, for he is giving something—he is exalting the unideational boys by sharing with them his "intellectual" picnic. But they give in turn the listening ear, the responsive eye, the wrapt expression—into the cockles of Harry's lonely heart they send a warming stream. The feeling for the play is now a prodding feeling like an endeared commitment which must be met. The need for that window is a lively need. Harry has touched it with human significance, has glamorized its purpose with the magic influence of his interpretive vision. There is an urgency—Come on, boys! Let's think hard!

Faces shadowed with unaccustomed in-thinking, the mad-genius look in eyes—it is natural that wild, deprecating, disinterested or ignorant youth stirred by the first vibrations of the human message should in the very dedication to reason swing out on flying trapezes to impractical heights. But this visionary soaring, this building of windows and manufacture of light not of this world is the returning vibration, the inspired human response! Irving is the first among them to come down to earth. He has a power the others lack—his factual mind and a small knowledge of carpentry. He says, "You're all too hifalutin . . . like babies." He is properly impatient; two weeks ago his tone would have started recriminations, three weeks ago a fight. Today they let him argue his point, follow the sketch he has made, listen to the minutiae of his plan. They talk figures, feet, inches; they talk dimensions, height, width, depth; they talk haltingly about color for slides and about directions and angles of light. Irving makes a natural error; he is too at home with his data, too glib in the choice of words for some to understand. But Know-nothing, who has slumbering in him an untouched artisan capacity, has been enlivened. Unfettered by Irving's little knowledge—and by Harry's fanciful trend—he has captured a synthesis of the plan, a simplification which step by step he gives over to the rest. He lacks vocabulary, depends painfully on gesture, perspires under the weight of this unaccustomed position among peers. The way Irving challenges him and the others want answers from him it could be believed he is Mr. Know-it-all!

In this intercommunication the mantle of status, like a king's beknighting sword, touches shoulders all the way down the line. In consequence the moment of its withdrawal is hard to bear like a new treasure lost. So Harry stutters more noticeably, and Irving feels put out. But this first wearing of the mantle is too elating, theatrical; more softly its pleasantness lingers in the psyche, starts up the drama of ego construction which in the heart of each needs to run its specialized course. This must be so to make possible a little later the boys' forgetfulness of this ego affront. Harry says to Irving, "You know, I just read a book about guilds and craftsmen proud of their trades; you impress me as that kind of a fellow." And Irving, to whom this is but faintly understandable except that it is complimentary, grins. "You're okay, yourself. Boy! you had me up in the clouds! You're a poet but you don't know it!" And then, having already remade his "blueprint" to Know-nothing's simplification, he thrust it out with a "Here!—this is what you were talking about—or is it?" The latter scratches his head, "I don't know from nothing. I listened to you and then I saw it all like real up there on the stage. I swear, this is the first time in my life . . . it was Harry's words, too, he got me all whoozy with thrills and my eyes popping."

The reader needs only to think of time as the piling up of such experiential moments, visualizing all the children as similarly alerted through discussion participation, to appreciate the psychic impulses and movements which are put into play leading to pattern changes or to the capacity for positive communication. In the above scene what was taking place? A window needed for the coming play was all but built and God's sunshine duplicated. Everyone had participated, gained a little status, lost out to the momentary status of others, had later recaptured his position through a give-and-take in human relations far outshining in effectiveness any original contribution of the mind alone. The planning for a window which had seemed a super-goal became a medium, a beginning for something much more meaningful to ego construction—"I'm okay"—and to social education—"The fellows are okay, we're going to get along." For long moments, in the rhythmic exercise of listening and speaking earnestly about an interest common to them, even the habitual need of the insecure for aggrandizement disappeared; the question of whose idea was to go into effect or who contributed an iota more than any other to the finished plan became less urgent since one was a participant in equality and therefore in effect its maker.

But this sense of worth and compatibility, the feeling of usefulness to and with others, is a positive inclusive feeling which cannot flourish without the accompanying sense that others are worthy and compatible with oneself. To this end discussion eased the psyche, making it receptive to outside impulses, not the least of which was the invasion into consciousness of the existence of good and sincere intention and traits in fellow beings. As for these in oneself, one's emotional accompaniment to arguing a point was challenged doubly—by the rebuttal from listeners impatient for concise, uncluttered thought, and by a new necessity in oneself to contribute responsibly, or as much as possible, reasonably in a mood of deference to the matter at hand. In this mood of dedication lay a marvelous reward, for as one receded from his self-preoccupation to rational effort one watched the plan building up. And one saw that it wasn't done by anyone alone, nor by any one language of fancy or of figures, or of smart talk or of specialized talk showing knowledge or aptitude; nor even by the sum of all of these. But by something which the total had brought into being—so ineffable a language quality that one began to listen with receptive senses and to respond with brand new aware sensations, directly without subterfuge and without emotional travail. Children became aware of the spiritual effluvia of their speaker-fellows, of the intention and purpose of their speech so that the tones of overenthusiasm, impatience, anxiety, zeal, haste, showing off, anger which is dispassionate and not personal, disagreement which is not attacking, etc., were recognized for their human meaning and responded to in kind without that inner stealthy drawing up of defensive forces habitual to them.

Of course a few discussions would not immediately wipe out Harry's deep-seated anxieties nor get absolute patience from peers for his enervating defect; nor keep Irving from stubborn insistence on making that window "by myself." But they could open long glutted sluices for the entrance and egress of beginning love streams whose exchange and change runnels would work gently against the backwash of sick and self-preoccupational flows. I would say that discussion, more or less formal, pertinent to the common interest and situation sets the human tone for the eventual natural communication or talk among children. Its directive—objectivity, reasoned interest instead of self-interest—has the virtue of engrossing children thoroughly in what they are doing together, hence in engrossing them with each other in reciprocal ways; both of which could not happen as completely and as quickly for emotional and mental leveling were they left to themselves to evolve and to discover the human message through merely casual speech. In fact, in the Group's early period, discussion was of life-giving importance, furnishing forcibly the only unifying tie in existence, the rational link, by which the mass functioned occasionally together *counter to actuality*—children joined in grouplets for evasionist reasons, speaking the specialized verbiage of esoteric activity, still attitudinally attuned to negative vibration.

Were a youth under irritable compulsion to turn upon Harry with, "Oh, shut up! I can't bear it!" this would be a living situation more important than any theater problem to talk about. Why can't he bear it? What makes people stutter? What has Harry to say about it? What can the others do about it? The hostile bundle of nerves who threw the taunt will relax a little toward the other if the discussion, immediately beneficial for taking both boys out of emotional embroilment into objectivity, gives him insight into a fellow's burden. Information about phenomena is always satisfying to adolescent curiosity about life, but impacts more on *these* children because curiosity has been too scattered and pointless. A firsthand human knowledge will give this boy, though also burdened and not able to become at once a kind person, a cathartic push—because of his involvement—a beginning reasonableness with which to question his own behavior whispering to him the wrong of blaming Harry for what he cannot help. In fact, he will feel responsible for Harry's welfare to the degree to which discussion of cause and effect makes him aware of his power of harm or helpfulness in the matter.

Actually, the by-products of feeling, attitudes, extended curiosity, and unexpected subject matter which spring from the practical discussions must be regarded as the real ground and substance for psychic nourishment. Time, so precious to a production group, must be spared for what often seems irrelevant to matters at hand. The choice must often be the window *or* the child, and eventually better windows will be made in quicker time if the child comes first. Much human learning and much of the universal aspect of living, as well as factual knowledge which the incurious, or unreading, or ignorant child would not otherwise attain, have their seeds in the incidental and often accidental throw-offs from the initial discussion about practical things. Time itself children must learn to respect and not to waste for helter-skelter motives; the showing off by the "brain trust" is not discussion, and these chaps must be told off as spendthrifts of time.

But if, for example, within the frame of reference—the discussing of pros and cons in the choice of a play—curiosity has been stirred because of what has been said by a committee of readers about the plays they have read, hence about the authors, and a boy gives the information that Russian writers are sad and another inquires why, nothing is more important at the moment than the answer to the questioner and the opportunity for the informant to elucidate his subject. Within ten minutes two children will have risen in stature for having begun something constructively engaging the entire group in a learning process. Within a half hour many others will have entered a discussion having the character of a bit of travelogue, a bit of national socialogy and history, and a little of an "Information Please" program. In the end a few writers' names will be added to the general store of knowledge and perhaps two children will actually seek in the library for Gorky or Dostoevski, or for Gogol, whom the director will have offered as proof that not all Russians express themselves sadly. The question of the Russian trait will certainly not have been answered, but Russians will have become flesh-and-blood people. To youths, whose own parents are strangers, the abstracted humans allotted a spot on the globe by all-knowing cartographers will have become intimates—palpable, vulnerable, aspiring, and alive members of an increasingly knowledgeable and *ownable* human world. That Milton comes from Russia and many of the participants' parents, too, will have given this talk an extra significance. It is speculation of course—but from the several introductions of "My father" or "My mother" it is possible that hostile sons will have had from their closeness with the Russians a first relenting insight into the ways of their parents.

There is a point to my italicizing the word "ownable." These children are being reeducated for mature living. Adult living is mainly the being *owned* by the world, by the family, the job, by the duties of citizenship, of social relations, even of friendship and of love. What makes it bearable, desirable, compensatory is the fact that one, in his time and in his turn, is also a bit of a possessor. That one not only gives of himself and yields to innumerable pressures but has owed to him some yielding and giving, too, just balances the scale in the daily striving of the average decent person. Then to the extent to which life is enriched—first, by the knowledge essential for relationships and for employment; second, by the broader knowledge which makes tangible and intimate the wider world—to that extent is the scale of existence tipped blessedly over with the compensatory sense of ownership in the world. To know is to invest the heart and mind in possessing meaningfully some part of the limitless and unattainable totality of the world of nature and of man. It is to be enlightened; or to be aware of, hence to possess, universal truths bearing on man's potentiality, revealing all men like one to have similar destiny, severally seeming cogs in the wheel of life but together a masterful race climbing always despite imprisoned and entangling roots. To know is to learn the nature of man's jailor, Life; and to discover, coexistent with bondage, the master's character of benign permissiveness allowing men to make something of themselves in human dignity. To be responsive to the *growth* force in the race, so to the force in oneself, is the highest enlightenment. Conversely, who respects this in himself feels himself in unity with all men. By this conscious act of the spirit, though one possessed nothing material of the world's substance, one becomes an investor or an owner in the world.

The delinquent child needs ownership in the world, all the more that he must *desire* to give himself over to being owned. The delinquent, like all people, only more so because he is just beginning to do what people normally do, loves that into which he puts personal investment. First he loves the things he does and the facts he learns because *he* has done and he has learned. Then he loves the deeds and the knowledge for themselves. Discussion is personal investment in the effort to understand, to know, to connect. In the end enlightenment is cherished as a beacon light. Mistress Theater with her laws and Master Life with his; children in the theater bound reciprocally, owned and owning, and general human living on its multitudinous levels; Russian sadness or another people's joy and universal human sadness and universal joy; things and feelings of immediacy and facts and attitudes for the future—the knowledge and insights through knowledge garnered in discussion total up a fluid comprehensive pattern of the whole of life. It is the disjointed universe being put together, and every fragment understandingly set into place is loved—first for the investment in its seeking and then for its own significance. Discussion reaffirms the human learnings from the work experience. Through the human communication with which it brings children closer it prompts the cooperative search for the larger comprehensions which will make life permanently meaningful. The tool, the bench, the project limit the child to the theater domain. The spoken word in the exchange of thought, contemplation, quests, brings in the limitless world.

I have a letter before me from Max which becomes more significant if we remember his rejection of me in his first year away from school after a talk about his political engrossment. It had been a wordless rejection, apparently after a debate with himself, for his visit with me had been entirely warm; merely a last envelope formally addressed lacking the usual ebullient "Her Royal Highness" before my name and within no personal note, only an item he had promised to return to me; afterwards no invitation sent to see him play in the YMHA theater and no regards extended through staff members or students whom he met. And then—the silence of two years was broken with a Christmas card from a war zone. On this he wrote: "I haven't forgotten. Thank you with all my heart."

The present letter is dated May 17, 1945, and bears the legend above this date, "India, damn it." But India, damn it! has as much gallantry in it as disgust, as much selflessness as personal preoccupation, and much more humor and consecration toward a cockeyed world than I have yet to find in letters I have received from maturer men, soldiers who had not been delinquents. The writer is disappointed in the news from the San Francisco Conference and sends me clippings, I suppose to be sure his old teacher keeps abreast of the times. But he sends to me this personal message, "Tell me—do you ever stop to think that perhaps your hard work in helping youth adjust itself to a screwy set of contradictions we call society is perhaps a thankless job? Personally I doubt it. But if you do, then remember that I, Max H——, former anti-social psycho-neurotic case XX thank you. You shall never know how much." He is unhappy about Poland and Palestine and disgusted over Argentina, but he adds, "I still have faith." Then Max closes his very rich letter with Kurt's farewell speech to his family in Lillian Hellman's play, *Watch on the Rhine*. And of course it is Max himself through Kurt Muller saying, "The world is out of shape. . . . All over the world . . . there are men who are going to make sure it will not have to be. . . . In every town and every village and every mud hut in the world, there is always a man who loves children and who will fight to make a good world for them."

What sustains Max who straight from the theater environment went into his postadjustment period of job hunting and job holding and then, barely secure in his footing, had to throw himself into a death struggle in a removed corner from his at last secure private world? He was prepared to sustain himself. He did not leave his theater experience without a buildup of a deep spiritual resevoir of attitudes and outlook whose essential nature was an identification of selfhood with universality or a responsiveness to the growth force of the race despite its turmoil, confusion, and despair—despite its "screwy set of contradictions."

Max had been prepared. Discussion—about peoples and individual people, about universal forces and small and big human hopes, about things insignificant and their vaster significance, about life and man and motive and result, about truth and falsehood and the relationship of all things—gave Max and his theater brothers the religion of humanity, self-arrived at and more solid to live by than the religion of God merely accepted on faith. The combination of play material with its generous by-product of discussion material brought to children incapable of wonderment or of childish simplicity a soul-filling appreciation for the living attempts of conscious man. "What is personality? Are God and nature the same? Are character and personality the same? Are children born with a bad or good personality?" These were the soundings of adolescent youth along with probings about the sad Russians, the whooping Indians, etc., and a thousand searchings into the future and concrete questions about this and that and everything. And their answers slowly emerging out of the mass questing for truth fed a wee flame—in each child according to his capacital being—into a self-perpetuating light to see by inwardly and outwardly for comfort, courage, rationality and faith.

Indeed, Max would be amazed how often his director questioned herself, not about the thanklessness of what she was doing but about the fairness of it to her charges; about the contrariness of her training "bad" children to be "good" adults for a world no less delinquent than themselves and holding out confusion to those attempting to live by the Golden Rule; about the contrast of the world she was sending them into to the one she was helping them build with its environment so basically sheltered, its orb so perfect a chain of understandable events, its atmosphere so warm with goodwill, its ground fertile with labors and rewards, its places resplendent with beauty, and its population exalted with dignity.

He would be amazed to know the connection between his clippings, symbols of his intelligent concern for the troubled world, and my seeing ahead to the disillusioning eventuality of his discovering its topsy-turviness—or rather his rediscovering it as unchanged, in effect unworthy of one who had himself changed. For I accepted with misgiving youth's mere snug adjustment to our precocious, rarified environment of theater. It could too easily become a retreat; despite the hectic life of its making it could be too much like a pleasant sleepful state in contrast to the encroaching, impersonally wakeful, testing world of unpredictable processes, the children had still to live in. Because despite every effort made to parallel the theater experience to real living, much of it was planned to serve as a recuperative lull or a vacation from evils—to let seep into the senses, as under a protective slumber, unexperienced moods of coziness and innocence to scatter the nightmare shadows of pangs and confusions habitually oppressing the psyche.

No one will deny the boon of a glimmer of light at bed time to an overwrought child, the peace it brings to the period of rest and the serene awakening on the morrow with the outlooking attitude that all is well. I have in mind sleep and wakefulness as symbolic terms for the balanced cycle by which normally growing children move forward to a sense of security despite the naturally insecure process of maturation. Night sleep under the aegis of hovering parents and day lull under protective guidance—both are a respite from trials and a needed soothing; the child rises in the morning, or in the day period after some trouble goes out to play, refreshed and reenchanted with the world. But the troubled child has no such cycle and sleeping and waking for him have always some shade or shape of darkness. In my responsibility I felt that the primary need of my charges was a substitute for this deprived cycle. Within circumstances one does what one can; under the realistic scaffold of the theater activities I tried most of all to erase the effects of time and tide on troubled personality, actually to help the children retrace their emotional steps toward what should have been their safeguard beginnings. I tried to return them to the state of ecstatic childhood, the aware time of self-discovery and the projection of the ego into the investigation of life; back even to an earlier period I tried to return them to the half-creature state of sensual well-being in the cradled certitude of ever present protectiveness and dependable love. This is why I was not satisfied with the mere fact of a child's adjusting to the environment. I had lit a necessary bedtime candle. For walking wakeful in the outer world there would have to be a torch which youth could keep aflame himself; for he would in the future have recourse to none but himself.

I cite Max especially because he was supposed to have been a waste of my effort by the advice of the clinic—I forget the specialized language which predicated the volatile explosiveness of his behavior as a hindrance to his social development. But I saw Max as a deprived infant of seventeen wearing his negative patterns like a blanket children drag over their heads to hide in a preferred blackness of their own making from the darkness they fear more around their beds. His overactivity and his emotionalism? Who knows what the shivering under the covers actually means? Emotional illness may conceal the life-force rebellion of leashed positive qualities seeking elbow room; for the delinquent is that unnatural being, a babe and a growing man, and if a youth like Max, one of vital personality, imaginativeness, and a swift intelligence. Until the babe is satisfied the thwarted ego must express itself in excess of what is normal. But because Max—and Hal and Harry—seemed so hopeless to the professional mental healers I felt all the more responsible for their future. I feared for their too-cozy happiness in our environment and their closeness to me because I had succeeded so well with the candle. They would have to step over the edge of our make-believe world and leave me a make-believe parent, for all their adjustment still dependent since none had accepted or troubled about them as I had.

What fortitude would sustain them in this abrupt separation from the fount of goodness which in the Group Theater gave joy to labors and balanced so pleasurably the being "duped" into the pattern of social harness? What fortification could prevent their looking back too self-destructively to our haven where one found unity in oneself and powers and confidence, and the noble happiness of fellowship with purpose and with goals sure to be applauded? What reserve force of a prompting inner voice could encourage the spirit to remind them in difficult days, "I am not alone in this. . . . Across the mountains, beyond the seas, next door to me or across the street, other boys, other girls, other people?"

It is believed that children who have had cherished infancies have the sustaining force to cope with life realistically and with a normal accruement of happiness to themselves. Normal adolescents have the suggestible memory of safety to encourage them in the dark moments when safety is not there; unhappy or frustrated, they do not totally disbelieve in its existence since it was an essence actually known to their senses. Similarly, whatever the pains of growing up or whatever the accidents of life, their capacity to love does not lessen; the cycle of being cherished and of cherishing in return has so well integrated the personality—with the loving as the expression and the proof of maturation in growing ascendancy. Because parents in the normal education of their children gradually wean them away from the shelter of all-safety and all-love to "stand on their own feet" and more and more to act or to give outward from themselves. But for giving—or loving—there awaits a limitless domain; and in this expansive expression of being, selfhood incorporates with universality. One loves mother, father, sister, God, heroes and heroines . . . the child around the corner . . . one's fellowmen . . . the marvels of man's hand and spirit. How much compassion for suffering, how much knowledge of the real state of the world a child gets out of the parental guidance to pray for the sick, give a penny for the poor, love little Red Riding Hood more than hate the wolf, identify with the striving figures of folk tales, history, and religion is inestimable.

Until one cannot breathe from an illness we take breathing and fresh air for granted. So we do not realize how much preparation for living there is in what seems simply the natural grace of affectionate beings—the reading of stories to children, the loving communication to curious youth of matters concerning nature and man, the transmission in the atmosphere of safety and love of an augmenting sum of things and ideas good, beautiful, and hopeful to cherish. With the stories, prayers, wonders, parents bring the world within the house, direct the way to union with it long before adolescents gird their loins to meet its unsafe blasts. This is the torch parents hand them, the perspective ingrained in memory of the essentials which count to illuminate shadows in bad times and to clear the mind for sifting and weighing daily trials.

This is what I tried to do for the children with discussion. Apparently by the grace of affection we talked about many things, but the purpose was the lighting of a similar beacon simultaneously weaning away the boys from the shelter of all-love and all-safety. When Max rejected me he was right for his moment's need, for he believed with a great hurt that I had rejected something greater than himself which I myself had helped him find. But so sure was I of his preparation for life that later I said, "He is a soldier now. In his loneliness he will have a perspective on things, his heart will renew its faith, he will write.'' And who but one prepared to judge nobly by the measure of essentials which count could have written Hal's letter on Americanism?

Elsewhere I have written that the director begins his job as the priest of Thespis making out the creative life to be the only good and true one. This was the fiction which induced the vacation period, which brought adjustment through the great pretense that love, justice, wisdom exist perpetually in the world—for in our environment they were phenomena so actually present as to be experiences of the senses like the feeling of safety in infants. And this despite the fact that chaos too existed as long as troubled peers made havoc in this perfect sphere. But the turmoil was an intrinsic part of the creativity, as watching the growth development in peers was part of it and the tie-up of both manifestations had personal meaningfulness in the self-conscious wonderment of unusual well-being. The closest connecting of this with the whole of real living lay in its recognized parallel to family life where youngsters are troublesome and all the children eventually grow up helpful to and fond of each other. For future sustenance the boys needed to know the real state of the impersonal world and to achieve within themselves as an expression of being, a compassionate identification with their fellowmen.

For this I had to finish my job as the honest spokesman for a nobler and more realistic kind of creativity which had little to do with the making of things with the hands and much with the conscious employment of the spirit in behalf of human affairs. I had to illuminate a truthful banner on which the ''cause'' theater was gradually erased, and indelibly inscribed instead was the concept: Life Is Human Striving. This was the parental guidance which had to go together with the parental love to teach children the facts and lead them together to arrive at the ideals which would give them a perpetual perspective for living gallantly, undisillusioned and warmly. And though it may sound exaggerated the endless discussions gave to Max and the others the opportunity, natural to untroubled children, to prepare themselves for come what may. These are the conclusions they were able to come to: Yes, man is a suffering creature, but behold! his indomitable spirit which is greater than his fumbling. Wisdom, love, justice are not present always, for man is imperfect, and in this is man great that he strives for these perfections. Man is ourselves. We built our projects and the process was not an easy one, for we built out of the chaos we brought into our little world; but we grew, found peace, had joy. For all men the process of living is unsafe, beset with troubles; but there is growth ahead and a measure of peace and joy. In the theater we learned trials were for men to grow strong by, to ameliorate if possible but if not to take in our stride. So in life we must be aware of the hard facts of our world, bow but not yield before difficulties, cherish despite the odds the essentials which give life enchantment, and dare to shape it by these measures in sympathy and union with other men.

Playwriting as Medium for Self-Expression, Catharsis; Revealing Subjective Material—Simple Dramaturgic Device for Children—"Noah Comes Again"–"The Mannequin's Revolt"

I had not planned playwriting as part of the theater activity. It came from the desire of the children in the very beginning to "write our own plays." Rather, two or three of the earliest Group handed me pages of dialogue, the writing inspired by our reading of plays and perhaps even more by the improvisations of scenes for which the players spoke spontaneous lines in the presenting of a mood, an idea, or a situation for the main purpose of getting to the core of the human story in dramatic material too literary for uneducated or unideational children to catch on to without simplification; or to prepare the ground for the interpretation of character and once in a while to clear up a situational problem in the Group reenacted for the children to see it objectively. This is not to say that children unanimously voiced the personal desire to write, but they enthusiastically supported the few in the idea of having home-created plays. A large number, when I agreed, looked suddenly wistful, fearful, withdrawn, conscious of inadequacy. I added on a special period for playwriting; gave the incentive that we would produce the good ones; convinced them that poor spelling and handwritings would not deter the working out of ideas and would in fact improve with exercise; that good ideas need not be one's own if they had an original twist, the greatest authors having done the same.

I was on the right track. Writing a play was better than scribbling notes, scratching initials on handy surfaces; it was an absorbing kind of self-expression, the weaving of a story, old as man and young as youth, making one feel mature in the attempt at intellectual activity and powerful as creators in having to make people alive

GALA EVENING
End of Summer Recreation Program
Thursday, August 26, P.M.

THE HAWTHORNE GROUP THEATER
Presents
A PUPPET SHOW—"TREASURE ISLAND"

Part One

Scene 1	A Tavern
Scene 2	On Board Ship
Scene 3	On The Island

For the Hawthorne Group Theater

Construction of Puppet Stage . . . . .S.
A.
Decoration of Stage Front . . . . .B.
Lights . . . . .A.
Props . . . . .B.
A.
H.
Construction and Costuming . . . . .A.
of Puppets . . . . .J.
H.
R.
L.
Scenic Design . . . . .N.
Dialogue . . . . .N.
Puppeteers . . . . .N, H, B, D

Part Two
Quartet Voice Band Cottage 23 boys

Part Three
Award of Prizes to winners in inter-cottage Skit Contest.
Dr. Papurt will make the awards
Finis

Community Sing
Director of Group Theater *Miss Celia Avramo*

more than in told stories. It was objective and subjective. One could think about characters and make them say things natural to them; but one could pick the characters for loving or hating them and could put into their mouths what one kept quiet about or didn't know how to say for oneself, or didn't dare or hadn't the opportunity.

The permissiveness about using known stories freed children immediately to make efforts and divided them into revealing categories. Most of them, the nonreaders, the less imaginative, and the less individualistic engrossed themselves in stories remote from personal experience. One could tell how much natural infancy a child had enjoyed by the choice of material, fairy stories or an imitation of a cops-and-robbers theme from the moving pictures; and one could tell from the turn of the material how emotionally infantile or mature a child was, how aware of himself and of his surrounding world. The readers, the more imaginative children, the individualists, varied in attempts at dramatizing remembered literature, a phase of actual experience or deeply impressed vicarious experience from the newspapers, the movies, from hearsay. All boys wrote first plays in which no boy or girl of their own age range were characters, except a handful who were obviously obsessed with their material as fantasy or actual experience and the writing served as a confused means of living something over again and cleansing oneself of a burden. In his first play Paul pimped.

Among the girls, much more sophisticated than the boys, most attempts were obvious imitations of screen plays, and these did have heroines their own age; it was clear that the basic theme was subjective and wish thinking. Generally the girl met her Prince Charming; the variation showed poverty in the home and the girl making good as some kind of public performer through the notice of a male—a working girl was never evoked as heroine, nor a daughter who helped her family out of its troubles. But in comparison with the boys there was more obsessive material. About a third of the girls had sex-delinquent heroines rising out of their guilty past, and from the oh's of the other girls—"Ts! It isn't nice to write such things . . . How could you! . . . Our teacher is a lady, you forgot!"—it was clear that the protestors were merely less obsessed or shrewder about guarding their problems. Whatever the children wrote revealed more in one page than numerous interviews might and was tremendously helpful in my knowing what to expect from them and what to do for them. First attempts especially gave personality clues often useful to the caseworker and psychiatrist and showed me how far I might go to motivate second efforts, or if not, at least to discussion leading to aware and cathartic movements in the psyche.

I should like to report that *all* the children engaged in the playwriting and especially that of those who did all made second and third efforts. But for one person I was doing too much to have time and energy to follow through when children dropped out of the active writing. However, merely being present in the writing atmosphere was beneficial to the mass. Through the concomitant questions and discussions which arose all were writing the plays, contributing to and gaining from the heterogeneous store of knowledge, experience, imagination, and insight. How do witches talk, feel, or act? And how—Satan, a king, a queen, a hobo, a parent, a butler, the winds, dwarfs, a man released from prison, a lumberman, the owner of an estate, Ben Gun in *Treasure Island;* God, Gabriel, Sherlock Holmes, Black Joe, a mannequin, a lawyer, and yes, even a psychiatrist? This is a partial list of only main characters arising from the writings of plays. One can see how far afield from the plays themselves these subjects could take a group of interested children, in cultural learning, in psychic airing, and in emotional education.

It was natural that the few rather than the many in the Group, as in life, should find a special outlet in the playwriting—first, because there was that in them which responds more vitally to stimuli so that self-expression is a must; and second, because the response to the dramatic, the ideational, or the poetic elements of existence has inherent in it a sensitivity to and a love for sound, color, form, mood, all of which are expressible through words. Thus a child who completed a first good play was more likely, soaring on the wings of his discovered capacity, to write a second and perhaps a third play. Nathan wrote two marionette plays, *Treasure Island* and *Noah Comes Again;* both of which we produced; his third was a stage play, down to earth, realistic, and at last about children his age which was barely completed when he left the school. Milton wrote innumerable skits—rather he evoked them orally until he learned how to write, by feeding lines and his basic idea to boys who worked them out on a rehearsal floor through error and repetition until they could be presented as polished dramatic material; midway between this and learning to write he began to express himself in poems. After many trials another boy did the major writing of a fairy tale in verse, "The Little Red Dwarfs," and some six nonwriting children added their bits with a rhyme here and there, an idea or a character exactly as collaborators would on a job with a major author. We produced this play and Abe had just begun another when he was paroled home. Max wrote *The Bargain* or *Three Men and a Chicken Dinner;* it was produced, and he, too, left shortly. Ben had his second practically ready before he left. Unfinished attempts were countless.

Consciously, but for the most part subconsciously, all the writing was a commentary on life, a revelation of attitudes, and with each succeeding effort showed greater awareness of the world or of one's own problems. No matter what the theme, good and evil were the actual protagonists, and it seemed that children were weighing matters and coming to some livable philosophy. Nathan's *Treasure Island;* chosen for the marionette project initiated for Sim's sake was infantile compared to this author's second play, a sincere adventure with the Lord pained over the world's misuse of the second chance He had given it. A profound sympathy stirs in Nathan; for though he judges through the Lord he begs from him through Gabriel to give erring humans another chance! Nathan's third play was called *Shanty Town;* and here he faces poverty, his own home world; there are bad people in the play, but the father of the family is kind, sacrificial, good! Milton's skits had social significance, war, politics; but his poems became more and more personal, tender in mood and outward reaching with disinterested love. *The Little Red Dwarfs* had the hostile and good winds, especially the tender South Wind that risked the wrath of the cruel North in order to protect the little people. Max's play was a summation of his thinking about his delinquency; he was determined to teach a lesson that crime does not pay. Six men had vowed to meet in a barroom on a certain date regardless of their lives and destinies throughout the year. Only one keeps the appointment. The script reaches a tragic climax when through word or telegram the one learns the fate—prison and violent death—of the others who had chosen against society. The reader knows Ben's conclusion of his first play, which I will give more space to later. His second play, *Dark Light*, in which he faces his world realistically, will also be spoken of later in the book.

But . . . children write plays! Unschooled, truant children master the so difficult problems of dramaturgy! The children had the example of the plays they were reading and rehearsing. No formal training was attempted: they were urged to go ahead. Make people talk about what they felt and thought. Rules would have had a sterilizing effect on children bursting with creative impulse, inspired to this urgency to put something of themselves down on paper. But the

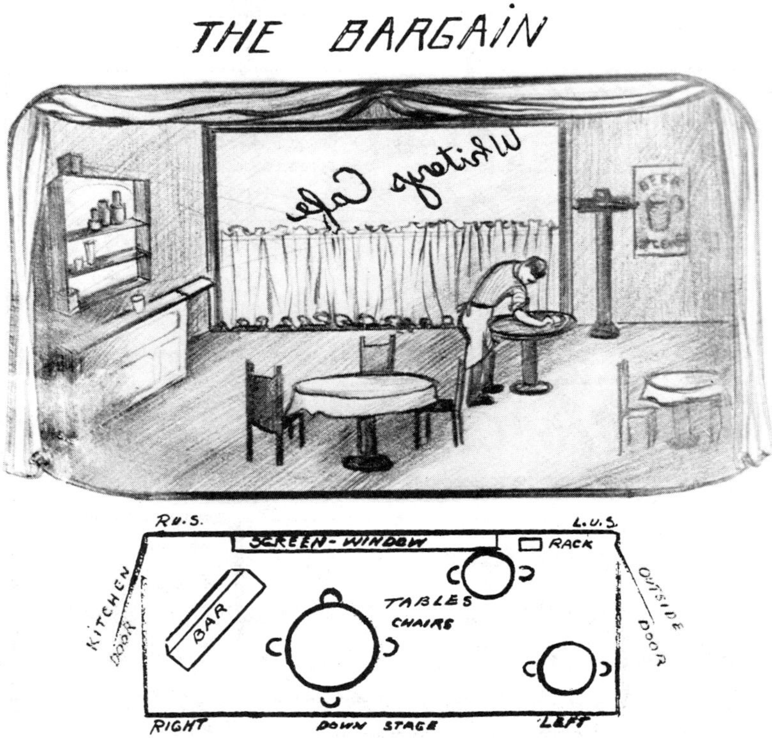

Set according to author's description. Max's play The Bargain

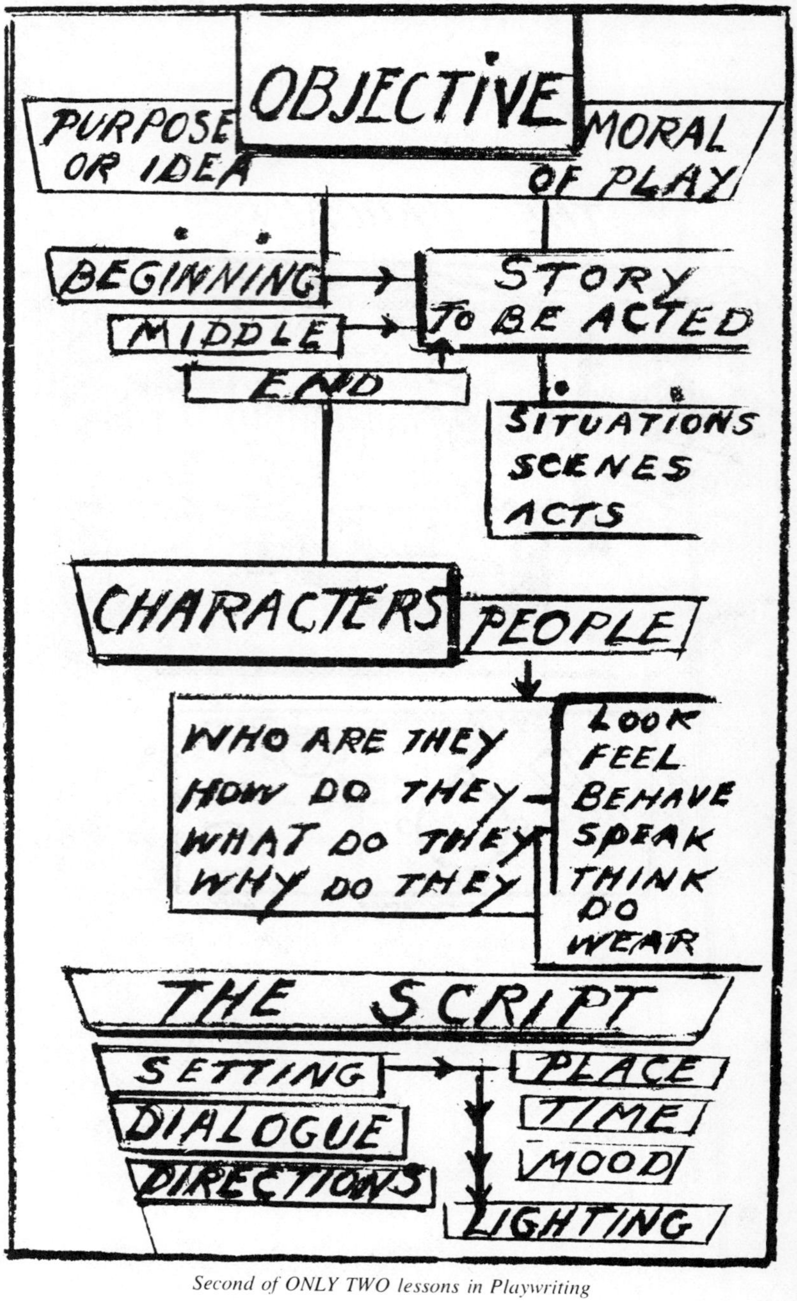

Second of ONLY TWO lessons in Playwriting

Puppet head for "Treasure Island."

more knowing ones were the least secure; they sensed the mystery of structure, form, movement, method, and wanted to be taught. I told them that the writing would be like the acting or building, they would learn with doing, there was no need to burden themselves with professional words or rules. They laughed when I listed them—dramaturgy denouement, resolution, etc.

But they needed something to serve as a guide or an inspiring directive to keep them vitalized and working. It seemed to me that playwriting could be understandingly simple if the young aspirant could *see* the structure of a play and could *sense* its dynamics. I thought of a chart which should graphically portray both the concrete and abstract essences of dramatic composition, a picture itself dramatic in nature with the power to impact difficult concepts upon the viewer via his imagination. And a word was needed, a fundamental symbol to cover wide ground—for direction into successful efforts; for purposiveness of character, story, and the play's movement; for a verbal tool useful in critical discussion; for a slogan because a slogan puts children on their mettle in the same way that shining armor and a sword might.

The result may be said to be the only "lesson" in playwriting the children ever received; all subsequent learning derived from a blackboard sketch which remained untouched for years. As the plate on page 234 shows, there were three steps leading to a door and over the door in bold letters was the inscription "OBJECTIVE." The children were asked to define the meaning and they quite understood the saga of the triumph of man over his destiny and the triumph of action over inactivity—in man's living as well as in the law governing dramaturgy. One look at the prostrate figure at the base with limbs tied and the children understood the basic principle of "the tying of the knot."

But these troubled children turning playwrights understood more—the skeleton figure was every child with his troubles and problems; the people in a play were like themselves, at the bottom somewhere, hemmed in by circumstances either of their own making or that of other people. From the moment they gleaned this there was identification with the necessary movement of characters in a play. They recognized that obstacles must abound and be overcome, for deliberately the first riser is steep and the tread wide; but the skeleton figure makes the grade and freed of external bonds looks forward and upward even though the arms held bodyward tell of awakening or awareness or activity which is still timid and incomplete. Because the second step in anything is easier to make and because the action in a play moves more swiftly with ensuing scenes the second riser is shorter and the second tread shallower. Now the figure moves with speed and purpose; but from the position of the head backward-looking children got the concept of complication-threatening progress. They understood quite clearly that midway in the plot the movement of progress is halted or misdirected for a poignant struggle which decides whether or not the character is to march forward finally triumphant. And discussion brought out the fact that much of life's complication is internal, in the makeup of the protaganist.

Thus the spiritual life—the driving feelings, thoughts, and moods of people—was established as the searching basis for creating true, interesting, and alive characters. Finally in contrast to this figure whose spirit and body express conflict, the last one expresses integrity, its inner and outer mien a complete totality; the body is the instrument of inner certitude, its head direct and purposeful, its arm stretched confidently forth toward success, the turning the knob of that longed for door. So children understood about internal and external action, about the necessity of a goal toward which to weave the elements of the play, about the serene unity in character when all is well at last.

In the study of this visual epic of a symbolic figure they grasped, beyond the lesson in playwriting the epitome of Man's living cycle—his obstacles, conflicts, and near-successes relative to arriving at some goal. This made them aware of themselves, for the parallel was quite apparent that their current status was similarly the knot which needed untying. Thus the playwriting began with a twofold joy: the pleasure of creating and the hope of being re-created. As the work proceeded this parallel showed up dramatically, for each child nervously nibbling his pencil went through his own turmoils and conflicts; the desire to give up, laziness, moodiness, disgust over failure vied in him against purpose, pleasure, a goal to reach. Merely finishing a play was the working out of an inner drama; and there was the blackboard chart prompting him, "What is your objective? Go on! Get to your goal! Finish your play!!!"

The other figures I jotted down one day when we spoke about people having different problems. The children identified them as follows: the first was a "breast-beater" who makes trouble for himself, blames the world for his ills—he would have to untie his knot by conquering himself; the second was the type who "hangs his head," waits for things to happen, lacks courage, and depends on others to do for him—he would have to learn how to face life on his own feet; the third was a "dope" who pulls and kicks vainly because he doesn't use his "noodle"—and it would be hard to solve his problem! The implications of this discussion relative to themselves are self-evident. But they got the point that one character's problems distinguishes him from other characters and that the knotted figure at the base of the steps had to be recognizable as a person who thought, felt, did, in a way natural to his own problem and that we would know him by the way he spoke and did things to other characters.

We called the two clothed figures the "Dress-up" as representing the complete "Person" whose appearance told something about him like habits, background, taste, station; whose face expressed feelings either substantiating or contradicting his words and actions; and whose gestures and movements revealed attitudes even when words were not spoken. We made these figures come to life by pantomimic improvisations and interpretations. The children now realized that they must *see* their characters clearly in imagination—how they look, sit, walk, feel—in order to create them through dialogue and write the directions which authors give for the actors. We took a phrase like "I am going home" and enacted it with varying emotional nuances as different people might say it under differing circumstances. Spoken happily, sadly, enthusiastically, rejectedly, casually, gently, angrily, spitefully—the writers saw that words are tools of the inner rhythms in people.

When the pages began to come, it was an amazing experience to hear children say to each other with intellectual challenge, "What is your objective?" and to see the earnestness with which the challenges floundered through to the core of their aims. What criticism I gave was in the form of questions which vitalized the blackboard sketch; for little by little my sparsely used technical vocabulary enriched its significance. Through repetition these words soon became the informal word tools of a dramaturgic formula by which the authors guaged their work. A play started with an *idea*; a play had a *beginning;* a *middle;* and an *end*. One jotted down a simple *plot* to go by in order to arrive at a *climax;* etc.

But the boss-word was "Objective," the open sesame to clear thinking and to creative invention. In *Treasure Island* Nathan brooded with the pencil in mouth—"I can't make Ben Gun *do* anything. He's queer and maybe he could make us laugh, but I can't make him *real*."

Question: Do you need him on the island? What is your objective in making the island scene?

Nathan: That's where the Hispanolo is headed. They're following a map. There's gold on the island. In the story Ben Gun is there.

Question: Does he have any connection with the gold?

Nathan: Sure. He was there when Billy Bones came back and hid the loot.

Question: But do you need him? Why can't they find the gold themselves?

Nathan: It would take them days, and you can't show that in one scene because then I'll need another for the battle. Ben Gun has to make it easy for them to find the gold. And he's important, too, to prove it is Billy Bones' loot. The audience wants to know, too.

Another Boy: But a man who lived alone so long would be suspicious of strangers. He wouldn't just pop out and say, "I have the gold."

Nathan: Gee, that's right! He'd hide first and maybe spy a little.

Same Boy: And make sure Jimmy was the right guy to talk to so he wouldn't be killed.

Nathan: I know . . . he'd see how the pirates are there after Jimmy and know he's the friendly one to take him back to England (with excitement). And that's another reason for Ben Gun on the island—to keep Jimmy from being killed—

Question: You have a number of reasons now. How are you going to—

Nathan: Boy! Oh, boy! Now I've got him doing things and something for him to talk about. But I still don't know how to make him queer.

Question: Who is he? What does he look like? How does he feel about things?

Nathan: An old-time pirate. Wild-looking. Gee! After ten years his hair must be long, and maybe he has a beard. And he must be lonely for people . . . and maybe for things.

Question: Like what?

Nathan: The things you get in a store. Tobacco maybe, and jelly (catching the reaction of his peers)—well, not jelly, that's sissy for a pirate. But beer—no, ale—that's what they drank in England! And cheese! Maybe hard cheese to get his teeth into after all these years.

Question: Go on. What about his being queer—how?

Nathan: Maybe he forgot how to use his voice. It ought to sound funny, cracked maybe, hard to come out, and excited. (Tries to speak like Ben Gun.) Sure, like this—making funny sounds and finding words! (Gets the applause of the others.) I have him now! Look! He could bend over, hunched like, as if he wasn't a man anymore, swing his arms, too.

Another Boy: That's not queer enough. Like this. . . .

Nathan: Gee! I've got my objective now—all about Ben Gun! He's gonna be good! Sad and funny . . . he'll be a wow of a puppet . . . Gee!

In this way the writers learned that characters must have a history—a past, present, and future. The questioning casually gave them a workable slogan which served as mentor: who, what, why, when, how? Without a formal lesson, without imposition of rules the mysteries of dramaturgy were cleared up, the children became initiates to an absorbing and satisfying activity. They took criticism with the attitude of craftsmen—weren't we, myself and they using, the same gauge arrived at together in discussion? It was fun of a lofty kind. the questioning based on the pictorial diagram and the professional-sounding but so understandable verbiage was like a game in which reasoned answering gave one not only a sense of mature responsibility but brought unusual returns in a job well wrought. In terms of personal adjustment this joy in the pursuit of exact answers to problems, this awareness of good creative results from the practice could not remain apart from the total personality already conscious of the cathartic parallel of all living beings whether inside or outside of the pages of a play. What mattered the scribbled sheets of paper, the crushed ones thrown into the basket, the nervous hours of hugging to a seat—there was the evidence of accomplishment, of slowly reaching one step and then another above the starting point of ignorance, incapacity, and the no-account delinquent state.

To make people tick and to remain unaware of one's own ticking is not possible. So the playwriting helped with the playreading and rehearsing began. The child's mind seeking answers to work problems made almost physically seeable and touchable by directive questions seemed like an interior abounding with candles where the lighting of one ignited the next and the next until a brilliant inner illumination took place. In its center looming clearer with time stood dramaturgy, a benign and effulgent abstraction of Law; and this essence bowed smilingly, "See . . .? How easy . . .?" But this was the seeking mind and the light heart of a living troubled child bound in strings like Ben Gun or any other character the mind had been creating; in translation the dramatic appearance became Life, a permissive abstraction who said, "See . . .? How easy . . . if you desire to re-create *yourself . . . ?*"

Who has ever tried writing a play, knowing all the rules, fights his major battle in the struggle to create good dialogue. This calls for a profound knowledge of the world and of the inner heart of human beings; for the capacity both to observe and to identify with many different people, for the power to verbilize emotion and to synthesize thought. I had a problem. I had promised that every good play would be produced, and there had to be "good" plays since an important aspect of therapy is the proof of successfulness, if not in oneself concretely then in hope through the achievement of peers. And a play is above all a creative form dependent entirely upon dialogue! This was the secret of the children's wanting to write their own plays—giving people speech is giving them the breath of life, it is being a creator of what has never existed before. The simplest thing I could do about it was to say, "Put it into your own words, but try to remember all the people you know; if they're a little like your character, how would they speak?"

But there was also the heterogeneous environment to help out, some twenty children of an age range of fourteen to almost eighteen who had brought into the Group their beginnings, backgrounds, knowledge, sophistication, experience. That constituted a vast apperceptive mass to call on for help to budding playwrights, to contribute to the *awareness of life* essential to the writing of dialogue for actable plays. Thus in *Noah Comes Again* Nathan had the Lord say "ain't," and the emotional quality of His speech was more like a boy leader dissatisfied with his gang. The boys rose up in arms. "God wouldn't say 'ain't'! *He'd* know better!" and "*He'd* not sound so bossy, but *strict*." One boy said with humorous disgust, "How can Nat know about God; he's a sinner! Then why do you write about things you don't know?" Another said, "The Lord wouldn't make long sentences; He'd be too tired after thousands of years"; and another added, "Anyhow, he'd be more dignified." But critical excitement was at its peak over Gabriel's line, "Go-wan, Lord! You don't know what you're talking about." Nathan's fellows argued with Talmudic finesse the affronting distinction between "You don't know what you're talking about" and "Do you know what you're saying?"; the protest was, "Gabriel is too fresh speaking to God the way we bums talk to each other." Nathan, individualist that he was and clear about his vision, refined the line in his finished script to read, "What's the matter, Lord? You don't know what you're agreeing to do." That the children were aware of their world and identified with it by this time was shown in their positive acceptance of God's disapproval of man because "It's true that things should be better . . . people are dopes . . . etc.," and the enthusiastic approval of Gabriel's defense of man.

So the children helped each other by thrashing out the pros and cons of the early drafts of dialogue. They were the first reactive, critical, and applauding audience. They helped also to test out the dialogue by enacting it. When it seemed unnatural, clumsy, or wanting they ad-libbed, the author participating but watching and weighing. And always there was the return to the question-answer method.

Question: Never mind the Lord. How would you talk if you were a king?

Nathan: High tone.

Question: Suppose our president were called king—how would he talk?

Nathan: Same as now. Good English. Grammar. And nice words. No slang.

Question: Don't you know nice words?

Nathan: I mean dictionary words . . . long ones.

Question: Do I speak that way? I'm your leader.

Nathan: (Alert) No. Simple ones—we understand you. But refined, words that mean a lot. I know! Okay, I know how the Lord has to speak.

I would say that the playwriting was a civilizing experience through which self-expression attained to social expression. Crude, jumpy, unlettered, and illiterate children stuck it out or encouraged others to do so, reasoned, sought dictionaries and other sources for help; but above all developed the mature faculty of taking criticism—from differentiated peers, of giving criticism—without ego-aggrandizement, of being self-critical—by sound standards and a tremendously enlarged apperceptive mass. The human language of good intention, identification, and disinterested giving was exchanged and appreciated and did its part to influence the basic human—and hopeful—mood of the play material.

Following is a page and a half of the beginning of Nathan's play. Despite its somber realistic substance the cadence of the dialogue rings an exuberant tone, the approach to trouble is mellow; the conception of the Lord pained rather than hostile, punishing rather than vindictive, is far from the prototype of the world's Master or the archadult which one might expect from a youth rejecting authority (but Nathan had been in the Group more than a year). And in Gabriel's simple plea there is so much epic pity! Nathan's objective is no longer hate the world but pity fellow sufferers.

NOAH COMES AGAIN

(The Lord and Gabriel are looking down the clouds upon Manhattan.)

Gabriel: See Lord! The boats are gliding in the water. Isn't it beautiful?

Lord: *(As in a trance)* Mmmmm. . . .Yes. . . .

Gabriel: What's the matter, Lord? You don't know what you're agreeing to. . . .

Lord: *(Coming out of the trance)* What? What did you say? I was just looking toward the inhabited part of the island—and what I have seen makes me turn away in disgust! Why, it's as if animals lived there once more!

Gabriel: I can't see. Show me where you've been looking. Maybe we can do something about it.

Lord: *(Pointing)* Over there. See? There's a man beating his wife—and for a little thing, too. *(Sound of crying)*

Gabriel: Why would a man beat his wife?

Lord: *(Dryly)* She didn't make his coffee strong enough.

Gabriel: *(Excited at something he sees; puts his hand on the Lord's arm)* Look over there, Lord . . . a suicide!

Lord: There are many these days . . . *(Sighs)*

Gabriel: This woman took her life because her daughter ran away from home.

Lord: Now the girl will have no mother to go to in her troubles . . . .It is sad . . . people do not know how to live. . . .*(Looks toward another part of the city—with disgust)* See over there! Here is a man promising riches to foolish people—and they believe him and lose their heads! And the worst of it is that he has no home to live in himself! Oh! If he could use his powers for good instead of bad he would be better off himself. . . .

Gabriel: Aha! . . .Just a swindler! What can you do, Lord? Look at Europe—wars all around you—you can't rest your eyes on a place that isn't havoc-stricken by war. You give them life, Lord—

Lord: *(Interrupting)* And millions of lives are snuffed out. Look down there—the poverty—the greed—the selfishness . . . .Fathers cannot support their families . . . poor waifs lead lives of crime to steal to get the bread they need to live on . . . THIS WORLD ISN'T FIT TO KEEP ON REVOLVING!!

Gabriel: What are you going to do? What CAN you do?

Lord: *(Thinking)* I'd like to start all over again. . . .Maybe a new world will fare better than this one. . . .But how? How shall I make this change?

Gabriel: *(Anxiously)* Don't do it, Lord! Give them a chance. They need another thousand years. . . .

I am sure the reader, like all fellow children, will want to know how the story ends. The flood comes again despite Gabriel; this time in man's history a crazy Noah escapes from an asylum on hearing the Lord's voice. It was something to see the crazy Noah-puppet rushing about beneath the clouds shrilly calling, "I'm coming, Lord! I'm coming! Coming!" The play does not show the new world; there is too much trouble on the ark which is a crazy upside down thing with the ceiling where the floor should be etc. But the play ends with a wiser Lord, this time in Heaven—is Nathan telling of the lesson he learned or is he giving the adult world a hint to be patient with the troubled child? Gabriel has turned tail, now he is disgusted with human events.

Lord: *(Very thoughtful listening to the voices of men. We hear Noah's drowning words*—"Hallelujah . . . Do you hear me, Lord? . . . I tried my best . . . I tried my best . . .") He tried his best. People aren't really bad . . . and for that I will let them survive.

God, Gabriel, and Some Human Puppets. *Creatures made for Nathan's puppet play,* Noah Comes Again. *In background is the asylum from which Noah rushed to save the world. Nathan (the author as spokesman for The Lord) chose an insane person to do what the sane had not done well enough. . .!*

Gabriel: Your ways are strange, Lord. I've lost faith myself. Look how Noah fared. My, but he was crazy!

Lord: The same as old Noah. Both meant well. . . . Gabriel! Wouldn't you say that was a good sign in man?

Gabriel: Mmmmm. . . . Lord! You are wonderful to behold! . . . I am very disappointed. But you—everyone on that ark had something wrong with him, yet *you* are satisfied.

Lord: *(Gently.)* What was wrong?

(There are several speeches about what was wrong with the people but the Lord sums up his new knowledge.)

Lord: But they stood for something, Gabriel, my boy. . . . One was too careful listening, and not so careful remembering. . . . One couldn't reach places because he was always mindful of his peg-leg. . . . And the other was too ready to laugh. And "Sherlock Holmes" even to the checks and pipe—he couldn't be what he might have been, so he picked himself a disguise.

Gabriel: You go so deep, Lord! Are you trying to make me feel good?

Lord: You have nothing to feel bad about. Because I am satisfied, infinitely satisfied. None were really bad. . . . None were really lazy. They all *wanted* to see straight and walk straight . . . *(Sighs)* But they didn't know how! *(With an emphatic gesture) That* is what man must learn—*(Pounding his fists)*—How, how, HOW. . . ?

(Three pages later the Lord makes his curtain speech and his decision.)

Lord: I shall go down to earth. I shall go among the people—high and low. I shall whisper in the minds of leaders. I shall show them the way. . . . *(His head is bowed over His hand which rests on His knee. Music sounds sweetly, also an occasional roll of thunder like a salute. Gabriel returns with a bundle of clothes and speechless offers it to the Lord. The Lord rises slowly to take them. Music is sweetest and loudest as*

THE CURTAIN FALLS)

THE HAWTHORNE GROUP THEATRE
PRESENTS
A PUPPET PLAY—"NOAH COMES AGAIN"

June 10th   4 o'clock

AUTHOR—One of our boys - Nathan
CHAIRMAN—One of our girls - Betty

The Puppet Cast

The Lord . . . . *Max*
Gabriel . . . . *Nathan*
Noah . . . . *Paul*
Sherlock Holmes Burns . . . . *George*
Peg-Leg . . . . *David*
Flap-Ear . . . . *Albert*

Hawk-Eye .... *Larry*
Scar-Face .... *Leo*
Laughing-Boy .... *Philip*
VOICE .... *Alfred*

Scenes

Scene 1 HEAVEN *Overlooking New York City*
Time: Sunset
Scene 2 AT THE DOCK *Noah's Ark*
Time: Evening
Scene 3 INSIDE NOAH'S CABIN
Time: Toward Dawn
Scene 4 HEAVEN *Another View*
Time: Immediately after

Scenes will be shifted and the stage set in view of the audience so that back-stage mysteries will be revealed to all.

Scenic Crew .... *Alfred; Leo; Sol Hy*
Lighting Effects .... *Harry*

FOR THE HAWTHORNE GROUP THEATRE

Construction of New Puppet Stage .... *David George; Larry; Sam Albert; Paul; Sol*
Design and Construction of Scenery .... *Nathan Bert; Albert Leo; Larry*
Construction of Foot-lights .... *Harry; Leo*
Posters .... *Maurice; Alfred; Leo*
Construction and Costuming of Puppets ...... *The Puppeteers*
Director of The Group Theatre .... *Miss Celia Avramo*

PROGRAM NOTE

Within The Group Theatre is a special group of children interested or gifted in playwriting. This Puppet Play is the outcome of the director's intention to motivate artistic expression in a lighter mood. But *as the play shows; our children are realists and need to express their own ideas about life. "Noah Comes Again", except for dramaturgic rewriting; represents the original thinking of one of our boys propped up by equally serious suggestions from the rest of the Group. . . . This play gave various skill and art labors to eighteen children. C.A.*

THE LOYAL PUPPET

The house was packed; the shades were drawn;
The footlights glittered;—then
The curtain rose on Nathan's
Noah Comes Again.

For three long acts the puppets lived;
The fourth had just begun.
The audience was spellbound
And soaking in the fun.

The final scence was ending
And the curtain coming down
Amidst applause, a puppet's head
rolled off and hit the ground!!!

And just when every thing seemed lost
The puppet took a trek—
He grabbed his rolling head and then
Replaced it on his neck!!!

They cheered the loyal puppet,—and
The other little men,
They'll still be cheering every time
That *Noah Comes Again.*—Max

Influence of Theater
Max writes for the school paper.

The cathartic potential of the playwriting is best examplified in Ben's play, *The Mannequin's Revolt.* (In the production Ben was the mannequin; Max, the witch; Harry, Satan; Nathan, the stolen boy.) In this "ordered" play Ben suffered to begin with; to a lad from the East Side, with intellectual pretentions, the subject was affrontingly

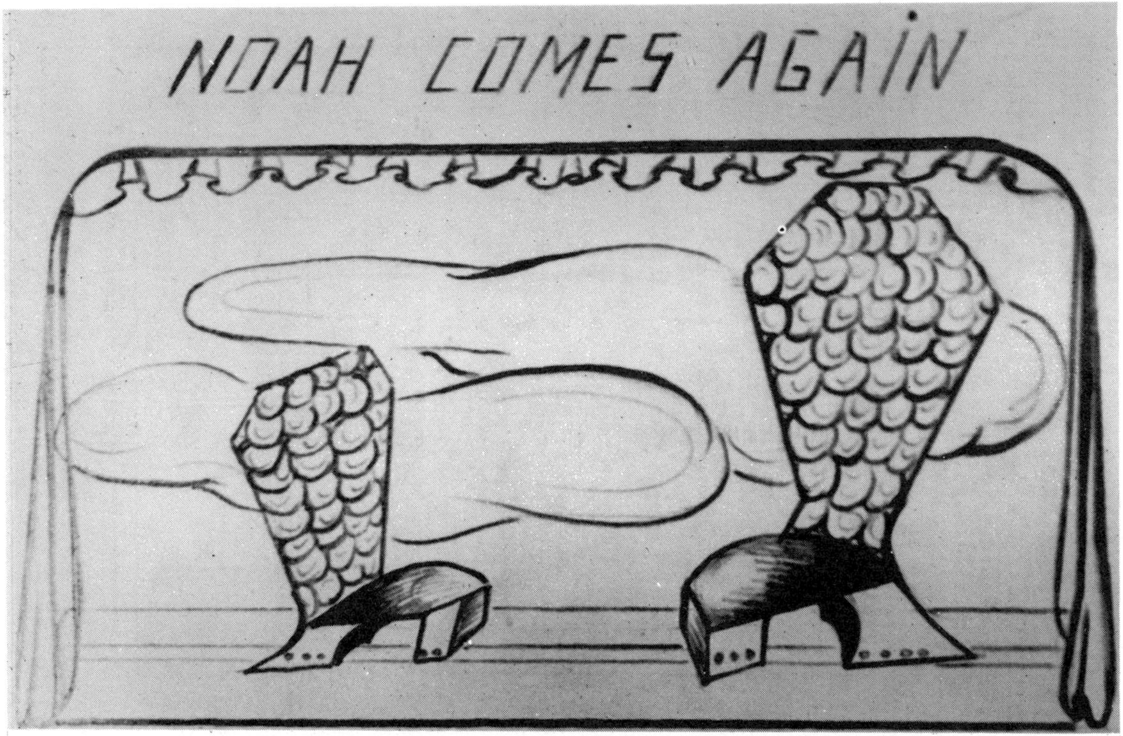

Heaven—Observation Thrones for the Lord and Gabriel: *Last scene in Nathan's puppet play;* Noah Comes Again. *The Lord decides that people mean better than they accomplish. One must imagine the puppet-God; to the accompaniment of Hallelujahs from below; voicing pensively his plan to go down to earth to "... whisper in the minds of leaders. . . . show them the way."*

NOAH COMES AGAIN

LIGHTING CHART

Scene	Time	Color and Objective	Where Placed
1	Sunset	Right - Red Spot on CLOUDS Right - Purple Spot " " Left - Yellow " " SKY	on top ladder, side of stage. on ladder, lower rung. from Left corner of backdrop at a diagonal.
2	Evening	Right - Red Spot on BOAT Right - Connect switch for Dock Light Left - Dark Blue Spot on SKY	on ladder, lower rung on footlights from backdrop.
3	Early Dawn	Right - Straw Spot hitting INSIDE OF CABIN Right - " " " " " Left - Light Blue Spot on SKY	turned on ladder, top rung, hitting through cabin door, downward. same as above, on lower rung. from backdrop.
4	Dawn	Right - Straw Spot on CLOUDS Right - Red Spot " " Left - Purple Spot on Lower SKY Left - Light Blue Spot on SKY	on ladder, top, turned as in Scene 1. standing on stage wing. " " " " from backdrop.

FOOTLIGHTS

1 RIGHT to LEFT ---- 1 Red, 1 Straw, 1 Green, 1 Purple, 1 Orange.

2 EXTREME RIGHT ---- 2 Red. EXTREME LEFT ----1 Green.

3 Same as Scene 1.,

4 Same as Scene 1.

BALCONY LIGHT - LEFT

1 Half and Half - Upper Flood, Blue- Lower, Red.
2 " " " - " " Deep Blue - Lower, Straw.
3 " " " - " " Light Blue- Lower, Red.
4 " " " - " " " " " "

childish and shallow. But my companionship in the library where together we sought the etiology of the festival was flattering; it gave importance to something which seemed inconsequential. Eventually the related knowledge he gleaned engrossed him and he was thankful for the experience which taught him how to search for material. But the folk data he accumulated complicated the simple subject he had started with. His poetic flight stimulated, Ben had the need to write something special and original, something loftier than about mere witches, goblins and candle-lit pumpkins. And troubling him profoundly was Hawthorne's story of a straw man brought to life by a pipe placed in its mouth—he rationalized its effectiveness as play material but did not conceal too well his driving sense of identification with this figure. An image of a curiosity shop was taking place in his mind to house this mannequin and now he had to invent, with Halloween to consider, episodes and characters pertinent to this protagonist's destiny. Let us follow—

THE MANNEQUIN'S REVOLT

It is Halloween Eve and the owner of the shop, about to close, has an unusual visitor. The Black Witch demands a mannequin, not any one, but that special puppet locked up in the closet. This the man does not dare open; his father on his death bed had sworn him never to let out nor look upon the figure within. Terrified, he leaves, throwing his key to the Witch and she releases Ozzie, the eventual hero of the play. With hideous glee she makes herself mistress of his soul which she gives life to with the smoking pipe she places in his mouth. And we have the beginning of an epic struggle between Good and Evil, man's responsibility and the dark forces of fate, free will, and predetermination. Though Ben had yet to become aware that he was throwing himself into Life, making a judgment on himself and coming to a decision, he was intellectually conscious of his theme as one can see:

> Witch: This key shall open the portals of Hell and set evil forces loose, for tonight is All Hallow's Eve. *(Unlocks closet. There will be an eerie, greenish light in it and a hideous mannequin will confront the audience)* Ah! A mannequin! Indeed 'twould scare even the minister himself! *(Helps it to chair.)* Sweet little doll, nice little

doll . . . *(Helps the awkward thing to sit; takes out a pipe and lights it.)* I light this pipe . . . I puff . . . I breathe life into your lungs. Take it and live. Live! Puff! Puff! Your life depends on it. For while you smoke you live! *(Watches the mannequin. Smoke comes from the pipe in his mouth.)* It lives! It LIVES! . . .But. . . .Has it a brain evil and cunning? Come, my darling, walk, walk to me . . . *(The Witch makes appropriate gestures. The mannequin walks hesitantly and awkwardly.)* Ah! Can you hear, oh, evil one? *(The doll nods.)* It hears . . . but can it speak? Your name, oh, evil one? Tell me your name.

Mannequin: *(Faltering)* My—name—is—Ozzie.

Witch: Ozzie, is it? Good. . . . Very well then, Ozzie, You can hear, you can speak, you can move. Listen then to the devil's instructions. This is what you shall do tonight, this night of All Hallow's Eve. . . .

(Lights fade out; curtain falls)

Act II is the home of the shopkeeper. A partition divides the stage to show the living room and a shadowy baby's bedroom. On the right the mother is peacefully reading by candlelight. On the left Ozzie, commandeered by the Witch, steals away the little boy. The mother shows uneasiness, looks in on her sleeping child, and discovers instead of him—the Witch's broom. Her prayer to God unanswered, in despair she calls upon Satan.

Mother: Then to thee, I pray for help, to thee, enemy of all that is good and kind! Return my child to me and thy price is yours. *(A puff of smoke from the fireplace. The Devil appears suddenly.)*

Satan: *(With a bow)* At your service, madam. You called me. Here I am.

Mother: *(Breathlessly)* The devil!

Satan: Yes. But I dislike the name intensely. I'd rather be called Lucifer. It is so much more becoming to my very, very mild nature, and so much more becoming to my features.

Mother: *(With genuine admiration)* Why . . . why . . . you are handsome. You don't look at all like the devil!

Satan: No. I dress with my mood. If I'm angry I'll appear with horns as humans know me best; but tonight is Hallowe'en, so I'm gay.

Mother: *(Bitterly)* Gay with the torment of others.

(They make a contract; Satan pricks her arm to seal the bargain with her blood. She promises to make a sacrifice "befitting a mother")

Mother: When does my soul become a member of your hordes of death? . . . only to see the earth on Hallowe'en when all forsaken souls are freed to revel in others' misery?

Satan: E'er sunset tomorrow I will return to claim thee. Is it agreed?

Mother: *(Looking toward bedroom)* For you, my child. . . .

The act ends with the meeting between a frightened husband and a distraught wife who tells the tale but attempts to keep the worst news from him. It is interesting to note the self-abnegation, the exaggerated guilt which Ben allocates to the mother in a blameless situation. One may say that after all it is a child writing a pretentious subject; but how much of his own feelings has Ben subconsciously put into the mother role! On the one hand she makes a sacrifice "befitting a mother"; on the other she tells her husband, "I sold my worthless soul to Satan, for the child. But I am from the gutter . . . my soul is no good. . . ." And Ben proceeds to his third and fourth acts in which he, the mannequin, grows up and reaches the sublime stature beyond mere manhood where both mother and child are restored through *his* sacrifice. Act three is laid in Hades, on the shore of the River Styx which separates the dead from the living. Ozzie steps out of his boat whose prow is a skull. He gazes into the river and sees his reflection. Ozzie-Ben faces himself and speaks his monologue:

> As I gaze into the murkey waters of the Styx, I see myself for the first time as I really am. . . . The Devil's offspring, certainly. By my troth! I look like one . . . hideous . . . ugly. Look how ugly my face is! Truly in keeping with all the evil things I have done—even if they were against my will. . . . Were I a messenger of good instead of evil, no doubt my face, my dress even would be pretty and enchanting to the eye. Fair lassies would stop to admire me and exclaim—(it is necessary to

> cut here and there for lack of space)—What lass would look at me now, to realize the evil I have done though I willed it not?—*(cut)*—To steal a child from its cradle, to carry it struggling to Hades, to fulfill a Devil's contract, is a devilish deed . . . *(cut)*
>
> Why shouldn't I be like other dolls are—sweet, bring happiness and good will into homes? Look at myself . . . Look at myself. . . ! (He leaps away from the image in the water) I hate you . . . I hate you . . . I HATE YOU. . . !
>
> Alone in the closet I was nought, and then—*(cut)*—Ah! only for the courage to fling this pipe from my lips and resume the peaceful slumber of death! *(He attempts to do so but puffs instead more heavily.)* Cowardly. . . . My entire being permeates cowardice. Courage to fight the Witch I have not. She commands, I obey. Courage to say Yes or No, to agree or to dissent, I have not. . . . Of what value am I now, a puppet moved by strings manoeuvered by the Witch? I am putty and they shaped me into the hideous, useless mannequin of sticks and rags without a will which I am now. . . . But why? Why do they exert a power over me which I cannot disobey? *Cannot* disobey? But why not?—*(cut)*—"
>
> Courage . . . Courage! What a costly gem thou art! (*His eye lights on something in a tree.*) Ah! What do I see amidst the branches of yonder tree? The spider has spun its web. The fly struggles in a web of evil and dread—helpless. *(He is struck with the similarity of their situations.)* Helpless? I . . . ?—*(cut)*—*(And Ozzie comes to the climax of his inner struggle with the words)* "I am a Man! I am capable of making decisions and acting on them. . . By all that is good and holy, I swear that I am making a decision now. I will fight the Master of Evil, Satan himself. Ozzie the mannequin has made a decision and Ozzie the Man will act on it! . . .

In this speech the implications of personal awareness and the inspired stirrings of a new attitude aiming at recreation are self-evident. The idea of a puppet's revolt against being possessed may have started from Ben's desire to invent an original twist to someone else's material. But this writing is not mere invention around an imaginary figure; it is soul tormenting with a cathartic resolution far

One boy's idea, a scenic design for Hades, a scene in Ben's play, The Mannequin's Revolt.

beyond the fanciful need for a Halloween story. As I read over the monologue I hear so clearly the touching tragic quality with which Ben as Ozzie spoke the lines; and I see again vividly their cathartic effectiveness on the spellbound youthful audience lost in complete identification, their feelings and thoughts, too, inward turned. As the writing of this scene progressed, Ben became aware of its subconscious significance and when it was no longer possible to contain himself he exclaimed, "I know. I am Ozzie!"

Act IV is a theatrical scene showing the inside and the approach to Hades. The Group had a wonderful project from this—recreating the Gate to Hades, snake encircled with guarding flames eating toward it from either side; experimenting with the mystical, otherworld lighting behind it, and constructing the crimson-carpeted steps for doomed mortals leading to it from below stage. The stair is the demarkation area between earth—the center aisle of the auditorium—and Satan's fiery domain in whose flames sport and writhe his evil, unearthly cohorts. A climactic conflict ensues over opening the Gate to its Master on his return from earth escorting the shopkeeper's wife. Ozzie seizes the key from the Witch after an insane, choreographic struggle for its possession. He next outwits Satan by threatening to hurl it into the Styx if the woman is not released from her contract. Here a poignant distraction occurs; one hears the husband calling his wife and sees his weary approach in pursuit of his beloved one. At this point Satan begins to lose his power and his kingdom, his own creatures mocking him as the reunited couple wend their way earthward. And Ozzie again outwits him when pretending to open the Gate he thrusts out the Witch to keep her master company. But the mannequin who became a man has still a great deed to perform—to destroy the whole evil kingdom—and there is no way except at the sacrifice of himself through so doing.

Satan: Foul beast! Traitor! You have broken your word.

Mannequin: Aye, and because of it I must die.

Satan: Die, yes, and a horrible death. My demons shall torture you at my command. Evil goblins! Demons! Come from the blackest pit of Hell! Rush forth! Tear him till he pleads our mercy. *(Some obey the command but strength has left them. The Kingdom of Satan depends upon his inviolate power of malignant leadership; and that has been destroyed by Ozzie's courage)*

Demon: *(Weakening)* The red fires that burn in Hell grow dimmer . . . dimmer . . . Master, come back! Fan the fires and give us life! Brrr. . . . It grows cold . . . colder. . . .The inferno that is hell is cold. . . *(In anguish)* It gnaws at our hearts. . . . The cold ebbs our vitality. Master, come back, come back . . . save us . . . for we die . . . die. . . .

Mannequin: *(With triumphant laughter as Satan's cries; "My kingdom disappears before my eyes . . . Let me in . . . Let me in . . .* LET ME IN!") Satan cringes and begs . . . ! Ha! Ha! Ha! . . . The Devil, Ruler of Hades pleads! *(Points him out to the Witch)* Look at him, Mother of Evil, Look at your master now . . . begging. How unbecoming the King of Hades! Ha! Ha! Ha! *(Pause)* Brrr. . . . It's getting cold. . . .cold. . . *(cut) (He falls to one knee and the waning flames seem to imprison him. His voice falters with physical weakness but rings triumphant until he dies). . . .*

No more need mortals fear Hell because of their evil deeds, for Hell is gone. Ministers need no more preach that Heaven is for the righeous and Hell for the sinners . . . because they lie. . . .Hell is gone. *(Cut)* Mothers! No more need you tell your children of evil goblins, horrible monsters and ugly witches . . . and say, 'Now sonny, be a good boy or the bad witch will carry you off' *(cut)* . . .

And Ben-Ozzie's exultant cry, his brave new attitude, if we are in doubt, comes with the jubilant lines—

Mortals rejoice! Rejoice, make merry. . . .For Satan and his kingdom shall be no more! *With his last strength he throws the key into the River Styx. The Witch and Satan are transfixed with hopelessness as they realize his triumph). . . .*My mission of good is fulfilled . . . I am happy . . . *(Holds aloft the pipe which gave him life)* This, too, I fling away . . . *Pause. He clutches his breast)* My heart . . . my body feels no more . . . I grow cold . . . cold with the frost of death . . . *(Begins to crumple; half lifts himself and cries out)* I Ozzie, a mannequin of sticks and rags . . . die. . . .die. . . .happy. . . .*(His body falls over and seems to be enshrouded in dying flame) (cut) (Outside on the paled crimson carpet Satan stumbles beside the Witch as*

THE CURTAIN FALLS)

In the play's dramatic finale, note how the author disposes of the ideology of Hell as a traumatic experience for children. About hell Ben knew from his reading; also he had the heritage of his Judaic-Christian culture. He came from a religious home where a

Teaching Device for Playwriting

Graphic device—a complete lesson in playwriting, incorporating structure, characterization etc. Perpetually on the blackboard, this sole lesson was the guide for writing and the inspiration for discussion and impersonal criticism. Also it effected an identification with growth and struggle out of initial problems or troubles—children talked about the knot that had them tied and visualized their unravelling it *and* climbing to the open door.

How Ben looked as Ozzie, the central character of his play, "The Mannequin's Revolt."

"bad boy" had surely been made aware of the concept of eternal punishment to sinners. He had been confirmed at thirteen and so carried the weight of personal responsibility—and guilt—for his deeds. Child of immigrant impatient parents, and of poverty, he had repeatedly rebelled against admonitions to be good. But this same boy who had been sent from home for ungovernable behavior now does not blame mother for anything (his, of course) and is gracious to fathers (the shopkeeper is worried about his son, tender to his wife). Instead parents are unhappy, unfortunate people, victims; and Ben takes it upon himself to remove the cause (the evil kingdom apparently, except that Ozzie is a weak, spineless creature and good comes only after he faces and recreates himself).

Ben has traveled a great distance in adjustment. In his home it was he who had made insatiable demands on his mother. Now it is Satan who does this and Ben who is outraged. Second in theme to the mannequin's facing himself is this new tender protective feeling toward her. . . . One may, of course interpret the phrase, "A sacrifice worthy of a mother," as another harsh demand on his part as if there were still a conflict in him. But by his own creation she makes the sacrifice willingly, lovingly, and it is he finally who makes the actual sacrifice for her.

Certainly Ben's preoccupation with morality throughout the story, especially with Ozzie's internal struggle and conquest over self, cannot be an accidental expression of a detached though rich imagination. And this is substantiated in his second play in which the figures are actually himself and the members of his family.

Director as Group Playwright

In the final polishing of home-written plays the director assumes the role of collaborator. But what a collaborator! Player of the game, "I believe in you," whether the original is worthy of attention or not. Angel treading lightly, delicate critic sensitive to his necessary empathetical—detached role in helping jealous authors with their work. Rewrite man for several reasons: rewriting troubled spots is practical teaching and argument by showing; the writers ask for it as for guidance, are reinspired by this adult proof of interest; it eases the periods of anxiety or fear of failure; it gives that needed sure touch to potential plays promised production, to assure artistic success, that is, to inspire the working interest of the whole Group; it

Gate to Hades: *A door of writhing flame guarded by a snake for Ben's play.* The Mannequin's Revolt. *Flanked by flaming sides, before it the red-carpeted earthward path (steps leading to auditorium); and behind it Hell's contorting Demons; all imaginatively lighted; this made the dramatic; even tragic; setting for Ozzie's sacrificial victory over Satan (Evil).*

places the theater children into a real world—no one does a perfect job, rewriting is done in real theaters. But if the rewriting shows the painstaking devotion of the busy adult, tampering with the intrinsic meaning of the play, its essential feeling, quality of dialogue or basic form is to break faith and to destroy stature. . . . Thus my correcting pencil always went gently. Spelling, punctuation, sentence structure, the shifting or tightening of a scene but not its withdrawal were in the domain of my superior knowledge. All else had to be touched with a humble regard for the author's intention and only if the changes were acceptable to the child as something he might have done himself were his skills better developed.

Nathan's anxiety about the Lord's last speeches is a good example of this. He had used a good device in exchanging the roles of God and Gabriel whereby Gabriel's disappointment in Noah brings about God's defense of mankind. Nathan said, "Something isn't right; we ought to know what He saw in the men because otherwise their actions seem loony." It was too much to expect a youth of fifteen to synthesize into crisp speeches his lengthy dialogue on the Lord's conclusions. I made him happy, I crystalized it for him.

Often the director has other writing to do to fill children's needs. In earlier pages I have mentioned changes written into the play material to effect individual problems: like fitting extra children into plays calling for too small casts; emphasizing or clarifying characterizations for greater self-awareness of children assuming specially cast roles; simplifying the give and take of dialogue to help a stutterer, etc. But sometimes more sweeping changes are necessary. One day, for example, the boys brought a play to me which they wanted to do. It was O'Neill's *Rope*. When I say they *wanted* to do this play I simplify the emotional, even morbid and driving currents with which desire was charged. The attraction was profoundly subjective. Old man Bentley was a lunatic parent; the prodigal son was a delinquent; fear, suspicion, mental sickeness was the atmosphere of the plot. I had no reasonable argument against the choice. How negate a great author's work to five outstanding youths in the Group, proud of their intellectual stature in seeking out the best of literature? And if the attraction related to personal father and son trouble did not this play have cathartic value? Nor was I too surprised to find the five supported by the other children in the clamor for this play. I interpreted their excitement that at last papa was discovered for what he was and sons were right in hating them, running away from home, taking money which they should rightfully be given, etc.

We gave that play beautifully with Harry as old Bentley—but drastically rewritten. I explained to the boys our duty to our youthful audience. We could not give them a play which showed an unnatural father by whom to parallel their own troubles, so learning a wrong lesson of life. We talked about the human value of theater, its responsibility to enrich the meaning of life and to give insight into living situations. As we wanted to help the children "out front" to adjust themselves and as O'Neill had not written his play to suit children's capacity to understand hidden springs in character I would have to rewrite the material to make Bentley understandable as a bad and lunatic father for obvious reasons; and similarly for the sake of truth beneficial to the audience, to clarify the personal problems of the prodigal son. As my pages came off the typewriter the morbid interest in the play changed to an engrossing curiosity in what made old Bentley tick; little by little he lost stature as the prototype of offensive, hostile fatherhood and gained stature as an interesting crabby old man living out his special pattern—and offering a grand opportunity for enactment and a good job with makeup.

One season, rewriting Shakespeare—*Julius Caesar*—helped vitalize the curricular literature of the English class. This was an experiment which I offered the English teacher who for some twenty years, twice a year, had had to repeat the "taking up" of *Julius Caesar* with delinquent and neurotic children definitely hostile to this academic study. A number of the Group were in this graduating class, and I thought I might serve the remainder as well and see meanwhile if acting the play instead of "studying" it would not vitalize an uninteresting subject—and teach much more English thereby to indifferent pupils. Briefly, I came into the classroom, took over as a director and proceeded with the enactment of the scenes, scripts in hand, using the classroom like a stage. Scenery, lighting, and costumes were made a project for the Group Theater in the spirit of a community venture.

The problems of cutting the play, rewriting or writing in material, were contingent on answers to several questions—for a balance had to be found where children and the bard could meet on workable ground and where the teacher could be sure to cover the minumum curricular requirement in the study of the play. I had to answer the following: how much of the play must the class cover to pass examinations; within this limitation, what action and which characters will most interest the boys; can the children take from the play what the poet intended or must help be given by simplification and if so,

Flats for street in Rome.

As the stage looked for the scenes in Julius Caesar. *Sets done by the group theater for cooperation with the English class.*

how—by what lines, words or phrases paraphrased, thrown out or purposely created? Also—how make it possible for all the children to participate; and what, to meet psychological needs and the problems of staging, should be the practicable sequence of scenes in the new version?

A group of ten volunteers edited old textbooks, crossed the cuts, wrote in what I dictated, pasted in newly devised or drastically rewritten lengthy parts. The play now ended with Antony's funeral oration—I learned that classroom study seldom covers the scenes beyond this. For a climactic curtain Antony's final speech was lengthened with relevant lines from a previous episode, and citizens in the throng were given additional lines and business, not only to make the scene strong but to make it worthy of the efforts of youngsters otherwise jealous of boys having the big attention-getting parts. In the plot interest was centered in the conspiracy and its culmination, with all extraneous material cut, allowing for a cast of seventeen besides the extras for the citizens' throng. The movement was condensed into two acts which went logically from the warning to Caesar on a street in Rome to the orchestrated cries of the awakened populous at the funeral. There were several drastic changes for swifter action and clearer understanding of the logic of events and characterization. One of these was the crowning with laurels of the bust of Caesar instead of Pompey which stood in the Senate chamber. The reasons follow.

What would the children make of Brutus turning murderer? Not only is murder for political reasons not understandable to democracy's children; but delinquent and neurotic children should be getting positive experience, not confusion over a character whose delinquent act *history* was condoning through the bard. If then Brutus was to be a patriot with courage to commit a necessary but personally sacrificial crime for his country, the case *for* him had to be strengthened and contrasted to Caesar's unethical, unpatriotic ambition. I placed the Artemedorus scene as an introduction—before the curtain—to the assassination scene in the Senate. Thus the Artemedorus epistle followed by Caesar's indifference to his suppliants and the brazenness of the garlanded bust strengthened the case against *him*. But Brutus had to be pure, not humanly weak and exalted by a great patriotic fervor. He could not be instigated into the conspiracy by Cassius but had to come to his drastic purpose by his own anxieties over the destiny of the state. I used a device understandable to children given to anxiety—sleeplessness. Brutus simply could not go home to sleep after the crown had been offered Caesar; he walked the streets like a worried man, so meeting the conspirators and joining the enterprise not by the persuasion of Cassius's honeyed tongue but as a consequence of his own studied conclusion. When finally, at the graduation exercises, the curtain went up on the curricular play, not a stilted line was spoken, not a movement was made nor a costume worn but by an authentic Roman. (In *Juluis Caesar* Milton played Brutus; Harry, Antony; Wandi, the leader of the populace.) Cast and audience both understood the currents of personal and political emotion of the drama, pitied Brutus and Caesar for different reasons, enjoyed intellectually the fine shadings in Antony's speech. The teacher reported a marvelous thing—all the children had passed well in their tests and were English the determinant all would have rated graduation.

However, the *Rope* and *Julius Caesar* activities may be classed as incidental to a major kind of writing the director may have to do for the Group. This deals with a very special need which our children had and have, and which must be universal in racial sections where an aspect of delinquency arises from the conflict of cultures inside and outside of the home. At Hawthorne the children are predominantly Jewish; they come mostly from the East Side of Manhattan, the crowded sections of the Bronx or Brooklyn. Added to other factors making for delinquency is the strain in the home environment due to disrespect of American born or Americanized offspring for their alien parents whose way of life adds confusion, insecurity and shame to children before peers in the American milieu. The normal rebellion of adolescence against parental control, the sturggle for independence which is part of growing up, here becomes a revolt against ideas and ways of feeling and of doing things. The rhythms of the life force in parents and children clash; both speaking Yiddish or English lack nevertheless the human language for getting along together. Parents rejected for what they cannot help being, and themselves insecure people for belonging to a minority race, cannot rise to heights of wisdom to cope with the situation. And Jewish anti-Semitic children are lonely children, deprived as they are of the pride of home, family and race or nationhood from which universally youth takes confidence, an outlook on life and the necessary secure beginnings for dignified selfhood.

Had I been working with Italian, Black, or Armenian, etc., children I would have felt it necessary, as I did with the Jewish children, to do something through theater to alleviate the situation;

through play material to inspire the youngsters with the unique traditions, history or folkways of their people. Ignorance is a fundament for hostility. Knowledge, especially knowledge through the emotions and the senses, has the cathartic force to bring about identification. To attempt this with the far away Russians, the Romans, etc., is a nice abstract handling of human problems. But there was something concrete to do, of the moment, and related directly to the problem of adjusting delinquent children for living happily in their environment. Let them know of the contributions their people had made to the world through the centuries—nay, let them make these contributions themselves through enacting them; let them *be* their people's heroes and heroines, their fighters and thinkers—and their sufferers, for suffering has been and is real; and children are not lonely nor feel inferior when sharing the moods of glory and defeat, when they feel in themselves the pride of belonging, in space and in endless time, to an identifiable flow of life having roots and traditions, and historic grandeur and continuity into their own time. To be able to identify with lofty figures in all phases of past and present life is to lose the pariah feeling. And to lose this feeling is immediately to build an inner sustaining bridge between being an American and a Jew.

To effect this kind of therapy I planned extrabeautiful productions for the religious holidays whose legendary or historical episodes centered around noble, strong, glamorous figures; or for important school celebrations because then the factor of public interest and the magnitude of the event lent the value of social correctness and approval to a project through which the children acclaimed after much preparation, "These heroes and heroines, our parents and we, we are one people." I found that it was best to write the play material myself. I do not know which was the foremost reason; that my doing this for the Group awakened an enthusiasm in the subject which a library play could not, because the evidence of my devotion to the children and *to the subject* was a live thing conquering emotional bias *against* the subject; or that I found the existent plays wanting for language too classical, or characterization too simple to effect the cathartic identification I aimed at, or lacking fuller historical content, or failing in the opportunities for children to build projects rich in pageantry for the meaningfulness which costumes, experimentations with lights and settings would have for them. And what modern plays there were centered around simple home life, and this would not be exciting enough to elicit interest; or had the biblical stories written in sophisticated language. I could not see, for example, how I would awaken in the girls the feeling about the beauty, courage and loyalty of Esther to her people by choosing a script I found in which she says about Ahasuerus something similar to *"I Made the King."*

The Banner of the Jew is an example of how I used a Channukah celebration to acquaint the children with their people's history and mainly their struggle to keep inviolate their spiritual values. This holiday commemorates the fall and rise of the Temple and the mystical legend of the untended oil burning its beacon flame on the Altar throughout the struggle. The special heroes are the fighting Maccabees; and the heroine, symbol of maternal fortitude, is Hannah preferring death for her seven sons in Jehovah's cause to their life without the spiritual freedoms for which most of us rallied in this recent war. A chosen play would have had isolated significance unrelated to a more distant past and without continuity into the present; and it was this reality of undying forces in the existence of a people, tangible only through continuity, that I wanted for the purpose I described. I had an unusual advantage in the writing of this piece—Milton, the only child through all the years to have of himself a positive racial feeling urged in a vague way that he wanted to act out Israel, *stylized*. Somewhere he had seen stylized drama and also he had participated in short dramatizations of poems I had used for their combination of human content and their teaching of Judaic ethics—for examples, *Abou Ben Adam* and *The Rabbi and the Cripple*. Peer initiation of a project is the best contagion for enthusiasm in the mass. I had the children impatient for my developing scenes.

The ground covered was the exodus from Egypt, the Channukah episodes, the Spanish Inquisition—the epical settlings and exiles of the race, with history brought up to date in Nazi Germany (no brutality, but the burning of the books symbolizing the recurrent struggle for a culture), Palestine and the United States. In episodes before the curtain a discourse between a Greek philosopher and a Hebrew prophet brought out the gist of Judaic ethical teaching; and a drunken Cossak after a pogrom gave an inkling of the experience of parents in the old country. I made every effort not to arouse chauvinism but to awaken historical identification with one's beginnings; not to inflame racial hatred but to give insight into human problems behind painful occurences. Thus the Cossak was depicted as an ignorant pitiable human being instigated to evil, believing himself right in obeying orders "to save the fatherland" and in his cups anguished, confused and remorseful as any of the boys rehearsing or seeing him on the stage were themselves apt to be when guilty. The emotional rhythm of the play was rise and fall, rise and fall—of a people and of the mood—ending with a crescendo Hymn Of Joy in song and chant of spirtual faith, and in dance. While relevant to the theme this finale was written with my mind on the psychic impressment of the rhythm in long time rehearsing. In the end the children were to experience over and over again, related to themselves, the fall-and-rise moods of individuals regressing and picking themselves up again in the upward movement toward personal adjustment.

It may be argued why not leave it to religious education to accomplish the entente between children and their people? Because sermons, rituals, and told facts are outside of the person, entering the ear but not the heart unconditioned to receptivity. To participate completely is to receive and to give, to identify. When Milton, weary and threatened by Egypt's lash dragged his burden of bricks before a background of sun-baked pyramids and the VOICE reverberated "She-ma Yis-ro-el"; or when he knelt before the Altar in an underground in Spain or suffered before an enthroned Inquisitor the conflict of yielding his beliefs to survive or of not yielding for something dearer than survival, then Milton and some two hundred children were actually body and soul alive in Egypt and in Spain suffering, aspiring, and hoping with their people. "Gee! The Jews have great people, too," a youth voiced at the end, the indescribable joy of this knowledge which shone in the eyes of all his peers. When at another date we produced *The Jewish Contribution to American Life,* and every child on or before the stage lived through the achievements of scientist, poet, philanthropist, musician, scholar, thinker, doer, etc.; there was no mistaking the sense of romance, worthwhileness and position in the world which the children felt about themselves in belonging with such people. In this piece Lillian Wald affected a deep impression especially upon the girls. There is no romance in poverty, in difficult parents. But Lillian Wald touched this off with her consecration to the environment and to the people inferencially the children's own. Such people must be worthy for so great an interest and the dedication of a life! So the connection was made between the little people of the race and the great, between the past and the present, and the outlook on life brighter, between enlightened children and rejected parents.

Memoranda

Taking notes on the children—first impressions, analyses of needs, attitudes, progress in relationships and work, unusual and revealing behavior, conversations, remarks or writings—is a helpful part of the director's job as therapist, in order to maintain a complete and individual handling of the members of the Group according to their problems. But I suspect, too, that I am including this sine qua non to authenticate the source of my inspiration and memory of material for this book. I pick at random from my notes.

Dec. 10th—Milton said tonight, "I get a chill (thrill, by further explanation) when I see something done perfectly." Refused to give up reading a poetic passage to whose meaning and cadence we were arranging pantomimic action. Reads with difficulty being a foreigner and needs glasses, too. Doing *The Rabbi and the Cripple*. R—and F—followed example, were embued with the desire—new in them—to thoroughly understand meaning and to conquer the problem of expression. All the children enthusiastic over the story, specially thrilled by Rabbi's catharsis. Ordained rabbi, proud, young, handsome, honored for learning and saintliness; on way to rabbinical seat, his inturned mood spoiled when on road misshapen beggar crosses his path; Rabbi in pride of self scorns the lowly. Conflict. Passing throng, adulation, public accusation by beggar; change of feeling in the throng and the Rabbi purged asks forgiveness. Heightened moment when Rabbi kisses hand of beggar and clasp hands in brotherhood. The populace exalted in background, humanity uplifted through fellowship. Children ask for shortening this poem and simplifying the language, the talmudic phraseology too difficult. Casting suggested by the boys and good choices, critical, for the first time without a thought of self.

January 9th—S—second month, entered for "bum-out," surprised at self for industry on miniature stage, working with Irving, in self-critical, cooperative spirit. Both removing poor work and remaking. Progress in Irving in skills, patience, control of obstinacy, tonight made "foreman" of enterprise. Eight children cooperating, making tiny furniture, tinwork for lights, etc. Irving mixing paints first time. Yesterday he looked at first batten he cut, burst out laughing at uncouth work, remembered refusal to take advice, etc.

May 6th—Have succeeded (refusing attention to Milton's poetry, if not written in his own hand). Results from his study with remedial teacher. Handwriting more intelligable, vocabulary improving, now anxious for education; showed me written poem. Milton now doing carpentry, painting; behavior controlled, acting like big brother to two new boys. "Sure, I'm going to graduate, I want to." . . . F—in regression, morose, idling. "Nobody says anything good about me." Made efforts after conversation. Happier before leaving, pointed out sunset. Joseph cheerily singing, working with Leo, etc.

PART THREE

10

In Resumé

A Stutterer Speaks—"My Sincerest Thanks to the Group Theatre"

I was considered as being hopeless. I stuttered, was shy, awkward with tools and with my hands, and in other ways I was unpopular with my fellows. Since childhood my stuttering had made me self-conscious. It was my greatest handicap. Once a fellow said to me, "Harry when I hear you, I feel like taping your mouth. It is so harsh to listen to." This hurt, it rankled deep. My not being able to converse, made me a butt of other people's remarks. I escaped to books. Soon I became wrapped up in my reading. I created a world of my own, surrounding it with an almost impenetrable wall of seclusion, by going off, alone, into corners. . . . Life had been pretty hard on me, stuttering had made me an outcast. Since early childhood I had been bullied by other boys. I never joined their play unless when bullied into it. I was, and still am, afraid of being hurt, but to a much less degree.

My efforts to escape made me an omnivorous reader. I am very imaginative. What I read, later on became something to daydream about. I always was the chief character in these dreams. Also, I became vindicative, and after being hurt by someone, either mentally, morally or physically, I would creep off to one side and in imagination, subject my tormentor to every torture I had ever read about.

But now I am proud of being a successful example of the

> help we get from the Group Theater. In my first summer at Hawthorne, a list of activities was called out. I signed up only because the name Group Theater had a nice sound to it. But though I wasn't aware of it at the time, this proved to be my salvation. My speech has improved, I should say eighty-five percent. Conversation is a fairly easy matter. I no longer shrink from contact with others of my own age and intelligence. I have visible proof of what I can do and it has instilled a certain amount of self-respect in me. I have friends. I am on the way towards being able to take care of myself and I have acquired enough confidence in myself to ask for lessons in the manly art of self-defense. . . .
>
> I have become a star actor in the group. I do not stutter at all when I am on the stage. People applaud me now when I speak. My parts in plays have been important ones, like old Bentley in *Rope* and Anthony in *Julius Caesar*. I won the prize for the speaking contest given by the Public School . . . . Three cheers and a big Hurrah for the Group Theatre.
>
> Harry B——

The above is a written statement which Harry put one day on my desk without comment. I hadn't asked for it. Like the handshake, writing out an evaluation of progress had become a Group Theater ritual, the outcome of tradition. It was a simple, dignified way of saying thank you and also of being helpful. This is how it came to be. Questioned on some notes on himself which I read aloud to a boy, I answered that I was checking to see if we agreed on his problems and progress. "Are you going to write a book?" "Would you mind if I did? I would like to spread the news of what you are accomplishing. In that way you would be helping other boys and girls." "That would be wonderful . . . . everybody knowing about us . . . and we helping . . . you may use our names if you want to. . . ." Oddly—now all the children were in on this talk—it was I who had to point out why I would not use their surnames *if* I wrote a book. Later when Irving waxed so eloquent on the meaningfulness (see p. 184) of his Group Theatre experience I asked if he would like to put it down on paper. Afterwards once or twice I had appealed, "I have been asked to tell in a little talk what we're accomplishing here. . . . If you could put it into your own words for me . . . .otherwise I cannot be sure that I'm telling the truth." Irving's writing was the start; thereafter children after a cathartic pinnacle, self-aware and thankful, or children leaving for home and completely aware and already in a nostalgic mood, handed me a paper or quietly placed it where I would see. It was a repayment and an offering of love—and a gesture in tradition handed over by one group generation to the incoming one.

Three facts about these papers are of interest. They represented the reverse side of a gesture already in the pattern of the children—in hostile, (Bob's letter, p. 135) disgruntled, and/or insecure moments they tossed on my desk or thrust at me or sent through a messenger scrawled poorly spelled notes showing even in the handwriting the emotional upheaval which prompted them. They were neatly written, usually in ink with obvious painstaking as to spelling and composition, as a serious statement for posterity should be; and as with the bad notes the writers conferred mysteriously with pals, but now the heads put together had the bright-eyed quality of youngsters planning a birthday surprise. And third of all, what the writers said of themselves, besides honesty, showed personal insight and checked with my own observations. Discrepancies were slight, insignificant differences in evaluation, as for example Harry's percentage of eight-five about his speech improvement. I would say that on the stage or in secure company his speech had become normal; in insecure situations his loss was fifteen to thirty-five percent with however a quick recovery to normal speech through the trick he had given himself to stop and whistle—actually through the poise he had acquired in handling himself when insecurity assailed him.

Reeducation of a Stutterer

"I was considered as being hopeless" says Harry. How could he know this except through people's deliberate bypassing him, and his own sensitivity to human cold or warmth? The "Don't bother me" of adults, the vacuous look, the ripple of annoyed expression is basically more rejecting than peer cruelty; a child does not anticipate safety and guidance from other children. Harry suffered on both ends possessing neither the hope of adult haven nor the hope of sharing the cosmos of peers. Harry had a caseworker and such people are very careful about using frustrating words or impersonal attitudes with children except where these are part of the treatment; the boy could not have gotten the idea of hopelessness from him. Nevertheless he felt all around him what he had felt all his young life, the indifference of people later echoed to me with sober finality in the clinical diagnosis. Both the caseworker and the psychiatrist agreed about his stuttering; ''Hopeless—an organic defect''; about his personality, ''Hopeless—an institutional personality.''

I didn't know Harry; I doubt if I ever laid eyes on him though he must have passed me often in the throng of children identified by cottage groups, until he joined the Group Theatre because it ''had a nice sound to it.'' I had never known a stutterer; perhaps this is why I made myself the personification of the adage about fools stepping in where angels fear to tread. I felt challenged. How could I help the boy? How, with the odds against him so clinically outlined by people who *knew?* The information I received about him was frustrating, or would have been to anyone better schooled than I in such things and not consecrated to battle windmills. The organic cause for Harry's stuttering had been an infection in infancy which had raised so high a fever that certain nerve ends were burned away. The permanent result was a fluctuation in body-behavior; at times he could speak fairly well, be attentive, almost brilliant in intellectual discourse, exude a lively interest in and an enthusiasm about his surroundings; other times he was extremely absentminded, sluggish, forgetful of responsibilities, seemed stupid and unreachable. How much of this was postencephalitic, how much was functional could not be determined. I decided to ignore all this—I had no scientific attitude to encumber my human attitude toward the unhappy boy.

He himself described his behavior as due to rejection and to the compensations he had achieved by surrounding himself ''by a world of my own.'' It seemed logical to believe that giving him a friendly environment in which to participate, an opportunity for speech and confidence through intellectual interests with other boys, also bodily activity through acting as well as through manual skills, would make him happier and as a result might help to modulate his psychic and physical behavior. Were he given a long enough time for living his daily patterns differently, perhaps what was functional in the old pattern might disappear gradually.

The improvement for the first six months was very slight. Here, naturally, the boy had to face the situations he had run away from all his life. His eccentricities were accentuated in group situations. His attempts at speech were blocked. It was too hard to listen to him, the other boys showed signs of irritability. But although Harry had to suffer the cumulative rejection from a large group, he was not unhappy. The books he had at his disposal were more interesting than the miscellaneous reading material he had had to pick up willy-nilly from tables or garbage heaps around the cottages. His interest in the work was keen. His opinions were asked for when never before did anyone care what he thought. He had the attention and care of the director.

But the situation in the group often took on a climactic effect. Instead of Harry the boys put the director on trial. They pleaded—"He makes us nervous. We can't stand it." Then either the group, en masse, threatened to resign, or Harry, aware of the trouble he was causing, pleaded to be let go. Neither thing could be allowed to happen.

Harry was impressed with the facts—in private conversations—that to drop out would be cowardly, also that it was the nature of boys to react to signs of courage with a sporting acceptance and respect, that these would be his eventually if he did not yield. The other boys were spoken to, singly and in groups, about the power they had to help this boy. They were asked to be patient with him. It was pointed out that if they did not humiliate him, his speech would flow more readily and sound less harsh. They were appealed to on the basis of kindness to a boy who never had a chance and were definitely told that Harry would stay. For a long time, however, his pattern remained the same. He sputtered; the boys, on nerves' edge, mimicked him; the director asserted authority—only to find when the boys had a change of heart that Harry had disappeared. He remained deaf to the call of his name and later would be found in the lavatory reading, or behind the curtains on the stage asleep! Or he was doing a crossword puzzle, forgetful that all the commotion had started around him.

Nevertheless, responsibility was thrust upon Harry in devious ways, but together with other boys. He was sent along with the stage crew though always given a detail for which he alone was accountable. Wherever a group of boys sat at a workbench he was given a task commensurate with his lack of skill, but *necessary* to the project the others were engaged in. Boys working together must necessarily converse—thus spontaneous conversation would, in the course of time, include him, too. In this way, the stuttering boy was kept in busy contact with the others. The others, by the close proximity engendered through a common interest, began to accept him.

Little by little, he relaxed, became more attentive, proved himself useful. With relaxation, there was revealed an endearing charm, a good humor which brought from the others friendly laughter in place of the former ridicule. Even his use of big words became acceptable. In fact, they became a challenge which took the boys to the dictionary to seek their meaning. Of himself he discovered a way to control his defect; about to stutter he drew in his breath, let out a whistling sound, and with an air of conquest continued speaking. Also in our friendly environment he learned to play. Now despite anxiety from past bullying he would find himself engaged with the boys in skirmishes, giving as well as taking hearty punches, in short, enjoying himself.

With this development in the group relationship, the director could put him out a little further into active participation, on such work in which speech was a major requirement—in discussion and acting. He had capacities the others lacked. He had intellect; they had manual skills. He had a mind and imagination and the ability to express ideas; they could carry out a plan once it was formulated. If the group could learn dependence upon him for an aspect of the work in which they were less capable, tolerance for Harry would turn to respect. With complete security within the group, the nightmare of his past might be obliterated, he might be helped to a pattern of purpose in his daily life.

Harry was given the special task of reading a number of plays and reporting on them. This called for telling the plots, making analyses of the characters, giving an opinion about their value for production. The group picture changed. The stutterer had his first attentive audience! He expounded; they listened. Around the table, Harry led the discussion, gave his ideas, and defended them against those of opposing thought.

A new problem presented itself! As his speech flowed more freely, his relaxed mind knew no bounds. All his unexpressed musings, questions, ideas were verbalized. Harry could not be stopped from speaking! His was a mind released—free association swamped the original subject and side tracked his point of view. What was apparent to the director was "nutsy" to the boys. *But;* by this time the group had a pride in him as an example of their own handiwork! They were awed by his progress, which they had made possible. His sincerity and imagination, and his style in oration, held a glamor for them. Their reaction was a mixture of awe and banter, but he had gained their respect; also they had an investment in him, felt they had a job to do with him. They pulled him down to earth! When he meandered, they good-naturedly reminded him they were waiting to hear a report on a play. They plied him with practical questions which demanded practical answers in relation to themselves, to the workshop, to the stage, to the casting of roles. It was the leveling process. If his intellectual qualities were furnishing *them* with a richer experience, opening their eyes to unknown vistas, *they* were teaching *him* to be logical, matter-of-fact, realistic.

Eventually, Harry began to handle tools—no longer as a makeshift apprentice to the others—as a workman, with a project of his own. This was also an adventure in design. He worked out a plaque of masks with the words "Hawthorne Group Theatre" carved on wood, painted and polished, to be hung on the proscenium of our theater. The industry, pride, and purpose of those following months! The plaque has its face in comic and in tragic expressions, for having no other model, Harry studied his grimaced face in the makeup mirror, made sketch after sketch until satisfied. This was not an isolation into one activity. Simultaneously, he was giving his share in crew work for productions; he was writing a play about a tailor—"A character like my grandfather. A swell guy, poor fellow, he was a diabetic tailor." He also, was taking important roles in plays.

It is hard to remember, that Harry could not speak, shunned people, could not draw, paint nor work with tools, had lived in an unreal world of his own, had been dull and listless, had been avoided by boys!

To the amazement of the campus, boys and staff alike, a miracle was happening. Harry was becoming the leading actor in the Group. The discussions on the campus were about Harry's latest characterization or about his forthcoming one. A new personality moved among us. A clear look in the eyes, a self-possessed poise, an ease of movement, expressive use of the hands, a remarkable ability to hold an audience, an even more remarkable ability to control his audience!

There was the occasion, when he stood before the curtain, demonstrating "How an actor makes up for his part." He had to change into an old weak-eyed, crabby, New England Farmer—a character from *Rope*; the author, Eugene O'Neill. It is easy to see the reaction from an audience mostly made up of other boys—the remarks, laughter, and banter. If nothing else was a proof of the profound change in his personality, this performance was! He matched wit against wisecracking, poise against the rowdy abandon of his audience. He never stopped in the serious business of his demonstration, and when the time came, used a simple gesture of his hand to gain a respectful silence from his public. The sportsmanship he had had so little of from boys, he was able to give to them!

Harry, in the graduation play *Julius Caesar*, gave one of the sincerest renditions of Antony, difficult role for any actor, that the director has seen. This opinion was voiced by many who saw a Broadway production of the same play at the time of our production. I feel no immodest note in my statement; it is used as a substantiation of a just pride in a boy who was considered a hopeless stutterer and an institutionalized type. In the declamation contest of the year—an affair having nothing to do with the Group Theatre—Harry won the first prize! He became somewhat of a hero on the campus.

Let us see, in résumé, what happened in his case. It is so simple. Affection, understanding, a controlled environment to give him a chance for reeducation, a director challenged by a diagnosis—and a helpless, hopeless boy, a pariah, became a person who was able to be paroled and sent back into the world with an equal chance to fight the battles of life. His disease could not be cured, but the functional results of that disease *were* profoundly mitigated. A boy was made happy, self-confidence was established, and through group experience self-discovery pulled this boy out of the morass of past patterns and attitudes and set him new, on sound pinnings, to walk normally among his fellows.

The theater experience opened up for Harry a realistic world, smaller than the one from which he had sought escape, but parelleling it in its demands and differing only in spiritual climate. The big world had been cold to him; he needed warmth, an all-embracing acceptance, a friendly prodding and patience—infinite patience. He got what he needed!! The world had rejected him; he in return had rejected the world; but in his subconscious hostility he had inverted the punishment upon him. His excessive stuttering was a pattern of fear-withdrawal-projection—"I am afraid, I can't talk, you see what happens when I do talk, so I won't ever try to talk." His absentmindedness and forgetfulness, his irresponsibility and laziness were all of the same weave—"I'm afraid, I'm confused, I'm tired—Why do you bother me? . . . Please, it is so hard to make the jump from my world to yours . . . I'm at peace with my books and my private thoughts . . . etc."

In the Group Theatre there was an incentive to effort. First, the theater appeal somehow spanned the distance between his dream world and reality. Plays were richer reading than jokes or dime novels. There was an adult who *protected* instead of demanded.

Later on there was an audience who did not jeer, and the pleasure derived from being listened to outweighed the negative pleasure of withdrawal. At the same time he wasn't given the opportunity to withdraw! In the past, he was either scolded into attentiveness or let go in disgust. But in our Group, he was held on to and kept attentive by interesting, vitalizing stimuli. Responsibility stemmed from the same stimuli. And social approval came on its heels with the pleasurable warmth of surrounding smiles and words of praise. And amazingly—it must have been so for this boy—all this well-being came because he spoke! What an incentive for taking oneself in hand! No more reason to fear, no purpose to withdrawing, no cause for rejecting the world at large!

Harry had become an aware person. Characterizations in plays had been more than a medium for improving speech or for gaining a place with his fellows. They were identifications with the trials and sufferings of others, they were an enlargement of emotional capacity. They took him out of the isolation of his own self-pitying and enlarged his own humanity.

When Harry began to help other boys with their problems or came to the director to discuss the needs of a fellow student, or when he became aware of disorder in the workshop and assumed the humble task of straightening up, or when he searched the grounds for stray materials to fill a workshop or production need—then it was certain that Harry had left forever his compensatory dream world and was prepared to live in our real one for which he had been successfully reeducated.

ROPE *CHOSEN BY THE BOYS OUT OF SUBJECTIVE NEED; ALSO EXAMPLE OF PROGRAMMING AROUND THE PLAY. SEE HARRY; "A STUTTERER AS SPECIALIZED SPEAKER"*

THE HAWTHORNE GROUP THEATRE
PRESENTS
THE FOLLOWING PROGRAM

Tuesday Evening, April 20. Assembly Hall

Part 1

Talk by Harold .... *How Stage-Sets are painted.*

Part 2

Talk by Harry .... *Analysis of the play; "The Rope"*

Harry will show how an actor changes into his role.

Part 3

A Drama- "THE ROPE"

This play, written by a world-famous author, has been re-written to be actable on our stage at the request of the boys who were enthusiastic about the chance it gave for character portrayal.

Cast of Characters

Maxie .... *Sidney*
Annuk .... *Hymie*
Pat .... *Jack*
Luke .... *Jerry*
Their Father .... *Harry*

SCENE—Farm district in a northern state where the natives work hard to eke out their living from the soil. A backward country where the people are quite ignorant and queer characters are not unusual. Action takes place in a rundown barn.

FOR THE GROUP THEATRE

Scenic Design—Harold
Stage Crew—Wandy, Ike
Stage Construction—Irving
Assistant Artists—Oscar, Hymie
Lights After Experimentation by the Group
Stage Manager—Abe
Director—Miss C. Avramo

The following statement by Milton over which he had put the title *Confession;* is so thorough a case history of "before and after" and so authentic that I am saved the trouble of adding my observations to it. Instead I include also a conversation we had which I jotted down almost simultaneously with the give-and-take between us. Milton's unburdening himself will serve not only to check with the evidence of a tumultuous cathartic moment some of the material he gives us in the calmer much later written analysis of himself and his problems, but to bid the reader entrance to a private interview, one of these talks resulting from a child's request to see the director "alone."

"Confession"

> I was a boy of very selfish thoughts, only satisfying myself, and truly, I came to the school not for robbing; the main reason being that I was ungovernable so that no one could control me. I would not, if I got into arguments with older people—even if I was wrong and they told me things best for myself—admit it to give them the satisfaction. I would always try to get out of my difficulty by lying and sneaking around and trying to patch things up—in other words CONNIVING. (This word was used by the boys to mean exactly what Milton's definition says. New boys looked to the conniver for leadership in "fixing" situations, expecially in manipulating staff members so that punishment was withheld or boys in mischief were not caught. When a sense of ethics had finally taken root, the same boys became suspicious of the conniver and parted company from him.) Well, I did the same things home, to my parents, but they understood me as all parents do understand their children.
>
> Before I came here I spent two years at the orphan home. I was in the habit of smoking, so I used to sneak down, with the smaller fellows, to the engine room, where they caught me about a hundred and fifty times. It wasn't the pleasure of smoking when I was younger; it was the thing of showing the smaller boys that I was a bigshot; in other words I was a nice big showoff, and I enjoyed myself doing it as I didn't know any better.
>
> At Hawthorne, I ran away the second week, from the hospital where I was sent because I said I was sick. Being a con-

niver, I made believe I had a headache and I was trusted to go there and to return alone. On the road, by luck I bunked into a man who asked ME the direction to New York. Instead of helping him I asked for a lift. I told him a sob story that I was hiking because I lost my companions and they had my fare. He even gave me a quarter when we got to New York late in the evening. My mother was mad at me for coming, but I gave her a sob story too, but since she knows me, she understood that I couldn't stay long in one place and I like to run around free and do as I please.

I did thirty days line for that runaway, then Mr. K—— called me in and told me he'd put me on the farm if I would stay out of trouble. I was away from the campus all day, being on the farm, so I got away with a lot. I got no line tickets because I was tricky. I was still unstable and I ran away twice when I finally got into trouble, because I couldn't face punishment.

I began to run around wild on the campus, getting tickets left and right. Then a lady by the name of Miss Avramo came. She said we were going to do work we had never done before, that we would build a theater exactly as in New York, and there would be no cheap stuff like our amateur skits, but real plays. As I was trying to be a wise guy, I made attempts to become acquainted, and I used to say "Hello" in my boisterous voice which could be heard ten miles away.

At that time I was stuck on the porch of my cottage, with a bandaged foot, because I had stepped on a rusty nail. What a sight I was then! I was a wreck, my hair all mixed up, my face unshaven, and I used to call out when she passed by and almost frighten her with my voice. She answered me so friendly, sweet and quiet, and if I had been smarter I would have taken a hint not to yell so loud. By her answers I began to have confidence in her, and I tried to know her better. I asked her questions. I tried to advertise the fact that I had been born in Russia. She realized who I was from my first speech. She later told me that her first impression was that I was quite hopeless but very interesting. But she said it though, as if she really believed in me. After winding up a number of conversations, I asked to join the Group Theatre.

We all took it very seriously because of the way she spoke to us. She told us she wanted to help us improve ourselves.

She didn't care what we were up at Hawthorne for, but she thought we were gentlemen inside of ourselves, and she wanted to build our self-appearance and our diction. And she said the Group Theatre is a place where you must give, and we could get a lot of enjoyment out of it, too, and we would then also improve in our general work in Hawthorne, and in our character. In other words she made us feel we would be a big family building a theater and she would be a mother of all the boys—the way she one day said in fun when the boys were too much for her, "You make me feel like a mother of nineteen terribly big boys."

I was a big nuisance for a long time, being stubborn, and not knowing how to read well and afraid to write because I am left-handed. But I got the thrill of my life acting, and she also let me act out my poems which I wrote when I couldn't sleep. And I loved to think how a character in a play would be in real life, and I got a deeper understanding about people that way. I began to look at the movies differently to see if the acting was good and honest and if the scenery was artistic. Soon I began to be interested in building and painting our own acts. I'll never forget how I couldn't get over it when I painted the log cabin for *Rope* even if I never had used brushes before. It was paint, but the walls looked solid like real logs, because Miss Avramo showed me on the rungs of a chair how the light falls and shadows come on round objects.

And I found myself changing all around. She had to chase me away from the Group Theatre because when I found myself slipping I had to come and cry on her shoulder. The tables began to turn. I used to be a conniver and instead I began to be annoyed if a boy interfered with our progress, or if he was lazy. And I began to help Miss Avramo when a new boy came in. I showed him the "ropes," and helped him rehearse his lines, and sometimes I even spoke like her and told a boy—"You can do it if you really want to. There is no such word as 'Can't' in the Group Theatre." I began to look nice. I combed my hair and saw about my clothes.

And then a crazy fit took me to run away again. But I waited until the play was over because I had to be loyal to the Group and she would have been let down. All the same, I told her I would run away, because I had to, and I asked her if she would take me back into the Group Theatre after I would be caught. She wouldn't promise me, and she looked serious, so I didn't enjoy that runaway very much. When I came back I couldn't face her, so I sent a boy to ask her. But she made it hard for me purposely; I understand now, she gave me a chance to act like a man. She sent back a message that I would know where to find her if I had to ask her anything. I couldn't stand it. I loved the workshop, and the plays and I had to get back. So for the first time in my life, I found myself apologizing and acknowledging to somebody that I had been wrong. But she appreciated it because I ran after the play was over, even though she saw I was restless and she knew I was heading for the runaway.

Gee! She made it hard. I had to promise I would not run away again for six months. I never stayed put for six months in all my life. And I had learned not to give a promise because that would have to be kept and I knew I couldn't keep a promise; no, I made a rule not to promise anybody, anything. But I wanted to be in the next play and I didn't want her to lose faith in me, and anyhow I told the gang in New York before I went back to Hawthorne, that I was through. This was January and according to her, she wouldn't take me back unless I promised, no runaway till June, and that I would work more in the workshop, and that I would let the Remedial Reading teacher train me in reading and writing, and that I would try to be graduated. It was a big number, but at last I took it. I gave her my hand on it and it was serious just like in a church.

Six months! Sometimes I was tearing myself to pieces—to stick to my word or to break it. But I knew she was watching me and it would hurt her to know she couldn't trust me. And she did a trick to me, too, said I wouldn't get a part in the play if I didn't read the lines myself—because I was ashamed of reading badly and always let the boys read for me on a pretense that I couldn't see. She sent me to the hospital to get new glasses, too! So I let Mr. R———give me private lessons in reading, and I began to write my poems down on paper, because Miss Avramo no longer let me dramatize them if they weren't on paper so other boys could read them.

When June came, I didn't know if I was coming or going. Because I really was on the graduation list! I was in the graduation play, *Julius Caesar*. And my teacher Miss Avramo was writing a pageant for Chanukkah because my idea inspired her.

She didn't think we could have a program for this holiday because where would we get a play, and then I told her I could do something to represent the whole race; I would be Israel and do it in modernistic movement like a dance I saw on one of my visits. So Miss Avramo was reading to us every night the scenes she kept on composing and I was already rehearsing the first scene where Israel is a slave in Egypt.

Funny, after all that which happened to me, after June 30th, I didn't WANT to run away. I had learned so much and I had friends; and everybody on the campus was saying what a gorilla I used to look like, and now I looked clean, and they said my eyes looked different. And it is true. I am now starting my second year in the Group Theatre. I am happy to write my confession because I do not think I am the same conniver and showoff I used to be. I am getting ready to see Mr. S—— (the director) and to ask him to trust me to form a social club so we could have parties Sunday nights, the boys and girls to plan everything and take the responsibility of good behavior. Miss Avramo thinks it isn't a bad idea if I am sure I can be responsible, because parties can turn out into trouble for everybody.

Milton S——

Milton Unburdens Himself

I am at my desk writing when Milton appears his eyes feverish from a sleepless night. He has not come to me about the play, his work, or a Group problem. Merely the weight of his personal problems is too heavy. He has reached the stage of personal and social awareness and his coming is due to the announcement of his name on the list of boys to be given home visits for a religious holy day. I take down our conversation as quickly as it occurs. I seem merely to be continuing with my work while giving him a hearing. I want this on record, for it is a culmination of many talks of the past two weeks.

Milton's voice breaks; he is near to weeping. He says, "I suppose you think I'm a big baby, weeping on my teacher's shoulder . . . I decided not to go home for the holidays, even if I *am* on the list." I suspect from many signs that his mood may be due to sexual disturbance and try to assuage him with the statement that spring is a trying time for adults, too. But he answers—"I am going mad.'' He attempts a gesture of nonchalance, glides down from the wall against which he has been standing, onto the floor and remains sitting throughout our talk with bowed head. ''If you are disturbed, why don't you go in to see Mr. S—— (the caseworker)'' After a silence he answers, ''I do not want to disturb you. Just let me sit here''; then as if he had remembered, ''I'd rather speak to you.'' There is nothing left to do but let him have his confessional hour:

Director: What is wrong, Milton?

Milton: It is something inside of me.

Director: Is it the spring?

Milton: (After a silence) I feel dissatisfied. There is something in me troubles me. I'd like to do things . . . Look at Cottage 2. The boys there work together, they're a different crowd. In my cottage they have no spirit, I'd like to build up the cottage, but there is no one to work with.

Director: Have you spoken to your cottage parents? Tell them your plans, I am sure they will help. (Silence) You're not having trouble with them?

Milton: They're very nice to me. They try their best; but I'm not happy there.

Director: Do you feel guilty about something you have done? In trouble with the boys? (Silence) Have you been—you know, the old trouble with the boys, and you feel guilty, and do not think you deserve to go home? (This boy's history shows homo-sexuality of an aggressive nature for many years. The practice stopped after a year in the theater activity but at the time of this conversation, it had not stopped altogether. I would not have mentioned it had not Milton himself spoken of it in an earlier interview.)

Milton: No, I'd tell YOU the truth if that was it . . . (After a moment) What does my case worker mean when he says I'm up here because I'm ungovernable?

Director: It means you are not able to control yourself, that you do as you please—

Milton: But I'm different now. In Russia, well, I did whatever I wanted to, since I was a little boy. That is because I saw my father do things; I thought, if he may, then I may. . . . Sometimes I see him, how he died in my arms. I think I am a fool just like my father. I do things for people. I could die for people, but people are selfish.

I learned that when he was dying. My uncle and aunt came only once to see him, then they stayed away. They didn't even come to the funeral. They were afraid of their skins. Why wasn't I afraid? My father had typhus; I kissed him while he was dying. Why didn't I get typhus? . . . I loved my father.

Director: And your mother?

Milton: My mother, I love her, too. But she is different. She always wanted me to be educated and to be different, and she suffered because of my father, and now because of me, because I am like my father. My sister used to be a little wild, running to meetings; now she is settling down and she, too, wants me to be something. My brother-in-law told me he'd break my back if I didn't behave up here . . . . But sometimes I can't sleep. I recall the scene in Russia when my father was sick and the relatives stayed away. It makes me very sad. You know when I sing, I am really crying. I try to hide it by singing and by making up poetry. (I took advantage of this boy's flair for making up poetry which he could not write down by refusing to listen to it until he learned how to put it down on paper by attending the remedial reading and writing class.) The trouble is, I can't sleep. Ideas keep me awake, and *thoughts* about everything. I feel that I am going mad sometimes.

Director: But you ARE sleeping better these nights! (In the last conversation, I had pointed out to him; one, that sleep would come if he didn't worry about it so much; and two, that his not sleeping put a burden on his cottage father because his lagging in bed mornings affected the cottage schedule.) Your cottage father tells me, he no longer has trouble waking you on time.

Milton: Yes, I understood how I was a trouble to Mr. K—— and now I do not lie in bed. But . . . I can't eat, I have no appetite.

Director (Casually) Very well then, maybe I can help you. I'll have to give you the hardest work in the theater, tire you out so you'll need to eat. (He attempts to smile, but ends by shaking his head.) In love with a girl up here?

Milton: No. I'm funny that way. You know what the girls are up here for. I couldn't do it just that way, when they ask me. Some girls, like R——, I feel like a brother to. She gets fighting and tries to boss everybody. I teacher her how to behave. I do just the opposite and tell her she mustn't be that way. . . . I used to worry about sex. That's why I ran away in January. I ran away with S—— because I knew we couldn't get far. You remember, I didn't want to run away; I told you then, though, that I was going to run. Just running, helped my feeling. I knew we'd be back quickly, because S—— is a coward. He's smooth, but inside he's slick and cowardly. I wanted a girl badly, otherwise I didn't want to leave. I felt sorry about it, remember? You understand me just as I understand you. You just lift an eye or open your mouth to speak and I know what you mean.

Director: If sex doesn't bother you, as you say, what is the trouble? Why do you bother boys?

Milton: It really was an accident. I didn't understand what I was doing. When it was explained to me I stopped. (It took years for him to stop.) That is one thing about me, when I know I am wrong, and I make up my mind, I can stop. (Which is true, but it is only a recent fact—the making up of his mind.) I never went out to do it purposely with a girl. But in the East Side the boys go on rides, their fathers or brothers have cars. And girls are invited . . . all kinds of girls . . . . You talk, and afterwards there is nothing to do,—so—the first affair I had, I remember I kissed her and I was so happy, I trembled . . . and then I enjoyed my satisfaction . . . and afterwards I felt ashamed.

Director: And all that bothers you— Is it your responsibility that bothers you? What if there were a baby?

Milton: There are ways to prevent that.

Director: You have been doing this for a long time? (It is hard to connect this history with that of aggressive homosexuality.)

Milton: Since I was thirteen. (Quickly). But not as often as most fellows. I liked the girl I told you about. But afterwards, I became spoiled. . . . But inside of me, I am choicy. The others drink, but I won't have it. I take ice cream. They make pigs of themselves. Most of the time I talk like a big brother.

Director: (Aware of the self-dramatization. Time almost for his school, too.) Look here, get yourself together and face what is troubling you. I have no time, you have no time. I am willing to help you, but you mustn't spend so much time and so many words.

Milton: I'd like to go home . . . and I don't want to go home.

Director: Let us get at the reason.

Milton: I can't find the words. . . . It is that I owe something to someone.

Director: You mean, you have stolen? (This in fun)

Milton: (Good-naturedly laughing) No, that would be easy to make up. I owe a debt to two people. I'll never be able to pay it back.

Director: You mean your mother—

Milton: And you, especially.

Director: Me? Well, I suppose as your teacher, I have taught you several things.

Milton: You taught me to love someone outside of my mother. That is a selfish love. (This is the second time he tells me this.) You taught me to be unselfish. . . . And you taught me to know myself.

Director: Good. You are growing up.

Milton: (Abruptly and with a sadness) I don't belong anywhere now. You believe in me, but I know myself, the real *I*. (Bows his head) I am like my father.

Director: You're afraid to go home, because in these few days you may fall into past habits?

Milton: I'll always be like my father. I know myself that I am putting on a bluff and I can't live up to it. Every time I progress I fall right back again.

Director: But we all are like that. Progress isn't steady and uphill in a straight line. (He raises his head willing to be convinced.) And you're not like your father really, since you suffer anxiety about being like him. . . . It's only the HABIT of being like him that is in you, because you had him for an example and imitated him. (Of course, it wasn't so simple, but a simple way had to be used to help him over his anxiety.) You say yourself that you have learned control.

Milton: But I'm afraid. . . . When I go home, I sit and sit, and stay with my mother. I sit and read. . . . How long can I do that? If I go home for good, I'll begin to run around. The worst of it is, my mother understands that. She knows I stay home not to make her suffer the way my father made her suffer.

Director: Of course you will run around, Milton. You must get used to running around and facing temptations. It isn't healthy to hang around your mother. You have no responsibility to her that way. Your responsibility is to yourself, to be natural and yet look out for past habits.

Milton: (Diverting the subject by some driving logic of his own.) But I feel if anything happens to my mother while I'm up here, I'll murder. . . still, I ought to remain up here.

Director: Look here, Milton, the trouble is you assume responsibility which is not yours. That is what brought you here, interfering in family affairs which concerned your mother. Now listen carefully—Your mother is a grown-up person. If anything happens to her, if she gets into trouble, it is HER responsibility. She is supposed to know what she is doing. She is ready to pay for what she is doing. You cannot blame the world for anything she brings upon herself, it is no concern of a growing boy like you. (Milton's mother is an emotionalist who runs to rebellious congregations, get herself mixed up with the police in rallies, deliberately courts this trouble.)

Milton: Yes . . . still . . . (And he continues to speak of hurting her as did his father.)

Director: Look here—you see your father as he was, you criticize him. That means you are outside of him enough to dislike things in his life and character. Why don't you get him entirely out of your thoughts? He is dead. You are alive. You can live happily, you can make your life. Why don't you face the fact that you hate, if not him, then what you don't like in him?

Milton: I have—I have hated him very much.

Director: But you've been ashamed of that. Don't be. A good strong feeling like hate may help you more than sentiment about a man who is gone. You are the only person that counts now. Hiding up here, afraid of yourself, will not help you fight out your battle. I think you are lazy, you don't want to make the effort. You hide behind a dead man, you identify yourself with him, because it is a very easy thing to do. . . . You have got to go out and face things squarely, and fight them out with YOURSELF. (He remains silent for a long time.)

Milton: I am a different S—— (Uses his last name.) that's why. I am different since my last runaway in January. But I don't know if it is the REAL S——. Maybe it is because you are my backbone.

Director: Then it is time you were your own backbone. Then you must go home and find out for yourself what you are like. It is better to get into trouble over again than to sit here in fear. How does a fighter become a champion?

Milton: He fights in competition.

Director: Is his opponent a weakling?

Milton: (Grinning) No, it's a stiff match. You have to give everything to win.

Director: Does one become a champion "right off the bat," to use an expression I learned from the boys?

Milton: Most of the time you go into the ring year after year. You have to take a hell'v a lot to become a champion.

Director: What is the discipline imposed on a fighter?

Milton: (His eyes wide open in understanding) I'll say, it's stiff. You got to live clean . . . exercise . . . that's control, I guess. I know all that, but . . . in January, I knew I do not belong to the past. I *used to* be a little thing who was never ashamed about anything. I used to get quickly acquainted with people. I spoke without thinking. I did anything and everything I wanted to. . . . Now, I have no pleasure with the old crowd . . . instead though, I'm afraid to meet new people. . . . At my sister's wedding I understood that. I'm afraid just like a baby, to walk or to talk. It began in January; I felt it first in my feet, then in my belly, and now in my head. . . . Funny, now that I have more love in me—you know, unselfish love—I don't belong anywhere . . . I don't know where to turn . . . I want to be somebody, I want to do big things—and I ask myself, "HOW, WHERE, WHEN" . . . I owe you a debt I can't repay. I say to myself I haven't any backbone to do it.

Director: But you have. Look at your progress. You have learned how to read, how to write. You are a good actor, you now can paint and you can build with tools. You have done all this in a little more than half a year. Compare your accomplishment in such a short time against almost seventeen years of the rest of your life! You have gone further than any other boy up here. . . . More important than these accomplishments is that you have learned to face yourself—that is what you are doing now when you are speaking with me. Let me show you. (I draw a little figure in boyish contours) You were this little fellow—let us be honest—this little no-account.

Milton: (Interrupting, doggedly) I was happy.

Director: And now you are growing up. You are this tall fellow I am drawing. This up and down line is your backbone. See! Your head is high. You are seeing the world and yourself in this world, for the first time. That hurts, of course. Growing up hurts in many ways, so you feel unhappy.

Milton: I don't mind being unhappy this way. I am not unhappy because I changed, but because I don't know where to go from now on. If I go back to live in the city, I will be lonely.

Director: (Drawing another picture) Look, this is a slanting line like a mountain. At the bottom is that little shaver you used to be. Here not too far above is Milton three months ago. Here, nearer to the top, you are there again. . . . You have been climbing. When you climbed the space between that little guy and the Milton of three months ago, and then you fell, you hardly noticed it and it didn't trouble you. But the climb between this middle fellow and the one higher up has been quite steep. Now, if you look back from near the top, it makes you dizzy. You know if you fall now, it will be a greater fall. You feel lonely because you have left your past behind. That happens to ALL OF US while we are growing up. Naturally you will be lonely until—

Milton: (Interrupting with feeling) That's it. I don't *want* to fall back again. (He takes the pencil and draws in dots as symbols) See, these are my footsteps. I must go on climbing. I want to. Something in me tells me I *must*. (His symbols have parallelled the mountain line, but he stops abruptly) but WHERE am I going? WHAT will I find?

(He draws again, a curved line, starting with the top figure and looping around to the figure at the very bottom.) This is what I'm afraid of, I'm going to fall straight back again, because it's lonely where I am now.

Director: Suppose you tell me everything that happened to you since you entered the Group Theatre, everything you've learned—besides acting and such things.

Milton: Every time I got into trouble with you, even when I forced you to scold me, that made me grow. I find it hard to acknowledge it when it happens; sometimes I walk out on you for that reason.

Director: You walk out on yourself.

Milton: I know. I don't have the guts to apologize. But all the time I know you are like a big hand, a big hand stretched out to forgive and to take me in again. You know me pretty well. Most the time I stay around because I know I have been wrong. I don't acknowledge it, but I know if I will keep quiet and sweep the place or finish some work, you will understand. . . . I have to be right in reach of your hand until I pick up the guts to come into it again. You have been like a knife in my back, pushing me up that mountain, that is the debt I owe you. . . . I learned plenty. I don't answer back to people the way I used to, I stop to think, maybe the other fellow is right. . . . I learned to see beauty and to look for it. . . . I suffer when the other fellows don't understand the lines they are acting, because then the acting isn't rich or real. . . . I learned that everything isn't what it seems and that one must weigh things instead of acting quickly and getting excited . . . and I learned the most important thing you taught us—that there is no word like CAN'T. I learned that I can do anything I *want to do;* and that when I *don't* want to do it, that is the time I make an excuse by saying "I can't" . . . I don't know, now, why I am so afraid. Because even in January, I told the old crowd that "we're through." Maybe I'm not used to being lonely, that's all. I think to myself, I told them that, I can't go back to them, I mustn't, I don't want to. But what will I do in the city? How will I get new friends? Who will want to bother with me? Also, I keep remembering your lesson—"There is no such word as CAN'T."

Director: What are you going to do about it?

Milton: (Jumping up) Gosh! I'll be late to school! (A grin grows on his face) I think I'm a big baby. Maybe . . . maybe I'll sleep now. Maybe that's what I needed, to talk myself out. It was on my mind so many nights. (Puts out his hand for a clasp) I give you so much trouble. Maybe you better give me the hardest work to do today. When I'm busy I feel happy. Goodbye . . . (He lingers) I know you believe in me. Don't worry. I'll make you proud of me. (He runs off at a leap to school.)

This conversation needs little comment. What real consolation could I give the boy? His confusion was the natural outcome of the beginning of adjustment. The worst about it is that his fears were real. How many adults could face the aspect of returning to old haunts, old family environment and the same poverty, the difficulties of job-hunting, without fear? It was later when Milton was more sure of himself that he wrote what he humorously called "My confessions about myself and the Group Theatre."

In contrast to the interview with Milton is the following one with Ben, who did not ask to see me but barged in without the consideration which usually crossed other children's minds that I might be busy and would not want to be disturbed. The contrast is one of personality and of the problem under discussion. Ben, more egocentric and less introspective, has no concern here with the future and his seething is due to a situation arising directly from the theater work. I jotted the interview down the minute he left. Following I include the major part of a closely typed eight-page statement composed by Ben after his leaving our community. I have made no corrections, have left out none of the contradictions or searchings of the boy unable to pin down what he owed to the Group Theatre and what to his other Hawthorne experiences. It is interesting to see his growth in introspection, the looking into the future, the counterpoint movements of rationality and emotion with which he makes humble acknowledgments and then detracts them with the insertion of a begrudging note; also the facts of experience he leaves out or interprets through incomplete reference. Trying to be honest, it costs something of his proud individuality to yield the fact of his not becoming what he is all by himself; also evident here and there in the writing is the self-consciousness of playing the autobiographical author.

I had not reread his paper put away for many years. Thus I am all the more struck with his tongue-in-the-cheek analysis of my motives and reactions and his I-am-I necessity to tell the teacher some truths after all the truths he had had to hear from her; these notes seem to be the painful echoes still lingering from our interview. Also I am struck by the concepts "dream" and "catharsis" applied to his Hawthrone experience; they conform with his teacher's thinking and planning as expressed in the pages on discussion; and it clicks that Ben should have been the only youth, as he was the only natural playwright, to epitomize so neatly in dramaturgic language the awareness I aimed for in all the children. However, Ben's composition leaves out much which is pertinent to his development. "In A Talented Boy" I will try to fill in what material I have which may enlarge what he himself has touched upon and what material he has avoided or has not been aware of.

Ben refers to his movements and relationships in the larger community outside of the Group Theatre. It is a reminder that I owe the reader at least one fuller interweaving of a boy's history than I have been able to give until now because I had other purposes to fulfill. Thus, I will not be closing these pages with a somewhat askew picture of theater children having a one-sided life because I had to concentrate on pointed facets of their problems and growth to elucidate my thesis of theater's power for therapy. In fact, the larger picture is necessary for the meshing of problems and events so that at least one case history may be followed per se for the better understanding of troubled children, of the help they need from us, and of the paramount service adults render when they plan together in behalf of them with the purpose of initiating and/or assisting their movements of growth.

Ben Straightens Out His Complaint

The author of *The Mannequin's Revolt* rushes into the workshop. His face is drawn, his lips tremulous. It is the day after the performance of his play in which he has also been an actor, portraying the major role. His first speech without greeting comes emotionally straight to the core of his trouble, but not with direct words.

THE HAWTHORNE GROUP THEATRE
PRESENTS
THE MANNIQUIN'S REVOLT
A HALLOWEEN PLAY

Scene 1 ....A Curio Shop
Scene 2..........................The Shop Keeper's Home
Scene shows living room and bedroom
Scene 3..........................The River Styx Hades
Scene 4..........................Outside the gate to Hades
The auditorium represents Earth

PROGRAM NOTES

This play has been written by one of the boys in the Playwriting division of the GROUP THEATRE. Sets and Props were planned by the entire group and various ideas co-ordinated.

Cast of Characters

Shopkeeper ....*Sol*
The Witch ....*Max*
Pretty Manniquin ....*Bert*
The Manniquin, Ozzie ....*Ben*
The Mother ....*Jacob*
The Child ....*Nathan*
The Devil ....*Harry*
Leader of Demons ....*Irving*
Demons In Hades ....*Arthur*
Michael, Nathan
Paul, Isadore

FOR THE HAWTHORNE GROUP THEATRE

Author of play ....Ben
Scenic Artists ....Seymour, Irving
Props (Conception and Execution) ....Sol
Paul, Irving
Harry, Morris
Hyman, Isadore
Arthur, Bert
Costumes ....Doris, Lillian
Construction Crew ....Hyman
Bert, Rubin
Stage Crew ....Al
Harold, Milton
Lights ....Harry, Morris
Director of Group Theatre ....Miss Celia Avramo

Ben: I don't know how I am going to live these days. I was so happy writing the play.

Director: But you're writing another. I purposely had you start the second before the big night . . . to help you against such reaction. What is wrong?

Ben: I don't know. . . . It's as if I were dead. Maybe I thought I was a bigshot, maybe I expected—I'm ashamed to say—

Director: To be called on the stage last night, to be fussed over.

Ben: (Brightening) Maybe—I guess you've hit the nail on the head. The play ended, there was applause, but *I* was forgotten.

Director: For whom was the applause?

Ben: A little for me perhaps, but mostly for the Group.

Director: Who did the play, who built the scenery, who did the lights, who acted?

Ben: Everybody . . . (With desperate protest) But I wrote the play.

Director: What did I do?

Ben: Well . . .

Director: Could you have written it without me? Without the hours I gave of training, criticism, advice? Without my correcting your lines and scenes? What about the directing of the play, of the training given in the workshop and on the stage? *(Silence)* Suppose I claim the play as mine? It may be mine as much as yours. . . . Aren't you forgetting the details which had to be organized? The problems which were not your bother, boys who had to be kept interested and working for your play? What would you have thought of me if I had rushed up on the stage to make a bow?

Ben: Well, you should have. You deserved it.

Director: But when the last curtain went down, and the applause rang out—where was I?

Ben: You were backstage. You made us go out and take a bow.

Director: Yes. And I was already moving the scenery out, putting things away.

Ben: You shouldn't have. We would have done it.

Director: You did—the rest. But there wouldn't have been time enough if I had waited. The stage had to be cleared for the morning assembly. The point is, if I were thinking of acclaim for myself, could I have cared—and acted on it—about the needs of the school for the morrow? You see, a play isn't an isolated thing for which the movements of life can stop. It is a great moment, yes, but smaller ones just as important must take place. . . . (long SILENCE. Ben is thinking it over and at last gets the point.)

Ben: I guess I'm upset about nothing. Still . . . I expected important guests. . . . I thought I would be called out, that I would feel like—well, like a hero. . . .

Director: Aren't you greedy, Ben? I did introduce you, privately, to my own guests. (He drops his eyes) . . . Ben, lumber, paint and paper, lights and costumes, your typewriter, were supplied you for all the needs of your play. Everybody's talent, effort, and ABILITY were bestowed upon your play to give it life. The printshop publicized your success through the programs where you are named as author; the entire school gave ears and eyes, and gratitude through applause. Without fussing about it the actors sacrificed their free time, their hours for recreation for the much-needed extra rehearsals. Your director gave up *her* free time—and all that wasn't enough to make you feel "like a hero" as you put it.

Ben: But you don't understand. It's altogether different . . .

Director: Do you really think I do not understand?

Ben: I tell you it is a terrible feeling to be let down, to feel so unimportant, after all these months when I was living for my play.

Director: Oh Ben! Actually you never really believed that one day you could write a play which would be done before an audience? But it did happen. Haven't you, now, a greater faith in your ability to write?

Ben: I am sure of it, now.

Director: Then this is the time to be very honest with you. You should be able to "take it." You must recall, this isn't the first time you have come to me like this. Every day, after playwriting, you have come with a protest of *not receiving enough attention;* or of getting *less credit* than you deserve.

Ben: I don't mean it that way. I know you have given me special hours, by myself every day, when you could have taken it easy or you had other things to do.

Director: Which play have I been using as an example in class, of *how* to write dialogue, *how* to build situations, etc.?

Ben: Why . . . mine. Both of mine.

Director: Is there a lack of great plays which I might have used for the purpose?

Ben: Of course not.

Director: Then why *yours?* If I used Shakespeare, what do you think would be the effect on the boys?

Ben: Too highbrow?

Director: No. You recall, the boys did *Julius Caesar.* I always remind them of the plays they have given because their own experience helps them to understand what I am teaching them. But nevertheless, I stuck to yours.

Ben: (Thinking) Because I am one of the Group?

Director: Of course. If I show them how well one of their own can do, how is it going to help them?

Ben: I don't know. Maybe give them hope that they can do as well.

Director: Now you are beginning to see things. You are one of them. They identify themselves with you. But now tell me—do they really believe they will write a play as good as yours?

Ben: Judging from myself as an actor, I've tried my best, but I know I haven't the ability that Hal has. I watched him and I was thrilled. I really think that helped me to want to try, even though I told you I never would take a part. But actually we *look up to him for his acting.*

Director: And whom do the boys look up to for their writing?

Ben: Several of us, Max and Nathan.

Director: Whom do Max and Nathan go to for help when they are stumped? Whom do I send them to for working out a problem?

Ben: (Blushing) Well—*we're* the three boys who really—

Director: You know you're proud of it. Say it!

Ben: They come to me.

Director: Of the entire group, who gets the most attention in that special field?

Ben: I do.

Director: How do you think the boys feel about it?

Ben: In the beginning they were jealous. It was my fault, I really didn't mix with them, or talk to them so easily.

Director: Then we read your play. Did it help the situation?

Ben: It brought us together.

Director: Think for a minute and answer this—what has been your complaint all this time?

Ben: Don't rub it in. You think—well—I always felt that you weren't giving me enough credit, you were showing me up. You always put it something like this—"When Ben first wrote it." Then you tell them my problems and my changes and our conversations. Then you ask me to read the scene as it was changed. You never praise me . . .

Director: Suppose I stopped work to make a speech about how wonderful you are—how would the boys feel about you, and how would they feel about themselves?

Ben: I suppose they would not feel so important themselves.

Director: You're avoiding part of the question.

Ben: I guess it would be natural for them to be jealous; they wouldn't like me.

Director: Then as a leader of your group, I have two problems. What are these problems?

Ben: To make them like me, and to keep peace in the group?

Director: Suppose I change the question. What have you gotten from me besides the knowledge of playwriting—something, I believe, much more important?

Ben: I feel like somebody; I know I can do things; I have something to look forward to.

Director: Can you put that into one word?

Ben: (After a moment) Confidence?

Director: All right. I must give them the same faith in themselves that I have given you. *How* did I give it to you?

Ben: You were friendly . . . You didn't laugh at me about my ambition to write. You helped me *learn* to write. You really gave me more than you did the others. Everybody knows that.

Director: Very well. You have talent so I've gone out of my way to develop it. *But not at the expense of the others!* Now, there is left *you;* the boy Ben who aside from his talent, must live with other people, other boys especially. First, I had to find a way for you to live with them—you had been unwilling to find a way yourself. Second, I must give the other boys the confidence they need. Remember, it isn't their fault, and it isn't your credit, that they were not born talented. However, their *needs* are the same as yours. They think they can write. So did you. I took you on your own evaluation. I must do the same for them. If they cannot write they will recognize it themselves. Meanwhile they want to write; they have something to say. They have the right to express themselves just as much as you have. Talent has nothing to do with it. My giving them security and a fair chance has everything to do with it. How can I do both things, help them and help you?

Ben: I understand now. You can't throw me in their eyes and make them feel inferior. And you got me to working with them even if I thought too much of myself. . . . But how can you have the patience? Sometimes I get the creeps, they have such childish ideas.

Director: Not more childish than your actions—your talking your head off about imaginary injustice to you.

Ben: I'm terribly sorry . . . I guess my success has gone to my head. It's the first time in my life I can talk about my writing without boys thinking I am queer. They listen to me now, and I have friends and we have common interests. . . . Maybe because I've been working a lot with them.

Director: I'll not be satisfied until that wanting-to-be-a-hero business is cleared up. In the future I can do one of two things. I can pat you on the back before the others and say what a swell fellow you are.

Ben: (Laughing boyishly) Don't do *that*. They'd call me a teacher's pet—

Director: Or, I can frankly acknowledge that because of your special hours with me your work has had the benefit of time, care, thought, criticism—that from these benefits the Group, too, has an advantage; since your finished work may serve as an example, for teaching purposes, to the other boys. But you do not like to acknowledge the help you've received. . . . How would you describe such a person in a play—characterize this attitude?

Ben: You say it so coldly . . .

Director: You are mature enough to understand. How would you?

Ben: Well. . . . Such a person wouldn't want to be honest.

He'd sort of want to believe that he did it all alone, even if he knew it was impossible. It would be like biting the hand that feeds him. (Blushing deeply, but smiling.) You always manage to make me see myself.

Director: Because I believe it is worthwhile. (Ben is pleased; the tension is all gone. He turns to leave but holds back.) Wait, Ben. Had you not come in, I would have sent for you. I have something to confess to you. . . . I knew you were disappointed last night. . . .

Ben: I—I was hoping you'd forget about it. I shouldn't have said anything.

Director: Ben, I'm going to shock you. I expect you will walk out of here very much hurt. I hope it will not impair our friendship. More than that, to understand, you will have to remember very clearly that everything I have done for you has been done thoughtfully, to help you. You are my charge—my responsibility for you and to you goes into the future, beyond Hawthorne days.

Ben: You frighten me. You never spoke this way. I was always pleased with what you did for me.

Director: You may not be this time . . .

Ben: But you couldn't—

Director: I did! The boys did want to call for the author. They pleaded with me. I didn't allow it.

Ben: You . . .?! How could you! You took away my happiness for the evening.

Director: I know, Ben. But I gave you something instead for the future. I purposely gave you a necessary painful experience. For the heady excitement of the moment, I gave you something as a lesson through which to be able to withstand future, and more real, disappointment. At the same time, I was fair to all the other boys in the Group.

Ben: But . . . I don't understand. I wrote the play. I put my whole life into it.

Director: Now we're back to the beginning. Who did the lights?

Ben: Jake.

Director: He was up on the balcony all evening. For two months he had been experimenting with the lights. Long weekends of tireless and wearying labor he had spent with me in the auditorium. How could you not remember to call him out, too, when you and the others took your curtain call? Without him, how would you have had your fiery Gates to Hades, your fireplace lit like a living fire, your effect on the River Styx? (Ben gives one long look and drops his head.) How many boys and girls labored on that production?

Ben: (Figures it out) Twenty-eight.

Director: How many talents went into it?

Ben: Acting, scenic design and painting, costuming—four.

Director: How many other crafts or labors?

Ben: Typing scripts, carpentry, electricity, printing programs, posterwork for publicity—six.

Director: You have forgotten the boys and girls who merely swept the stage or kept the workshop clean and tools and materials in order—necessary work which had to be done by those who had no other skills. You have forgotten the crew who carried the sets and arranged the stage. You have forgotten the ushers. Should these have been less praised because they were born untalented?

Ben: (Seeing the light) Gee! We couldn't have a play without them.

Director: Then you agree that *they* "put their whole life into" what they were doing? . . . . Isn't it terrible that for many of them the future holds nothing more than being sweepers—you know what I mean—people holding humble jobs without personal reward.

Ben: Everybody's work is important. There is nothing to be ashamed about.

Director: That is only true if all of us recognize their share and show appreciation. Would I give them the proper appreciation if I picked only you for glory?

Ben: I see what you are driving at. But only with my mind. Inside I still feel that you did something to me. (Hastily) Don't misunderstand me. I realize that everybody needs feeling important. Talking with you has made clear to me about the others, and how you work so hard to give everybody what they need . . . . I didn't sleep last night, but I will tonight. . . . I almost cried before, but now I am ready to tackle my new play. . . . I guess I'll get personal congratulations throughout the day, anyhow. And I feel better knowing the boys wanted to call me out.

Director: Ben, are we going to evade the important issue? You *are hurt*. I must so often try to understand *you*; will you now see if you can understand and explain *me?*

Ben: You said you wanted to prepare me for the future. You mean when I get home I mustn't expect too easy success.

Director: Not exactly—rather, you must know how to take failure, which is part of success. Real life is not a success story. This is a crucial day for you because last night you were not able to recognize your real success—instead you longed for praise, attention, even flattery. Unless you learn the distinction two things are likely to happen. Either cheap flattery will be acceptable to you, no matter where it comes from, and you will amount to nothing; or, the first disappointment will make you lose confidence and you will not even try again. You must decide whether you want to write because you must—that is, you are going to write because you have something to say and you enjoy saying it, regardless of the labor it costs, and without expectation of praise, and despite adverse criticism and—when you go home will you do everything to be self-supporting? Will you be satisfied with writing in spare time for what it means to you? In other words—have I helped you merely to make your place at home more difficult? Is your security in your talent going to give you an added weapon to excuse laziness and superiority in relation to your family? Are you going to sit around and wait for horns to blow?

Ben: Do *you* think I can write?

Director: You're not getting soft words from me at this moment. My responsibility is too great. I must think ahead for the days and years you will not have me to sustain you. It is very important that my words reach you so deeply that they cannot easily be washed away by newer influences which I fear will tempt you. If I wanted to softsoap you, I could be very *nice* to the "bad boy" Ben. . . . That is just what I am trying to make you see, the real reason why I did not let them make a fuss over you. . . . What do even the adults of last night's audience know of bad writing or good writing? Would they have clapped for your ability as an artist, or for the "miracle" of "a bad boy" who accomplished something they had not expected from him? Understand me, it isn't a bad thing for them to do even that. But it would have given you the wrong slant on things because outside praise is earned sparingly after much waiting and hard work.

Ben: Gee! You're right. I have experienced it already on my home visits. The way the girls hang on my words, and the fellows, too. It thrills me, but I realize afterwards that if they didn't know that I had been in trouble they would be more critical.

Director: Is that the only reaction you have?

Ben: I get bored with them after a while. The thrill wears off and I realize they haven't much to say. . . . I'd like to meet people who have ideas and can argue about them.

Director: Such people wouldn't praise you; they'd find flaws in your conversation; you'd have to be really good.

Ben: I know, but I'd respect them, and I'd feel thrilled because they bother to argue with me.

Director: Which group would recognize your worth more—the group that flatters or the group that accepts you as you prove yourself? Have you ever read the lives of writers, of playwrights?

Ben: Didn't I tell you what has been happening to me? Every time I go into the city, especially after a serious talk with you, I find myself going to the library. And I surprise myself because I read plays, and then I become interested in the author and I read up on his life.

Director: Are they success stories?

Ben: Except for Odets they seem to struggle for years before—

Director: And yet, you still identify yourself with Odets!

Ben: Oh well, that's because he was an East Side boy. I could be like him.

Director: Isn't it better to remember about the others? They're just as good company. They're there to show you the *truth* about life.

Ben: I'm more sensible about it now. Anyway, what I read is exactly what you told us in class—that mostly those writers who succeed all at once never amount to much later on. Well—like myself, they write mostly about themselves from their background. Like myself—for instance—I've been writing about things and people, but it's easier to write about my own feelings, even if I don't know at first that I'm writing about myself. It's harder when you have to write about others—you have to study them more, think it out, understand and live more. I know now, that in my play, I really didn't *write* the monologue—it just came out of me because even though it was the Mannequin talking, the Mannequin was myself, saying things about *me.* But take the scene between the husband and wife—I had to wait until rehearsals to see how stiff and unnatural my lines were. At first, I didn't believe you. But now I know the difference between writing that just comes out and creative writing. That takes time and patience.

Director: Then your play, last night, was no test of real creative ability?

Ben: I guess it went over because of the big scene, the monologue. So, maybe the rest of it, too, was noticeable.

Director: But a play reader and a theater critic would have come down very hard on you. . . . Not that they are always right.

Ben: I see your point. They may be wrong, but even then, I must know how to take it. . . . It must be terrible what writers have to take.

Director: The weak fall out . . .

Ben: Gee! You make it so clear, I feel *prepared* now for disappointments. I think I understand you better, too. You're more interested in *me* than in what I am doing.

Director: To prepare you for the time when no one will be interested in *you* but only *in what you are doing*. Then we understand each other. . . . What are you planning to do when you leave Hawthorne?

Ben: Look for a job.

Director: Then I haven't failed.

Ben: You taught me to think of things realistically. I have to support myself, first of all. I'm a man—I'm going on seventeen.

Director: The second thing?

Ben: I've learned a word from you—"click." I'm going to observe life, try to understand people, see what makes them "click," and continue to write.

Director: Easy writing?

Ben: (Smiling) No—you needn't worry—honest writing. . . . Gee! I feel so much better. You really must care about me or you wouldn't take so much trouble. Don't worry, you hit me hard last night, maybe now nothing will hit me so hard again. . . . I feel like a fool, like a baby who was crying for a lollypop.

Director: Don't feel that way too much. Let me tell you a secret. Directors also feel "let down." . . . There is always a letdown after a great labor, and there is always an emotional need for a special show of appreciation. But—most of the time you don't get what you need and—well, you learn to take it; this is the difference between maturity and childishness.

Ben: (Looks up suddenly, his eyes alight.) You honor me. You've taken me into your company.

Director: Into the company of all those who do a good job for *its own sake*. (Silence)

Ben: Thank you . . . (Hesitates) There's something I haven't had the courage to admit, but now I feel I owe it to you. . . .I just want to say, I'm *glad* I came to Hawthorne.

(Ben leaves before he has finished the whole word Hawthorne. It was difficult to make the admission—it was giving up his only weapon, the holding out against the adult world. But outside the door of the workshop, down the whole length of the assembly hall, Ben is heard whistling a cheery tune.)

Later in the day, the psychiatrist informed me that Ben had been in to see him. He came happily into his office to say that the disappointment of last night was forgotten, that he had straightened the whole thing out with me. This does not mean that Ben actually forgot about it. His behavior immediately afterward and continuing for several weeks showed evidence of alienation.

Ben Writes About Himself

I came to Hawthorne late in February two long years ago. The first few months, in the main, were spent in familiarzing myself with the school. Not that I wanted to so much, but the process is automatic and natural.

It wasn't long before I paused and took perspective of the

various activities offered to me. It was true that I liked to write. I made no secret of it, and it was soon that I acquired a reputation. I had heard of the Group Theatre, even saw one of their plays—a Channukah Festival I believe, which didn't particularly impress me, due more to an indifference on my part than to incompetence on theirs.

My entering the Group Theatre was a gradual process. Eventually, it is true, I would have taken the step, but certainly not as soon as I had if the psychiatrist hadn't spoken to me.

"Ben," he said, "you want and need a person who can tell you that your first scene is swell, keep up the good work, and in the same breath tell you that the second is rotten and needs to be thrown out! That person is Miss Celia Avramo!"

Fortunately the psychiatrist's suggestions had struck a responsive chord. A chord within me that recognized maturity and when one has attained it. Taking criticism of the sort he said Miss Avramo could give would be that, but now, as I look back, I think he was wrong when he said that I was beyond the stage of the uncriticizable. What he should have said was that I would take, feel hurt about it, yet profit by it just the same.

One afternoon I met Miss Avramo. She was petite, pretty, and certainly looked intelligent. I paraphrased my psychiatrist's talk to her. It sounded very grown-up-ish and I felt pleased. So did she, I think. Anyway I was in the Group Theatre.

I had entered the Drama Group with the thought only to write plays. This was something different to me. Everything I had written in the past had been some strange essayical hodgepodge which was really amateurish, believe me.

The more I think about how the Group Theatre struck me as a newcomer, the more convinced I become that it wasn't then a question of how the Group Theatre affected me, but how I affected the Group. An underlying wave of show-offedness greeted me. They all wanted to show me how good they were. I think then that I lacked the insight to recognize this, but it was probably my new teacher who pointed it out to me, and probably worried herself sick about the bad impression she thought I had received.

The boys treated me with respect. It was a kind of respect towards a thing very much apart from you. You are curious about it, wonder about it, and for the life of you cannot identify yourself with it.

I was to write a play—a Halloween play, it was decided. But what in Heaven's name could I write about? Reading last year's Halloween play—a childish affair—didn't help except to give me a higher standard to emulate.

Together with my teacher, I spent much time in the library glancing through encyclopedias in an attempt to find any ritual that one could base a play on. We met with no success. Still, I had become very much Halloween conscious. So, it was largely by accident that inspiration presented itself disguised as Hawthorne's fantasy, *Feathertop*. This tells the story of a doll being brought to life by smoking a pipe.

The story graciously supplied me with a good first scene but no play. During the summer every moment of my leisure was spent working on the play. I felt very much like a sculptor who creates something with only his tools. I'm sorry if this is old stuff to you, this creating business. I hadn't meant to be trite, but the feeling is a glorious one no matter how many times one has recaptured it.

The typing of the manuscripts was left to me, but this, too, was done with lots of enthusiasm, and understandably so, too. It was my play. Mind you, not the Group's to work with, now. It was mine.

Group work not only was the war cry of our director but also of every social worker on the campus. I once made an attempt to put it into practice. I remember I swept the floor of the workshop. My social worker came in and watched me. I realized that I had made a good impression.

I believe that realizing it was wrong. Wrong is not the word I want, for this question does not hinge on moral values. These acts have to spring from a deeper source to be genuine. The very fact that I was aware of it at the time proved that once again I had been only conscious of myself and the impression that I alone would create.

Miss Avramo had already told me I was to act in the play. An interesting sidelight happened one afternoon while casting. I read the play to the class. I learned later that unconsciously I had been acting the Mannequin while just reading the others. Later I was given the Mannequin's role to act. Who can argue with me when I say this is an infallible way to cast?

You must remember that you are not dealing with professional actors but with boys and girls—some of whom had talent and some who hadn't. Scene designing and prop construction, I may add, was not imported but done entirely by the boys and girls. This is s slap on the back of the Group Theatre, but I had not intended it as such. I am simply stating a fact.

Just before the eve of the play, I left for a two-day visit in New York. I believe this had much to do toward continuing my progress. Now I would put theories into practice and see how well they worked. I do not believe I thought this at the time for I was too wrapped up with the pleasure of seeing New York again.

Doing at Hawthorne what was to me important work made me feel superior, heads and shoulders over all of my friends in intellectuality. No, I don't mean it had approached superciliousness. It was a quiet reserved air in the midst of joviality.

Here was something curious. I didn't dream dreams of becoming so much a successful playwright as a "young author who shows promise." This phrase appealed to me. Probably then I could have explained it, but now time has dimmed my memory. Although I dreamt things not so much in relation with theater work, I talked about it enthusiastically to my friends and parents. I even got them to listen to the play. You dream dreams; they're not for conversation.

From the moment I stepped from the locked closet (my entrance) to the moment when I threw the key into the Styx and the doll of sticks and cloth crumpled up and died, I realized I had done well. . . . Congratulations were showered on me by almost everyone. Most important of all, the shiny happy glint in my director's eyes when we shook hands and I said hoarsely, or words to that effect, "We go places from here!" and her eyes nodded acquiesence. I was too happy to go to sleep and lay awake all through the night tossing, very . . . very happy.

How did success effect me? Was anything digested from the experience? How would I react to everything? All these questions were foremost in my mind, and for a while I was conscious of everything I said or did—not wanting anyone to feel that success had affected me for the worse. And I believe I acted so.

Besides acquiring a degree of poise, I realized probably, half-willingly, that others besides myself were involved in any venture. And here I learned cooperation. There were many other things but which I don't mention because they manifested themselves later on.

Still languishing over the success I made, my momentum increased and it wasn't long before I rushed into the work of a second play.

Miss Avramo had said to me, "Your last play was a fantasy, but the real test of an author is to write a play about real life. How well can you write a realistic play?"

This was a challenge, although not intended as such, and had much to do with the selection of my material. As a matter of fact everything I did was in a way an effort to please her. Some of the things I said or did, did not win her admiration and purposely so. I wanted to show her how versatile I was; write, act, wash dishes, tell dirty jokes with the best of them, and be a regular guy with the regular guys.

I owe a great deal to Miss Avramo for the writing of *Dark Light;* the realistic play, and also a great deal for what culture I now possess.

Once or twice a week she would devote an hour or so in discussing what I had written, talk about everything in general and especially the theater. She taught me how to look beneath the surface and not to be content with superficialities. After each talk I was filled with such zest and with a will to really write great things. True, a lot of the things went over my head, for I think my teacher overestimated me, and not to discourage it, I was flattered.

Strange to say, my dishwashing in the kitchen tied up a great deal with my work in the drama group. It's true that inspiration presented itself many times while working, often resulting in the shattering of a dish (much to the steward's displeasure); There was something else, however.

Even to the day I left the theater and with it the school, I left the impression that working with my hands would be to lower myself. For this I have none to blame but myself. I certainly gave evidences of it there. But this I believed was caused by my director in her never-ending search for behavior patterns unsocial in any way; she leaped upon my shying away from tools as unmistakable evidences of it. I encouraged it because I thought (foolishly, of course!) that it gave me prestige and dismissed it, never bothering to explain it. But now I will. I have never been handy with tools and dislike anything I can't do well. I think I was trying to achieve some sort of a balance which would take in the entire school, and so I did: Group Theatre, newspaper work, and kitchen work. Miss Avramo, on the other hand, was thinking from a Group Theatre basis, and so the conflict. . . . .

Parole is looked forward to by almost every boy from the day he enters to the day he leaves. Social workers are constantly confronted with the question, "When do I get out?"

I, too, asked this of my social worker and psychiatrist the first few months of my stay. Then as I gradually swung into the curriculum of the school, these discussions stopped and current topics took their place. Quite suddenly for myself were they resumed when the psychiatrist asked me, "Ben, when do you think you should leave?"

I was in a dilemma. I had wanted to go home so much. But I was in a play and I was writing and. . . . "Oh in about two or three months," I said as casually as I could.

Call this loyalty for the Group. It's very probable that I felt that way, then. It probably was a little selfishness, too; with the play, writing, criticism, I was taking in too much to throw it overboard like this.

Do you realize what this means? Four months back all the demons in hell, to quote myself, couldn't have stopped my leaving if I had the chance. Something tremendously important to myself must have happened in those four months (September to December) to change me. I will try to explain some of it later on.

My first serious difficulties with the Group were to begin. A Purim play had been written. It was the product of another boy in the Group. Immediately, I was told that I was to have a part.

I knew I was going home soon. I was ready to leave. *Dark Light* had been completed or almost so; I had already left the school newspaper, and I looked upon this Purim play as far as it concerned me as extraneous, as an intruder into my plans.

There was trouble from the start. I took no interest in the play and did nothing to help. Group pressure was brought to bear on me and I resented it. It made me not want to do anything more and more.

Then I acted like a child. I merely went through the motions in rehearsals, did not pay attention to lines, situation piled on another. Finally the entire artificial structure collapsed. I'm unable to remember how this was brought about except that the psychiatrist as usual had everything to do with it. Incidentally, he was one of the greatest helps to me at Hawthorne. Together we worked out my problems, giving me an understanding of them which would have have been impossible to attain otherwise.

Miss Avramo really had two jobs. She had to help boys with their problems, and she also had to produce plays which had to be of some worth. It was seldom the two didn't go hand in hand. When a boy's stay in the Group Theatre lengthened, the quality of the plays would improve.

Things in the Group Theatre went quite smoothly up to the very end. And with the play finished, the end was not long in coming.

One brisk morning, about a week after the Purim play, I finally left with unpretentious farewells to all of my friends at Hawthorne to enter a much different, much more difficult existence in New York.

New York! Here my growth is slow and often spasmodic. Growth here is a hit-and-miss method. Sometimes I hit and learn; sometimes I miss and learn more. But always the constant growth, more, I think for those who seek it. It is not the revolutionary change that took place in fourteen months at the school. Perhaps, the reason is that Hawthorne, to me, was that ideal environment where everything was, in a way, conductive to growth. A vast outlet of expression was mine, with teachers to watch, admire, and to learn from. It's like taking a concentrated dose of a drug and living through a dream where an individual's ambitions, desires, are crystallized and brought itno being for the community's use or for his own in a catharsis, a purifying of himself.

Then New York awe-inspiring, big, impersonal. What a tremendous difference.

Applying the culture and ideals which were brought out at the school to a practical world is a difficult task. Sometimes it seems easier not to have any. Then we would suffer no qualms over any muffed opportunity. Ours would be a very "black bliss" indeed! But I cannot do that. I have a drive for education. I want to know things and do things with my knowledge. I must run the gauntlet.

A great deal of the gains I received from the Group Theatre have become so much a part of my complete makeup that I find it impossible to isolate it from the rest. But they're present, a very tangible something which helps evaluate other people, to chart a course for oneself, a degree of poise, an ability to discard nonessentials, and a host of other things which make themselves felt on weekends because it is only then that I have the sufficient leisure to pause and to think about myself and others, to ponder regretfully over one's sins and virtues—to grow consciously. Then the maddening weekdays. Always hurry, hurry, hurry! No time to think about doing, but always do. The maddening rush, the swift tempo. Always the saving of time. How can I use the things the Group Theatre and the school gave me here? Tell me, and I'll be much obliged.

I remember how I felt when I first came into New York. Like a little microbe in a sea of bacteria. Faces cold and inscrutable. Each reflecting a life that I hadn't lived, backgrounds that were not mine. So utterly lost and alone! Then gradually the familiarization. I discovered that when reached these people were human like myself. Only they shielded themselves with an almost inpenetrable air of sophistication. Now that I thought I understood it, I felt more at ease. The struggle for a job. Working for almost nothing. Empty pocekts but too many dreams. . . the city gives you one swift kick in the pants and you're minus all of you're fancy ideas. . . . Either you have too much time being out of a job or none at all working. I look back at the school, now. I no longer see the trees as I did then, but a solid forest, always there, constantly growing, changing with the years, and always helping.

A Talented Boy

Ben was introduced to the Group Theatre actually by his caseworker, almost immediately on his entering the school. This means that in the fourteen months at Hawthorne, the boy was mostly influenced by the theater environment. It was his major interest, and he later told the psychiatrist, it had been the richest experience in his life! He was otherwise occupied with his high school studies and, in the class in journalism, he was one of the editors of the school paper. Since all the boys have a work detail, Ben's was that of dishwasher in the kitchen.

Except for truancy he was not a delinquent in the usual sense and among strangers was liked and considered a nice boy. In fact this was his misfortune, that opinion of him inside and outside his home was so contradictory that he was able to rationalize his rebellion against his family as altogether warranted. Another misfortune was the too mature impression he made for a lad of fifteen and a half. He was tall, of quiet mien, well spoken, and intellectually developed far above his years. The consequence was that adults expected grown-up behavior from him and blamed him unduly for emotional reactions of a boy of his age. On the other hand, on the social scene where it was easy to live up to expectations, Ben enjoyed approval unusual to youths of his age. The praise and the blame weighed perpetually against each other and Ben developed a boundless hunger for flattery—so that the bottom of his world dropped out when words of good opinion were not fed him. It can be seen how this developed from the urgent need for security and affection he was not getting at home, or thought he was not getting; also how his dependence upon approval from strangers aggravated the existent home situation and provided him with excuses for negative behavior. It was hard to believe that this shy, obliging, wide-awake, serious boy—as he appeared even to me—could be considered by his own kin lazy, impertinent, demanding, and a devil for harshness and lack of feeling.

What were the factors which had contributed to make this pattern? There had been a childhood sickeness from which Ben had come out with a minor eye problem and suffering from an imaginary rejection. There was the mixture of poverty, religion, and rebellion in the person of an older brother who flaunted his irreligion in the face of pained parents. There was a very sick sister. There was the consequent neglect of Ben, his identification with the sister and rivalry with the brother. And of course there was Ben himself—his childish emotions in conflict with his maturer intelligence, his intelligence seeking expression through writing, his resulting detachment labeled by the family as indifference to their problems and bringing down upon him resentment, the effect of which substantiated Ben's sense of rejection. The writing became the battleground for family conflict, the excuse for truancy and laziness, the rationalization for drastic demands on the mother expressed in temper tantrums and wilfullness, the pattern of isolated superiority which prevented contacts with peers and made him accessible to praise by older people not of the family.

Mentally Ben was precocious. From this can be explained, at least in part, his preference for staying away from school to write, and to read books beyond the curriculum of his classes. Also, we have a partial explanation for his exclusiveness; most of the boys of his age had not his intellectual interests. To top this, average boys consider bookish boys "highbrows" and "sissies." Unfortunately, too, Ben called forth this reaction without any intention to be snobbish. His walk was smooth, too graceful for a boy; he had not the ready wit and slaphappy vulgar phraseology of the boys of the street; his vocabulary was too good, his sentence structure too literary.

This was the boy who in the first conversation with me stated his ambition, to be another Odets! Indeed this was the richest conversation I ever had on a first meeting with any boy. Ben revealed a complex set of contradictory traits; he was shy yet outspoken; repressed yet warmly outgoing; he emanated intellectual assurance but questioned his knowledge and his power; he was diffident and withal demanding. Ben was versed in current events and in several of the new writers. He had heard of the Group Theatre and was going to get all he could get from his enforced stay at Hawthorne.

He practically demanded—echo of parental experience—to be taught how to write plays. He showed a barely concealed annoyance when told he would be expected to participate in the Group activity in order to do so. He refused to commit himself to the promise of being helpful in the Group in exchange for what he was going to get from it. He attempted to force an agreement that he would not be asked to act. Ben knew what he wanted, and that was to write! But he wasn't hard, really. It was the habit of making demands. His moist eyes were evidence of a deep capacity to feel. He expressed wonderment that opportunity should be here for him in the least expected place—a correctional school! The opportunity to amount to something, here in the place he had looked upon as a confinement and a punishment, so touched him that in this first talk his rebellious spirit yielded to gratitude. "Now I'm glad I was sent up here. They laughed at me because I wanted to write. Now I have found someone who understands."

It became apparent to me that Ben would have to be given individualized attention. Whether he was capable or not, the stress on writing had to be the focal point around which to work his adjustment. His hope "I have someone who understands" was too delicate a thing to ignore. But the boy could not be permitted to accept himself as privileged or the result would merely be an unadjusted writer. How this was handled the reader already knows.

I did not ask Ben to write a play for Halloween because we

Scene from staff play. The Valiant, *A* Group Theater *production. The group made the scenery, lighted the stage, acted as ushers. This was an act of reciprocation from the students, and actually a step upward towards adulthood.*

needed one. The subject was deliberately chosen to meet a problem in Ben. To understand this, we must look into that older problem of his, his inability to be a boy among boys. In the city he had avoided the rougher youths of the street; at Hawthorne, he had no choice but to mix with them. By virtue of their number this type symbolized the norm to Ben and accentuated his "not belonging" till he found a way through his writing to play up to them.

So on the school paper his style was a self-conscious sophistication, a conglomorate aping of the playboy style of several known gossip columnists. This was in his editorials. But in his attempts at short-story writing, Ben wrote in brutal realism; the dialogue was unvarnished, of the street. It was not accidental that James T. Farrell was the author he carried around with him, and read aloud to groups of boys who listened avidly. The appeal was obviously twofold. Ben had an honest curiosity about human beings, about what made them tick, and essentially he was aware of his own ticking—Farrell was writing about a background similar to his own! But chiefly Farrell was the compensatory bridge between himself and the boys who accentuated his difference. Farrel was the acclaimed writer whose pages were luscious with slang, vulgarity, the smells, talk, and actions of back alleys and whispered places! Farrel was the artist who couldn't be called a sissy! So Ben imitated him, wrote like him for the boys, but didn't write like himself. Ben got the acclaim he wanted. He said at this time, "I like it—I feel like a wild man." But he wasn't one; he was living in conflict. I had to find a way to build his faith in what he was, in what he did, in what he wanted to be.

How could Ben be helped to be his creative self? By my show of confidence in his ability through practical assistance. By social approval from a finished work actually produced. By continued writing, and his getting more and more approval, not on a false and borrowed style, but on his own! . . . How could he be led away from brutal realism in its copied form? Not by a realistic subject, but one in which poetry or fantasy would stimulate imagination and create the need for a different content and mood of expression. Hence the Holloween subject which required the departure from old habits of feeling and thinking and demanded a new orientation.

How could Ben be freed from the sick need for praise? By growth through his accepted artistic self. By the balance of severe criticism and earned praise which the art process imposes on the artist, and through which he becomes aware of the distinction between the true and the false. Professional criticism from a sympathetic adult—intrinsically the highest form of approval—would be a first and acceptable discipline for enjoying life without the gluttonous bidding for cheaply earned praise. The results in good achievement, leading simultaneously to self-confidence and self-criticism, would call forth pride and the critical attitude fastidious about receiving falsely won applause.

How could Ben be helped to be at ease with peers on his own terms as an individual person? The experience he was put through has been described in previous pages. Here it is interesting to note how Ben skims over, in his own paper, the rapprochement between him and the boys through his act of sweeping; how he explains the difficulty in the Group over his working with his hands as my attitude in being concerned only with the Group Theatre in contrast to *his* attitude—"I wanted to achieve a balance which would take in the entire school: Group Theatre, newspaper work, and kitchen work"—though in a previous page he says, "Some of the things I did and said did not win her admiration and purposely so. I wanted to show her how versatile I was. . . ." But note the follow-up, "Strange to say my dishwashing in the kitchen tied up a great deal with my work in the drama group. . . . I left the impression that to work with my hands would be to lower myself. . . . I have never been handy with tools and dislike anything I can't do well. . . . (After his play production) "I realized (etc.) others besides myself were involved in the venture. And here I learned coopeartion" . . . (and two and half pages before this) "The typing of the manuscips was left to me (etc.) it was my play not the Group's to work with now." . . . This boy's concealment of his emotional reactions to high peaks in his experience is amazing. He does not mention that he actually worked on his scenery; that he became aware of "the power in hands" after having finished the typing of his script; that his previous typing of the group's play brought him the first comrade warmth from peers; that every bit of labor he attempted attached him to peers with joy, laughter, and increased regard for himself as a writer; nor that he had friendships eventually in the Group and correspondence later with those who left before him.

How could he be helped to a realistic attitude toward life? He would have to go back to the same home and background where all the troubles began; he would have to work for a living! By placing more and more weight on his leadership activity in the Group as separate from his preoccupation with writing. By emphasis on the truth about success stories of writers. By his return to realistic writing, motivated toward the subject of his background and people, his home and his family, for the arriving at objective understanding of the home situation—the potential for this existing in the creative process which requires the sifting of material and the critical study of the development of character and situation.

Ben's stay in the Group Theatre may be divided into two periods, before and after the *Mannequin's Revolt.* Both began with Ben's all-out effort to be a "wild man," or to finish his statement about being versatile, " . . . tell dirty jokes with the best of them and be a regular guy with the regular guys." Both ended with the writing of a play, with development, satisfaction, and progress in adjustment. But the reasons for the beginning symptoms of both periods were different. In the first Ben was reacting to a conditioning in himself. In the second he was regressing on the rebound to a combination of conditionings planned for him: one, the pain I gave him on the night of his play; and two, the pain caused him by the decision made between the psychiatrist and other adults related to Ben through their work on teaching jobs. But let us follow Ben's history in natural order.

What happened through the writing of his first play? Contrary to my handling of less intelligent boys, I worked with Ben on the conscious level. Because discussion of play material and criticism for help in the creative process had the implication of intellectual parity between student and teacher, my directness, aimed at creative awareness, had the functional justification of probing for personal awareness. The one is not possible without the other; Ben was told what his imitation of Farrell represented in terms of his own personality and why he was being asked to write on a theme unrelated to life. However, in the search for material—the reading of Hawthorne's story, the cross-research in the encyclopedia of related words discovered in the paragraph on Halloween—Ben gleaned a greater reality—that of the human spirit as expressed in religious ritual, folk tale, and folk festival. At last the "silly stuff" of Halloween kindled his imagination; the given date, Octobert 31, for the production gave a realistic purpose to creative concentration, acted as a disciplining goad in the ups and downs of fluctuating mood and the general difficulties pertaining to writing. There was no time for seeking false satisfactions and actually no desire. From here on Ben's school paper items showed the influence, in style and in mood, of the honest job he was doing with the play and the headway he was making in relationship with peers. His editorials were sincere, simple, and direct.

He no longer attempted the Farrell-type short stories.

In the Group he was sharing his creative process. He read his scenes, listened to suggestions, elaborated his plot, passed on to the others his learnings in dramaturgy. He became more and more involved with the group of boys. In epitome the interchange could be symbolized by "How's your scene coming, Ben?" "Okay," or "Ozzie is writing me instead of the other way around; I better do a good job with him or he won't be worth that Gate to Hades you're making—it's beautiful!" Actually Ben was carrying sets between the workshop and the stage—tenderly, they were for his play—and using hammer and paste and paint awkwardly but actually. More than once he said with a gentle awe, "The boys are giving life to my play." He became aware of the creative process of the work jobs as fundamentally the same as that to which he was subjected; the inspiration and the slips between the beginning of work and the satisfactory result, the emotional giving, the sweating, the anguish over errors, and the final joy—these were a common denominator joining him with the boys.

And he had fun and frolic with them; the boys did enough droll, crazy, or foolish things for laughter without the strained seeking for it from dirty jokes or secretive nonsense. Physically Ben presented a more boyish appearance; as his spirit naturalized he looked younger; his walk took on a masculine stance not only because he moved more frequently with the others with the swift engrossment demanded by the manual labors but because I was putting him through the exercises of leaping, running, walking to fit the part of Ozzie in the big scene in which he determines, "I am a Man." Contrary to his belief, Ben was not given the role in the play because he read it well; he was asked to read as a trick for getting him to act. After his commitment to the part I told him privately of the use I was making of rehearsals to help him lose the characteristics which marked him off from other boys. As a consequence his voice gained power and assurance, his limbs lost their too-effeminate grace. The totality of new assets and deep satisfactions simultaneously straightened Ben's sense of individuality and gave him a secure place among peers.

At the end of six months no happier boy walked on the campus. Between the psychiatrist and the Group Theatre he was working out a satisfactory adjustment; though ups and downs existed due to new conflicts arising from emotional and intellectual experience. This is revealed in the interview; what was clear and acceptable to his mind was not so to his emotions. Another five months had to pass before the emotions caught up parallel with the writing of his second play. But immediately after the production of the *Mannequin's Revolt* Ben had a regression. The pain I caused him by not having him applauded as author coincided with a drastic measure against Ben taken outside of the Group Theatre of which I was not made aware until several days later.

With certain teachers and the adults in the kitchen where he was dishwasher Ben had been having difficulty. These adults had been acting out a dual and confusing role. In them merged the habitual reaction of parents and strangers to Ben's personality. They treated him like an equal and expected a return in mature performance. On the rebound to his poor work in the kitchen—they forgot that he had no work skills—or his childish behavior in the classroom—they ignored his youthful age—they came down on him harder than on any other child. In the city Ben ran from the rejecting adult to the accepting one. Here he had no such recourse; tossed between praise and blame by the same adults he countered, in rhythmic turns, with deference and disobedience, loyalty and abuse, warmth and demoniac unreachability. And his relationship with peers, too, in the kitchen and in the classroom differed from that in the theater environment. Heady from the parity he enjoyed with grown-ups, he kept aloof from the other children; in the grip of what he thought unjust treatment he behaved so unreasonably that peers withdrew from him.

However, for about three weeks up to the time of his play Ben's situation outside of the Group was working out well. The adults were uniformly pleased with him. His threater experience was showing its influence; Ben was making efforts at his work; he was taking criticism more genially and cooperating better with the boys around the dishwashing machine. The psychiatrist believed that now was the time to effect a major goal with Ben. He advised the grown-ups to put a distance between the boy and themselves or to pal with him less in order to establish his position in equality with peers. He thought that the abrupt loss of artificial prestige would prompt Ben to more intrinsic relationship with his fellows; that this could be done now because Ben had in the scale to balance pain the salve to his ego from his theater prestige and the experienced satisfactions from camaraderie with the boys in the Group.

But Ben's reaction to the new situation was more violent than anticipated, and the violence was in my direction. The seeming rejection from a number of adults coming immediately after my vanguard action of letting him down added up as an organized adult rebuff of which I was the leader. At the height of his success this made us out to be ungrateful, inconsistent, cruel; and myself more than the rest since I was his ideal person, the one he was closest to and the only one actually guilty of an overt negative act. Moreover, Ben's basic security with me freed him to make me the brunt of the torrential flood of his discontent—few "tickets" for bad behavior were given out in the Group; he was sure of my continued ministering, notwithstanding how he behaved; he knew I would care about his actions so flagrantly undoing my work with him and effecting the spiritual atmosphere in the Group. Ben reacted with more extremity than the psychiatrist had intended. He turned to peers with a vengeance.

He was back in the old Farrell period, but worse, much worse. Now he was running wild in the Group Theatre. He was deliberately passing dirty jokes, showing off, rejecting my teaching, and instigating disruptive behavior in the laziest and least cooperative elements in the Group. That he did this more in our environment than outside indicated his intended rejection of adults, of me specially. (At this time Ben avoided or broke appointments with the psychiatrist, too.) We lived through several difficult weeks interspersed with apologies, conversations, conscious-stricken attempts to soberize, more mischief and vulgarity, etc. If I ever questioned my analysis of this situation I am now certain from Ben's own skimmed-over mention of his mood of the time in his phrase, "I was still *languishing* over the success I made," though seemingly he is not remembering any of this at all, connecting instead with, "My momentum increased, and it wasn't long before I rushed into the work of a new play."

It is true that he was already writing *Dark Light* at this time, but not yet with momentum nor concentration. Actually, the play was in outline some two or three weeks before the curtain rang down on his performance as Ozzie. Before this beginning Ben was engrossed with other children in production preparations and in intensive rehearsing. So busy was he, and enraptured with this new experience, that outwardly he forgot about writing until I motivated the second effort. I had said, "You ought to think of another play, Ben. . . . After this is over you'll have a letdown. . . . You'll have an empty feeling unless you're already wrapt up in something else." He replied that he had no subject; he was himself worried about the matter. "Why don't you write about the people close to you? Once you told me that you hated your brother—and other things; but then you were also involved. . . . You are now removed from your conflicts at home. See if you can recall characters and situations. See them from afar and try to think out what made them behave in their special ways, what were the circumstances behind good and bad things at home." "But I can't! I still hate my brother." "As much as before?" "Come to think of it, I'm just repeating myself . . . actually he no longer bothers me. I'm changed. I understand him now." "That should help. . . . Writers do not hate people, only ideas, situations, the forces which make people unhappy or bad . . . for the sake of truth they make an honest, objective study of these things . . . will you try to write this way, re-create the life you know, approach it without bias and with the same human sympathy you wrote about the mother in your first play?"

Another aspect of his regressive period was his avoidance of our private work sessions. Ben was scorning my aid, spending his time in the Group between troublemaking and pretending to write. "I'll show it to you when I'm ready" or "It's coming all right" or silence were some of the answers to my inquiries. But this couldn't last; life was too aimless. He sobered up a bit. I let him alone for about two weeks. At this time I was busy writing the Purim play to which Ben ascribes another boy's authorship, though not without some verity. To interest the children I had asked if someone would volunteer to write a realistic introductory scene for it. "I am writing this in verse. Esther, Mordecai, Haman, etc., will step out of a large book. My idea is that a boy refuses to go to a Purim party, throws aside the story of Esther which his parents gave him as a Purim gift; he is alone in the house, falls asleep, and is thus visited by the characters whom he scorned to read about. It would be nice if someone wrote the family scene."

Thus Ben saw me working intensively with another youth and his subsequent refusal to act in this play had everything to do with this fact—that I was interested in another boy. Holding aloof from me it fitted his mood to translate this as my withdrawal from him. It is interesting how completely he ignores me as author, especially as the role he took was that of Mordecai, a major character posed with Esther, his niece, within the illuminated page of a twelve-foot book which had slowly to open up on the stage—and had nothing to do with the simple scene written by the other boy to open the play. Ben emphasizes the trouble he had and gave, but recalls nothing of his naïve rapture at the wonder of the lighting so much experimented with for the austere effect of his character person. He recalls nothing of the joy he had in the cadenced lines, nor the feeling of conquest in managing the courtly movement required for stepping forth to the stage escorting Esther—for graybeard and uncle though he was it was vicarious romance to a boy not yet at ease with girls. In these omissions lie the conflict and the guilt of that period, for despite the covering himself with mud he would have been unhappy to leave the Group. His recoil from a confusing situation was in the nature of a boomerang; the "wild man" had postured far too much before his peers, had affronted his adult friend; he wanted to get back into place but didn't know how.

Actually the play we were preparing now was *Bread* and was the one which Ben was being recalcitrant about. For his physical needs I had given him the major masculine role. It was in this that he was merely "going through the motions"; but since I had always to plan far ahead I was already working with Karl on the scene for the play to follow. It was in a moment of tension during a rehearsal of *Bread* that Ben flung the challenge which to save face he had to cling to—"I refuse to act in the Purim play." It was now that the psychiatrist worked so much with him; the later troubles at the beginning of this disliked play were the overlapping echoes of the earlier period, mainly of the front which the boy had taken and remained stubborn about.

Ben needed helping out from his morass. One day I said before the others, "I believe we're all interested in Ben's new play. . . . I'll tell you what's happened to Ben, boys—I've seen it happen every time a boy makes unusual headway. He goes through a period when he thinks he doesn't need help; he gets cocky, does crazy things and goes down hill a bit. I'm sure Ben knows this about himself now. In his case he went all the way back because he misunderstood something which I did—or he understood it until something else happened. (Humorously) Authors are funny people; they think they know all about human behavior, but sometimes they add up the wrong sum. The point is—and you boys understand each other well—Ben's gone so far afield he can't come back. Suppose we give him a push in the right direction. Make him write his play! You've been annoyed with him for a month now. Tell it to him to his face; shove him back to where he belongs." The boys knew what to do. They told him what a "dope," "dumb-cluck," and whatnot he was. In the direct lingo of boys this was a vote of confidence, of preference for his real self. Ben now threw himself into his play with "momentum" and "concentration."

He was working out his third major catharsis, cleaning up his whole inner house. Father, mother, sister, brother moved through his scenes—and Ben himself, too. In this play formal training was extended; it served in a threefold way—to substantiate my interest in him, to feed his need and capacity to learn more about his craft, to help especially to work out his emotional pattern of the past by a critical comparison between his subconscious writing and the demands made on a playwright by the logic of character and situation as initiated by himself. There was one scene which we worked over for weeks, over which the psychiatrist and I constantly checked notes. By no logic of dramaturgic movement could Ben, rather the lad who was Ben, shoot his father; but it happened again and again. With every redoing of the scene Ben so manipulated the material that this was the forced culmination.

That in the father character as written by him there was no instigation to this drastic act; that in the rebellious totality of the boy character there was but artificial intimation of a personality capable of shooting his parent; that the scene had no buildup for this violence; that it wasn't honest writing; that I could not be dramatically convinced, etc.—these were the technical arguments I gave to charge his awareness of himself in relation to his artistic expression. Finally one day I said, "Ben, you had better look into yourself. I am convinced that you are wish-thinking." He looked at me, and a slow flush suffused his neck. He *knew* that he was living through his home problems; that as a protagonist in the play he was struggling through his old rebellion with biased memory and with no attempt to study his subject.

Yet from the first he had the title *Dark Light;* the symbol of his general theme which he put into words for his father to say, "Life is like that—hard and much tragedy. And when a little happiness comes we must keep it forever. And the last lines of the play end with:

> Neighbor: Yes, yes . . . tragedy sometimes brings even a little happiness.
> Mother: You hear, Jake? Tragedy brings happiness.
> Father: Yes, I hear. May that God in his heaven look down upon our poor unhappy lives and bring us happiness . . . much happiness!

When analyzed this finale, too, is wish-thinking, but it has dedication in it; this last curtain is the climax of troubles in the family after Moishe has been sent to a reformatory, has run away because of homesickness, and, lost in the shadows of his apartment, overhears in an unguarded conversation the intrinsic suffering and well-meaning quality of his family.

That Ben takes blame on himself for his past is obvious in his re-creation as Moishe, not merely a truant but a monster, a gambling, gun-toting, and hard guy. But what a softy really as Ben reveals himself in the homesickness! In the scene he rushes out from his corner with a cry, "Ma!" and a moment after, "I'm homesick, please let me stay, I'll be good. I'll go to school. Give me another chance." He is not so sure of his father but yields when the latter says, "What do you want me to do? I cannot afford to pay for lawyers and courts." Moishe makes a decision, "I'll give myself up. Don't worry about me, please. You've worried enough." In this short play, in three acts, Ben makes peace with life; and this includes father and brother and the apportionment of responsibility to himself. He blames poverty for everything in such deft touches as the brother's political slant arising from the endless search for a job, the sister's failures, the neighbor's borrowing an onion or overhearing the family's troubles through rat-ridden walls. But the neighbor is the voice of hope! Her son had been bad, too, worse than Moishe; now he is an artist—Ben?—and has a job for fifty dollars a week; through him they are moving out of the rotten place, rising in the world. . . .

In this play there is much tenderness, and as he worked closer to its finish Ben mellowed considerably. He went through the Purim play beautifully and soon after a happy boy, with an upright walk and purpose in his eyes, said good-bye to Hawthorne. At the meeting I had with him a year after parole—when he treated me to coffee—the conversation was not about plays. It was over the difficulty of keeping well fed on his salary. Instead of a lesson in dramaturgy, I showed him how to shop for food to keep his health. Other things spoken about were the progress and affairs of the other boys, and the plan to join together—as the boys from the Group Theatre went home—into a group of friendship to continue the cultural interests they all had in common, and to sustain each other in the difficulties they must meet in the city.

Ben's talent had taken its proper place and Ben faced life with the normal planning and hopes of a normal boy. If one day he is heard from for his writing—as may happen because undoubtedly he is talented—it will be because his theater experience had removed the bee in his bonnet about his unusualness, and had prepared him instead for the whole of his life's struggle.

Conclusion

A formal conclusion will add nothing to this work if it has not already summed up the evidence that delinquent and neurotic children have been and can be helped by the use of theater subservient to specific techniques oriented to the purpose of helping them. In showing results I have checked myself carefully against wish-thinking or mere interpretation. My own need to *know* has cautioned me; also a projected vision of my young friends one day reading about themselves prompted, in looking backwards self-consciously detached and perhaps needfully forgetful, to seek flaws in truth, expostulating, "But this was not so." As much as possible for absent or unknowing collaborators they, too, have written this book. Throughout, their statements of mood and welfare, oral or written, pre- or postadjustment, factual or subjective, as consciously or subconsciously revealed have presented case material from its source and filled in the widening hiatus made by distance and time. Thus my growing friends will recall truth by what they have themselves contributed to it. As to the reader, especially that one mad enough and blessed with the necessary qualifications to attempt the difficult but rewarding job of theater as therapy, the authentic voices of the children, more than mine, declaring their aware and vitalized relation to the human world must substantiate the worthwhileness of such labor in their behalf. Now in these end pages I must tie up a few threads and speak of a number of things outside the major theme but pertinent to it.

Almost I was left in the position of closing with my task uncompleted and with that annoying superego which bothers one picking a quarrel. Ben's history had been left dangling in air, I had no answers to many doubts and questions. But Fate has been good to me if a special providence may be thanked for a continuous exact timing of events with the progression of my writing. For just as a visit, news or letters from Hal and Max, for example, happened periodically in the nick of my creative need for substantiating material to connect the tenuous past with the recurrently unpinned-down present, so a week following the last words written on Ben he appeared on the scene, dramaturgically timed like a *deus ex machina;* knocking at my door after a silence and absence of six years. The following statements stand out from this visit: "I'm flattered that you were wondering about me, but I didn't want to have a teacher-pupil relationship. . . .Why was the Group Theatre cut out? It was the only wonderful thing here—it's a tragedy! . . . . I'm planning a novel about Hawthorne—what's wrong with it is that it adjusts us and then sends us back to our old environment. . . . A year after I left Hawthorne I moved away from my house—my older brother has still not changed; he's as delinquent as I was once; my younger brother is a good kid. . . . The war hasn't taught me anything—there's chaos all around—but the hopeful thing is that I will be able to study for a profession; I don't believe the social workers did much for me, but I'm going to become a social worker. I'd rather teach but my subject would be English, and the way values are changing I might never get a chance to teach. No. as a one-time boy I haven't too much faith in social work techniques, but maybe for that reason I would make a better one—because *I am* interested in people. . . . My wife and I are very much in love with each other, and we have a nice little girl two and a half years old. . . . My present job is that of a receptionist, very uninteresting work, but it gives me time to write."

Ben was smiling, shy, adult in his knowledge and viewpoint of world events, well read, and reported that he got along well with his in-laws with whom he was living, by eschewing controversial topics or listening more than arguing. Having conversed with many returned soldiers I would say that his bitterness is mild compared with the attitude of others, one or two of whom had been Ben's teachers. "I discern a bitterness in you, Ben; do you feel it so keenly or is it an impassioned quality of speech?" "I'm really not too bitter, but I'm not satisfied. I must know what to do about my future, and we must all know what to make of the world situation." Politically Ben has not gone to the extreme Left. He has been probing with the help of Koestler, Silone, and other writers the position a man must take toward the unresolved problems of the world.

Without this visit and a letter which followed, because in him the facets of personality are so markedly discernable, I would not have been able to corroborate definitely a growing knowledge gleaned through years of meetings and correspondence with many young people who had shared the theater experience. All have remained as like themselves as I knew them originally; that is, nice human beings though they have become, the individual ego expression or basic character structure remained unchanged.

I would like it better if Ben had not kept silent for six years waiting for time to eradicate the teacher-pupil basis of our relationship unbearable to his ego. It is somewhat disconcerting now to receive his letter addressed to me by my given name. It is disconcerting because of my own ego, which cannot receive a gesture wrenched out of place; and this makes me anxious all the more about the faux pas this young man will still be making and suffering for in an unlenient world. But a rereading of his paper in this chapter shows clearly the early signals of this coloring in Ben's immutable ego quality—that inerasable directive of his personality nurtured, I believe, by the traumatic struggle with a family finding fault with traits, and behavior elsewhere applauded. The ego effect from the inflating acclaim by strangers for an authentic maturity of intellect could hardly be eradicated by subsequent learnings of how to be a boy among boys; since in this attribute definitely Ben was always above being an average boy, as now in maturity by the fact of his probing mind sensitive to life he is beyond being an average man. But he is not a delinquent man. As I listened to him, and afterwards read his letter, I was aware of a person with an egocentric quirk like a bulwark of defense desperately put up by one toeing the social line as husband, father, and citizen in order to hold tight, despite the struggle of daily existence, to that lonely inner identity which is life itself to people like Ben. . . .

The end of the war did not bring Max to me for a final observation, not even news of him by letter. So unusual was this break in friendly contact that I made inquiries about his fate to several agencies. But a rereading of his letters sums up the impression of a basic character structure unchanged throughout his service, actually its facets sharpened in the apocalyptic flame, tempered consonant with his ardent and volatile nature to a headstrong dedication to the *causa bellum*. On December 7 Max reacted to the world catastrophe by enlisting. The portion of his letter, the last received and quoted on page 198, surpasses in awareness of the war's meaning anything written to me from the various fronts by others who fought out of some vague patriotism or indifferently or rebelliously, having been caught up by the inescapable draft. From furloughs to Calcutta and elsewhere Max wrote feelingly about the poverty, disease, and the degraded status of the "people"; to his mind, rectifying this human degradation was to be a universal result, justifying the savagery and sufferings of the war.

How had Max-Don Quixote fared? He could have been a casualty—or? I remembered that in his behalf I, too, had been half-mad, fighting the windmill of clinical prognosis—eventually he would crack up, they had said. . . . Then from Dayton, Ohio, in 1949 an unexpected air-letter arrived! And in 1951, ten years after his having left the school, he wrote:

> ". . . Hello—surely you must have known that unless I were dead you would hear from me some day. . . . Four years of war earned me a few scars, a few medals, a wife whom I offered nothing but love and a pocketful of hope . . . took her to a cold-water flat . . . studied at Columbia, journalism, creative writing, poetry . . . she became pregnant, I had to lose two additional years of hoped-for study. . . . picked up a few dollars with occasional poems of magazine fillers, worked part-time as a waiter . . . not enough to live on. . . . Now three of us were living in a one-room flat. . . . Desperate, I joined my father-in-law in wine-distribution business and two years after Columbia found myself driving a wine truck. . . . No good! Accepted job as trainee-salesman for chain of furniture stores . . . studied hard . . . everything—advertising, interior decorating, salesmanship, appliances, carpetting. . . . I have been lucky—am now top-salaried salesman and also advertising manager. . . . Have a fine family, a car . . . just finished building my new home . . . specially proud of additional room, nursery for my second child arriving soon . . .
>
> . . . I intended this to be a letter of thanks and affection. Thanks for having helped me find confidence in myself and in the future. Thanks for directing my helpless hands and my groping mind towards creative and rewarding channels . . . and thanks for being YOU. . . . My love—Max.

My impression of Hal home from the war is that he was over-wistful. The reader may recall how this youth alienated people by what seemed a mocking glint in his soft brown, almost black eyes. This light in the somber darkness of his withdrawn face, when Hal had contact with adults, sifted through as from behind slits in velvety curtains and mocked the way an impertinent grin does. His look seemed all-knowing, harboring judgment and the clue to his essential expression of being, its soft misty anxiousness or wistfulness, was overlooked. When Hal left the Group Theatre the protective, sardonic expression had long disappeared and he faced the world with naked eyes warm with joy, enthusiasm, or wonderment—or when he was wishful, disappointed, or hurt, with the exposed contracted wistfulness of a small child. On his postwar visit to me I looked into eyes more naked than that, into vulnerable eyes which had seen and learned too much too quickly; but frank ones, nevertheless, harboring painful knowledge but no longer hostile judgment.

In his last letter after a furlough he had written openly with a calm poignancy but without trace of disillusionment, "I am ashamed to say some of our boys do not behave decently to the natives. In a disgusting case a soldier was given the right simply because he had pull with his superior officer. It made me ashamed to be an American. . . .In Havana everything was wide open to us. Strange to say a glass of gin cost more than the price of a woman. . . ." On his visit Hal told of his extra duties assumed in his soldiering, how he was sent to lecture to the boys on a subject in which he was proficient, how he organized and participated in the dramatic entertainments. "They were good if I say so myself. But I never got the rank promised me. I didn't do the extra work for promotion, just the same it hurt to be told by my boss that he rated me high and had put in three recommendations for my promotion. Even he was disappointed, said it was army politics and some got theirs nobody knew why. . . ." About the present and future Hal said: "I have no home; my family still is at odds, there is no place for me there. I want to marry soon—but I want to study, too . . . and yet . . . inside of me is still the love for the theater. You know I have talent. Sometimes I feel that I'd give anything to be an actor—but how can I do all of these things, they conflict so much?!" Three weeks later Hal made his major choice; he got married; he needed so much not to be alone.

When I think of the three boys I am mindful of three distinctly patterned totalities made graphic to me in what is best described as movements of being like streams with differing depths, tempos, and reflecting and fluid qualities. In my mind I salute each in his particularized, conditioned, reactive expressiveness toward life. I see the basic movements of reactive being distinguishing their character makeup thus: Max—emotional motor reaction; Hal—biding interaction; Ben—withdrawing emotional mental action.

Compulsive activity, like deep undercurrents riding upward, move Max and Ben; the one to act immediately on reaction, profound forces of heart and mind bursting through his surface and converging tempestuously upon stimuli; the other to be sucked downward first to muddy depths, the emotions mulling around facts and fancies for a buildup of a tidal wash in tart mood, or, depending upon the stimuli, of a slower tide in sublimated gently-bitter cerebration with the pleasurable anguish of renewing self-identity. But in Hal less turbulent currents have not the force to burst upward or to suck under; quieter midcurrents draw him ducking below, hugging to himself pain and frustration until counter stimuli of goodness or beauty filter through reconverging his powers into a joyous surge of outward action. Or tersely, the three may be differentiated as: Max—volatile ecstatic, i.e., accepting-balancing; Ben—rebellious ecstatic, i.e., accepting-subordinated; Hal—wistful ecstatic, i.e., accepting-predominant.

The point at which I am arriving is that here are three erstwhile delinquent youths, for general purposes representative of all the others, who shared soon after the kindly theater environment the most harrowing exposure to evil circumstance known to modern man—the uprooting, the hardships, and the disorganizing inhumane mood of warfare. Differing individuals as they were and are, they have in common two outstanding attributes: they are accepting in attitude and ecstatic in outlook. To them life is not meaningless nor without hope but in fact challenging beyond self-centeredness; they are, despite painfraught sophistication, citizens of the world. I believe the preparation they had through the theater living and treatment is a good deal responsible for this—that, manipulated by life more than is the normal lot, actually uprooted and anguished twice in one youth time, they still maintain the forward embracing attitude; they feel responsible beyond the horizon of self, they care, idealistically, whether caustically or poignantly about their fellow beings and a better world. . . .

And now if the reader wants to meet these boys as mature men, I am happy to present Harry who stuttered, Max who would "break up," Hal of the rejecting eyes, and Ben who vaguely longed to be a teacher—all four in their individual ways poised, youthful and humanly fulfilled adults.

Harry has the habit of calling me once every two or so years to ask to visit but the visits never materialize. I suspect from the conversational content that his feelings are too intense for an actual effort on his part to come to my home. The last time he said, "I am relatively happy. For *me* I'm doing well. I have a job where I do not have to talk, just do. I am an orderly in a hospital and so I am helping people. It isn't a bad life. I also have a son, as you know. I would not swear that I'm a good father, but I try."

Hal who wanted to be an actor, and made a willing soldier, became an entrepreneur! Hal whose eyes ever challenged the adult, Hal in a flourishing umbrella business! He writes, "Are there Hawthorne boys who need jobs? Will you find out?" He is not patronizing. He is trying to help out.

The years that separate the ages of Ben and Max from my years are not important now after the passing of time. We are tender friends. I smile to think of Max as a pillar of society—on a youthful visit to me after the war he called me *bourgeois* because I held a membership card in the Museum of Modern Art! In a distant city Max owns a house and a business and has two strapping sons, one just graduated from law school and the other writing his master's thesis on sixteenth century theater. Max still fights windmills, and successfully. He is interested in nutrition, is now a specialist in the field and has recently been elected as president of an outstanding organization dedicated to better nutrition for Americans. Max writes tracts, makes speeches, even has a booklet of limericks published on the subject. He hobnobs with notables we read about in the news. Theater is his avocation; he has given the bee to his sons. When a cause can benefit from a theater production there are the three of them! Then I receive the columns about their theater ventures printed in his city's newspaper. In a last letter he ends with," And now doth not thy cup runneth over?"

Yes, my cup runneth over! In Westchester, close by me, Ben owns a six acre estate. This is Ben born to sorrow, Ozzie who wanted to be a man! He has had more than the normal share of blows. He did his soldiering bit, went to college, had a wife and child, prepared himself for teaching. He got a grant to finish his studies in Europe. And then through unique misfortunes there was only Ben! This time he could not blame poverty. But there was Fate. Ben has survived the horror and the aloneness. He is a sadder man than the others, but there was no going down for Ben! He teaches English to children as difficult as he once was. And he remarried. After years of writing what he calls, "Ah, well—that was only homework," he has two-thirds of a novel stacked on his desk.

I wish I had influenced him enough for him to write plays. I think it is his forte, but—! I call him up, because I happen to open my pages to the description of Ben taking up a broom for the first time, and read aloud to the "gentleman farmer" about that unwilling boy of yesteryear. We both have a hearty laugh. Then Ben gives an extra chuckle. "Gee, people should see how I look now." Ben has a heavy mortgage. He also has a tremendous sweep of lawn to mow, seedlings to transplant and a hot-house to keep clean. I think that Ben "has made it!"

And after all that I have said the pertinent thing is what did the young people say about us and what today as adults do they say. Just before publication of this book I received the following two statements from Max and from Ben which seem a fitting finish to our life-long odyssey.

Dearest Celia:

Here is commentary from Max which you may utilize for your book and paraphrase as you wish. All from the heart.

> My memories, the earliest, are those of teenage frustrations.
>
> I recall the anguish, the bitterness because I could not change the world.
>
> I remember my silent screams in the darkness of despair.
>
> But most vivid is the memory of the doors opened for me at Hawthorne School so many years ago, the end of bitterness, the beginnings of hope and meaningful creativeness.
>
> And I remember the Great Beginning when I could look for enemies and see only brothers and sisters.
>
> I knew nothing of philosophy, of religion, of political realities, even less of psychology and psychiatry. But I gained new tools of learning.
>
> It was scripts and props and flats, paintbrushes, sets, blocking and Act One, Scene One; these were the tools and these were my new and real salvation.
>
> The name of salvation was Theatre and the architect was Celia Avramo Rabinow.
>
> Dearest Celia, guide and mentor, you bring to mind the words of educator Horace Mann: "Be ashamed to die until you have won some victory for humanity."
>
> Your book will be a record of many such victories.
>
> Like mine.

Max ——
June 20, 1976

I was a problem boy remanded to the Hawthorne Cedar Knolls School for "anti-social" behavior. I was fifteen years old. Looking backwards now, with the advantage of maturity and perspective, I can see that I was then searching for love and self-knowledge and self-definition. I was then dangerously close to an abyss. That abyss has reappeared from time to time. That I did not fall into it then or later was due primarily to a stroke of good fortune on my part. That good fortune was the fact that this school had two people on its faculty who became my teachers, and so changed my life. These two people were Celia Avramo and Barney Rabinow, later Mr. and Mrs. Rabinow.

Here I wish to speak of Celia Rabinow.

It was her genius to "know" what my heart demanded and needed and to make the theater group under her direction, and in which I was enrolled, work as a healer of souls. How can one measure this gift, or the genius that was hers and which she freely bestowed on her actors, stagehand crew, and writers? By some magical process, the plays themselves as produced had that special radiance, I recall, of all art. But first and foremost, was that special radiance in the hearts of all her boys and girls—still shining.

Ben ——
July 15, 1976

THE MAKING OF THE THEATRE

Half Man—Half Goat
Part I

It is a golden red autumn day in Greece, 3000 B.C. The skeleton of the trees begin to peep thru' the crispy leaves as the breeze carries them to the ground. Scampering down the mountainside comes a freak—with the body of goat and the head of a man. From this legendary creature came the theatre.

To the ancient Greeks he was known as Dionysus, God of Joy, Happiness and Harvest. With his coming wild celebrations were held because it meant the harvest was safe and that there would be plenty to eat and drink.

These affairs were unorganized, resembling the parties we hold on New Years' Eve. Wild dancing, singing, and drinking were the main events. The drama was born from these happy festivities.

An old Greek story tells that after Dionysus had visited the earth many years, Zeus, father of the gods, ordered him to remain at Mt. Olympus, where all the gods lived, never to go down to mortals again. When harvesting time came the people missed him. Somebody decided to act as if he were Dionysus. Others helped him. These first actors were the priests of the ancient Greek religion. The singers at these parties were known as poets. The others who watched the joyous dancing and singing were called the audience.

Legend tells that this is the romantic fashion in which the theatre began. In Part 2 the Group Theatre will tell how the early actors suffered because people were suspicious).

by M.C.
For the school newspaper

The Hawthorne Group Theatre, as all you boys know, is a dramatic group with our own workshop where we are building everything necessary for the stage in the Assembly Hall. About thirty boys and about twelve girls, most of whom have gone home, have been members. In less than ten months we have given five complete productions, that is eight plays; we have been building up the stage, and we have sent twelve interesting projects from our workshop to the Boys' Exhibition in the Commodore Hotel.

The following are the plays we have given: at the Halloween Party we make for the entire school in the Detail Hall, we presented "The Dentist's Den," farce; on our stage after we hung the new curtains, we gave three serious plays—"Little Heroes," "The Bad Penny" and "At Stake"; for Chanuka we presented on our stage which now had new footlights and a new floodlight, "Hail Chanuka Lights," a play in pantomime to music, with, readers, which we made up from five poems; for the Purim Festival in the Detail Hall, we gave a human Marionette Show about the story of Esther which Miss Avramo, our director wrote especially for us; our last production for which we had complete stage sets and a complete lighting effect and make-up was two plays—"The Brink of Silence," a tragedy, and "Lima Beans," a comedy.

The boys enjoyed very much getting the exhibition ready for June 1st. Henry —— and Irving —— built a miniature stage with others doing the best they could to cooperate. It was built on a scale of one inch to a foot in comparison with our big stage. These two boys also built the tiny foot lights and overhead lights which were connected to three batteries with on-and-off switch. The purpose for this stage was to experiment with lights and sets before we make them the right size for the actual stage.

Henry —— built the small furniture for this little stage; this furniture was exactly like the set you saw in the play "The Bring of Silence." Milton —— built and painted the log cabin, the enlarged copy of which you also saw in the same play. The tiny bunk has small mattresses and blankets. On the shelf there are books a half inch big. On the table there is a tiny built-in socket that lights up like a lamp (we couldn't use a candle here, it is understood). Henry —— built the stove out of a cigarette tin, with a little socket and a bulb inside and red gelatine behind the doors so you have the red glow of a fire falling on the floor. On each side of the stage he built in two little mirrors and dressing tables with lights over them. Different colors to resemble make-up lie ready on the table for imaginary actors. . . .connected all the electrical wires and fixtures. The overhead lights were an exact copy of the strip——make for our big stage. The girls Martha —— made the curtains and Mollie —— made the masks over the proscenium just like the big plaque which H—— designed for our own stage. R—— made a special table for this stage.

Another project of which we are proud is the motto plaque designed by D——. The boys chose the words many months ago. "There can be no harvest without first tilling the soil and sowing the seed." It is about five feet high and stands on its own legs and an easal back. All the boys and girls helped cut out the letters and polish and paint them. The frame was designed by F——, S——, and R—— did the most work on this. W. ——, J. ——, J. ——, H. —— and others helping, even the girls.

We had lots of fun carving and painting this motto because it means just what the Theatre Group is doing sowing the seeds and growing slowly into a big tree of many trees just like the tree we carved under these words.

You all know K——'s electric sign. Remember, it stood in Assembly Hall during one of our performances? The words Hawthorne Group Theatre flash on and off. It is finished now and beautifully painted.

Now the girls, too, working with us in our dramatic workshop. One of the stages—made of cardboard and frame was made by Dorothy ——. It had a stage design in it for "Little Heroes" made by N. F——.

You are invited to see our work in Cottage 17.

by Henry

For the School Newspaper

Index to Children Mentioned